HALO
HELLJUMPER

HALO: HELLJUMPER. Contains material originally published in magazine form as HALO: HELLJUMPER #1-5. First printing 2010. ISBN# 978-0-7851-4023-8. Published by MARVEL PUBLISHING, INC., a subsidiary of MARVEL ENTERTAINMENT, INC. OFFICE OF PUBLICATION: 417 5th Avenue, New York, NY 10016. © 2009 and 2010 Microsoft Corporation. Microsoft, Halo, the Halo logo, the Microsoft Game Studios logo, Xbox, Xbox 360, Xbox LIVE, and the Xbox logos are trademarks of the Microsoft group of companies. $24.99 per copy in the U.S. (GST #R127032852); Canadian Agreement #40668537. No similarity between any of the names, characters, persons, and/or institutions in this magazine with those of any living or dead person or institution is intended, and any such similarity which may exist is purely coincidental. **Printed in the U.S.A.** ALAN FINE, EVP - Office Of The Chief Executive Marvel Entertainment, Inc. & CMO Marvel Characters B.V.; DAN BUCKLEY, Chief Executive Officer and Publisher - Print, Animation & Digital Media; JIM SOKOLOWSKI, Chief Operating Officer; DAVID GABRIEL, SVP of Publishing Sales & Circulation; DAVID BOGART, SVP of Business Affairs & Talent Management; MICHAEL PASCIULLO, VP Merchandising & Communications; JIM O'KEEFE, VP of Operations & Logistics; DAN CARR, Executive Director of Publishing Technology; JUSTIN F. GABRIE. Director of Publishing & Editorial Operations; SUSAN CRESPI, Editorial Operations Manager; ALEX MORALES, Publishing Operations Manager; STAN LEE, Chairman Emeritus. For information regarding advertising in Marvel Comics or on Marvel.com, please contact Ron Stern, VP of Business Development, at rstern@marvel.com. **For Marvel subscription inquiries, please call 800-217-9158. Manufactured between 1/4/10 and 2/3/10 by R.R. DONNELLEY, INC., SALEM, VA, USA.**

10 9 8 7 6 5 4 3 2 1

HALO
HELLJUMPER

WRITER: Peter David

ARTIST: Eric Nguyen

LETTERER: Blambot's Nate Piekos

EDITOR: Charlie Beckerman

SUPERVISING EDITOR: Mark Paniccia

COLLECTION EDITOR: Mark D. Beazley

ASSISTANT EDITORS: John Denning & Alex Starbuck

EDITOR, SPECIAL PROJECTS: Jennifer Grünwald

SENIOR EDITOR, SPECIAL PROJECTS: Jeff Youngquist

SENIOR VICE PRESIDENT OF SALES: David Gabriel

PRODUCTION: Jerry Kalinowski & Damien Lucchese

BOOK DESIGNER: Spring Hoteling

EDITOR IN CHIEF: Joe Quesada

PUBLISHER: Dan Buckley

SPECIAL THANKS TO:
Kevin Grace, Frank O'Connor, Alicia Brattin & Alicia Hatch

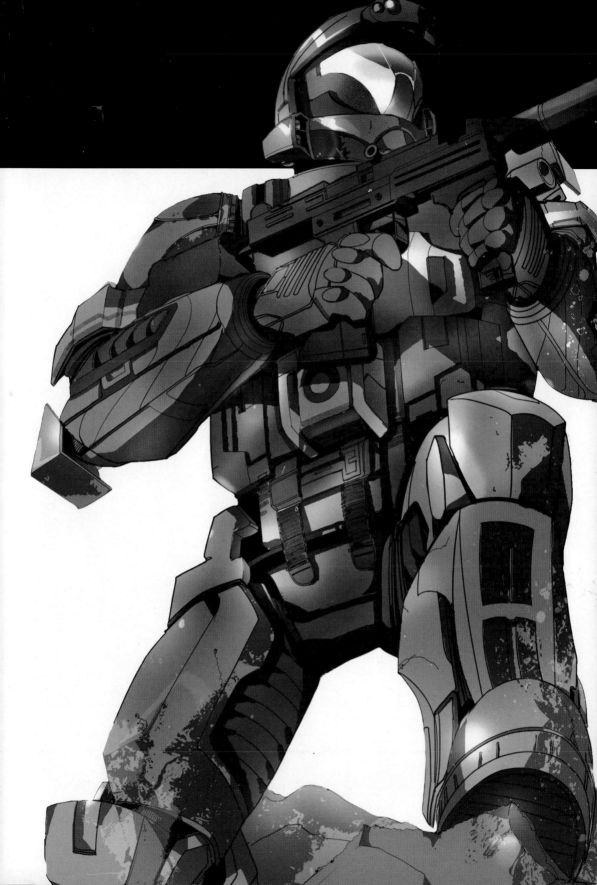

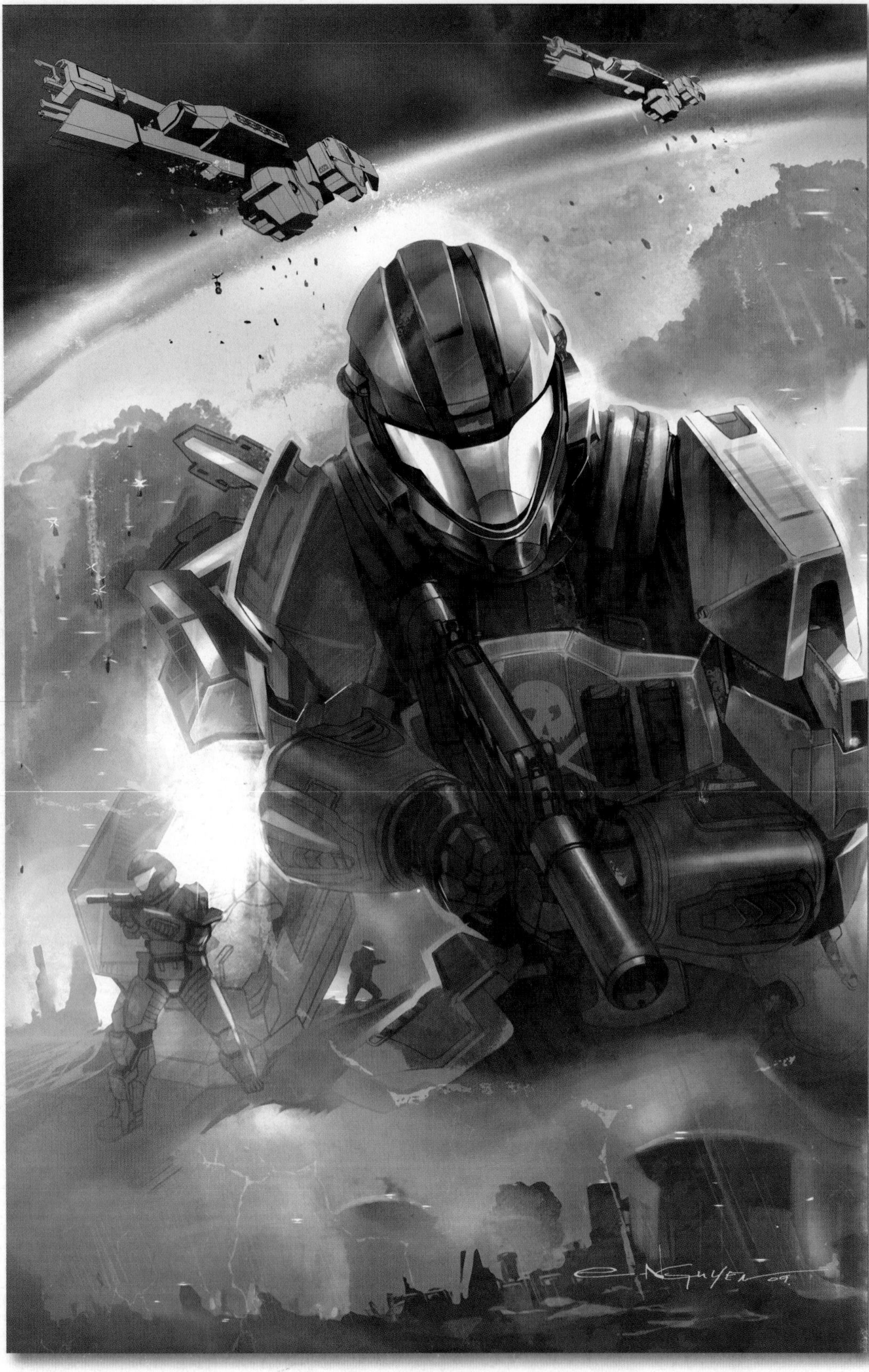

By the early decades of the 26th Century, Humankind
had settled large portions of the Galaxy. Under the
dominion of the United Nations Space Command and
with the use of Slipstream travel, it seemed man's
reach should always exceed his grasp. And it did, until
something reached back.

In 2525, contact was lost with one of the Outer
Colonies, a farming world called Harvest. Attempts
to raise the planet were unsuccessful, and the UNSC
soon learned that the attack came not from any Human
threat, but from a new, alien, and terrifyingly powerful
enemy.

This theocratically ruled alien collective known as
the Covenant declared their intent to exterminate
Humanity, believing us to be offensive in the eyes of
their Gods, the Forerunners. An ancient, disappeared
civilization, the Forerunner left many dangerous
artifacts strewn throughout the galaxy, including
several large ringworlds known as Halos.

The Human-Covenant war continues to rage on, and it is
in the midst of this conflict that our story begins...

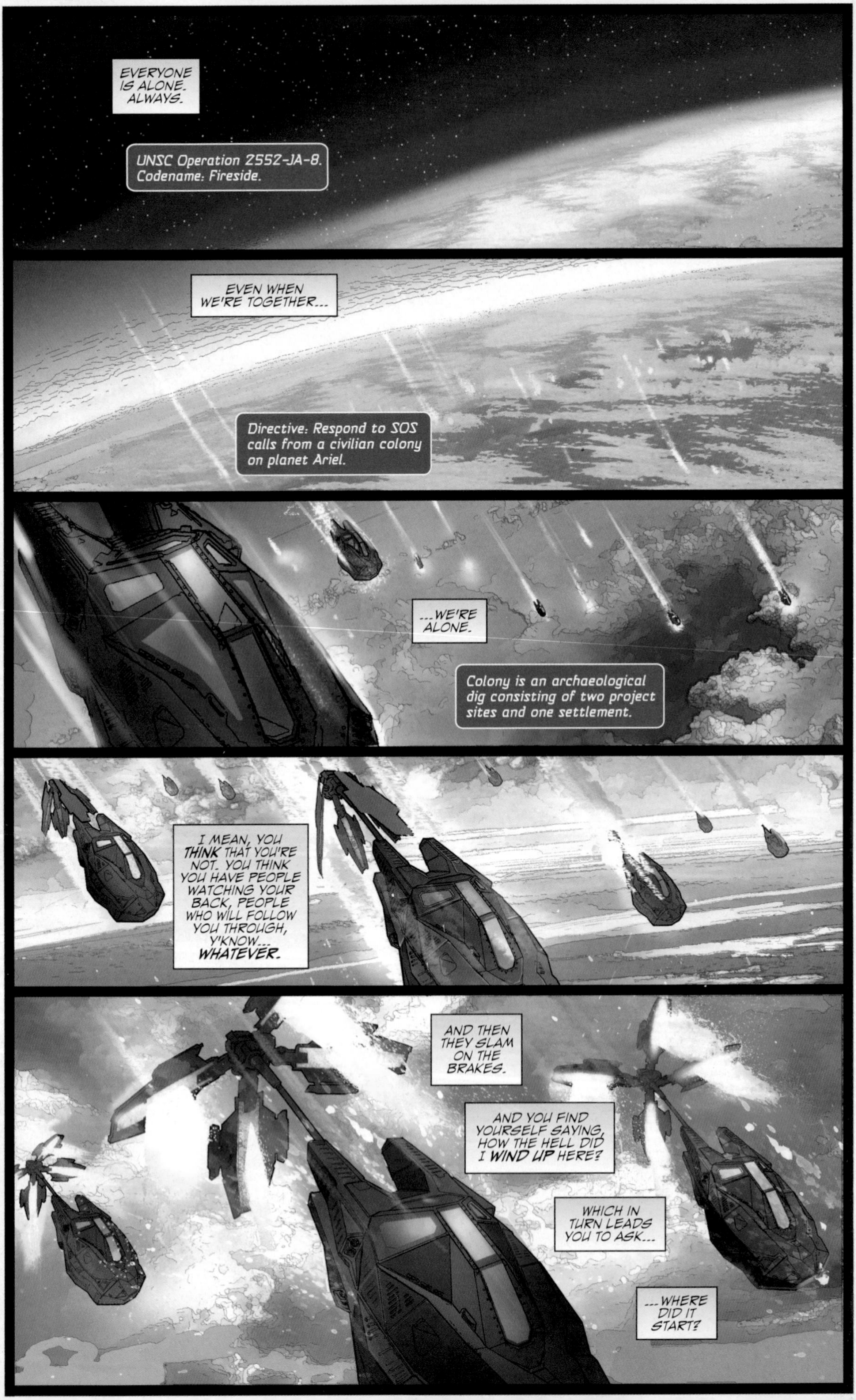
EVERYONE IS ALONE. ALWAYS.
UNSC Operation 2552-JA-8. Codename: Fireside.
EVEN WHEN WE'RE TOGETHER...
Directive: Respond to SOS calls from a civilian colony on planet Ariel.
...WE'RE ALONE.
Colony is an archaeological dig consisting of two project sites and one settlement.
I MEAN, YOU THINK THAT YOU'RE NOT. YOU THINK YOU HAVE PEOPLE WATCHING YOUR BACK, PEOPLE WHO WILL FOLLOW YOU THROUGH, Y'KNOW... WHATEVER.
AND THEN THEY SLAM ON THE BRAKES.
AND YOU FIND YOURSELF SAYING, HOW THE HELL DID I WIND UP HERE?
WHICH IN TURN LEADS YOU TO ASK...
...WHERE DID IT START?

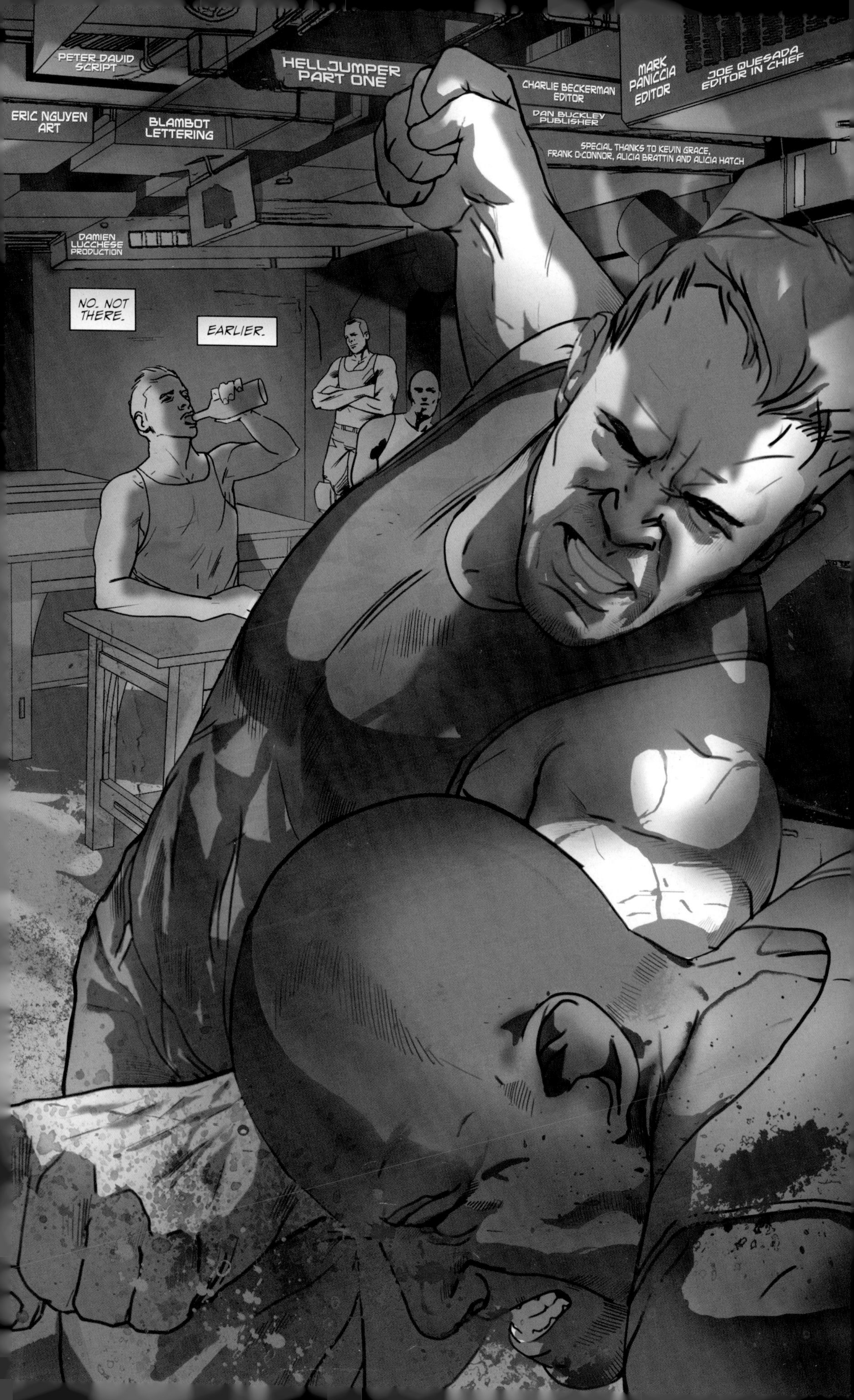

PETER DAVID
SCRIPT
HELLJUMPER
PART ONE
CHARLIE BECKERMAN
EDITOR
MARK
PANICCIA
EDITOR
JOE QUESADA
EDITOR IN CHIEF
ERIC NGUYEN
ART
BLAMBOT
LETTERING
DAN BUCKLEY
PUBLISHER
SPECIAL THANKS TO KEVIN GRACE,
FRANK O'CONNOR, ALICIA BRATTIN AND ALICIA HATCH
DAMIEN
LUCCHESE
PRODUCTION
NO. NOT
THERE.
EARLIER.

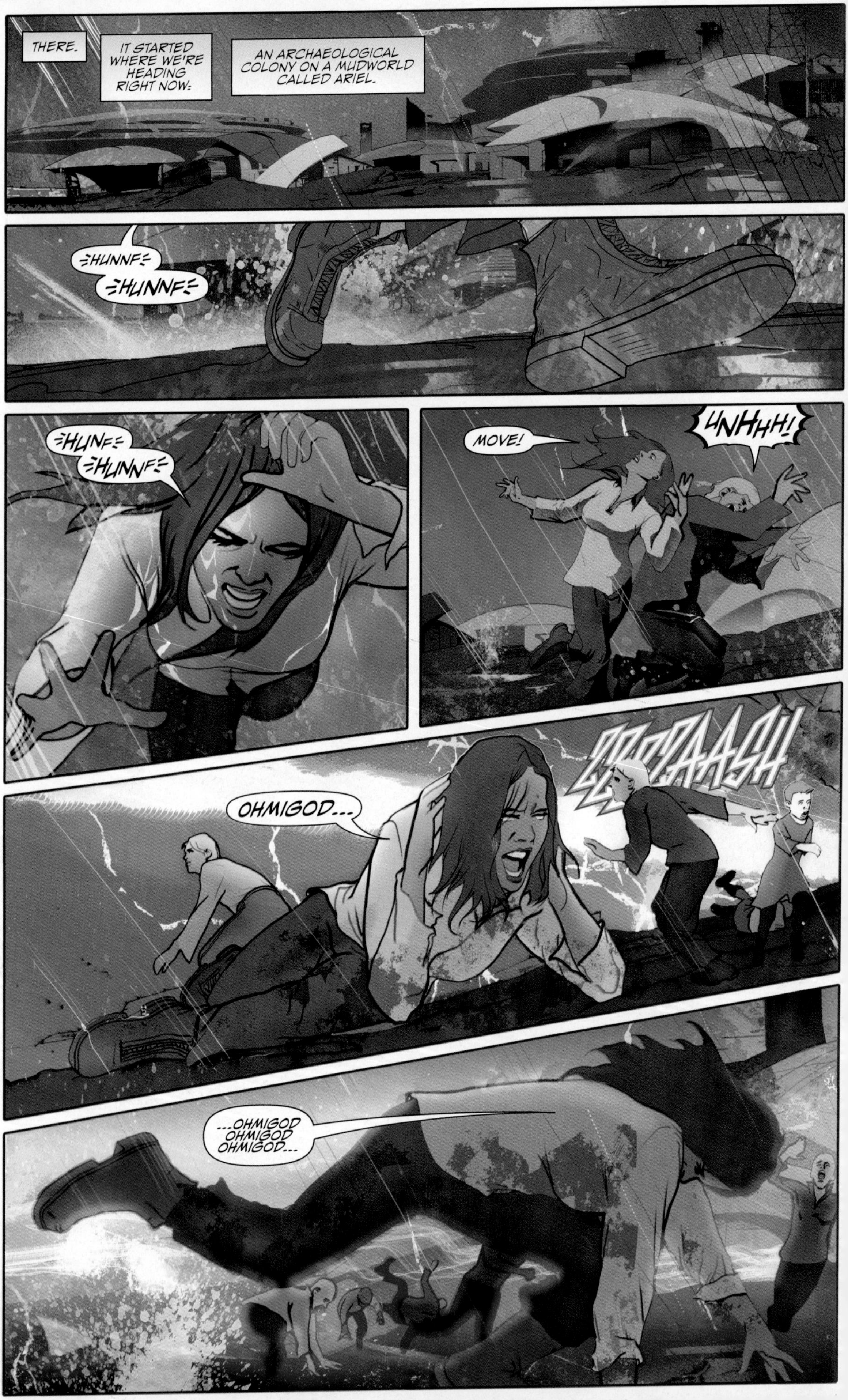

THERE.
IT STARTED WHERE WE'RE HEADING RIGHT NOW:
AN ARCHAEOLOGICAL COLONY ON A MUDWORLD CALLED ARIEL.
HUNNF
HUNNF
HUNF
HUNNF
MOVE!
UNHHH!
CRRAASH
OHMIGOD...
...OHMIGOD OHMIGOD OHMIGOD...

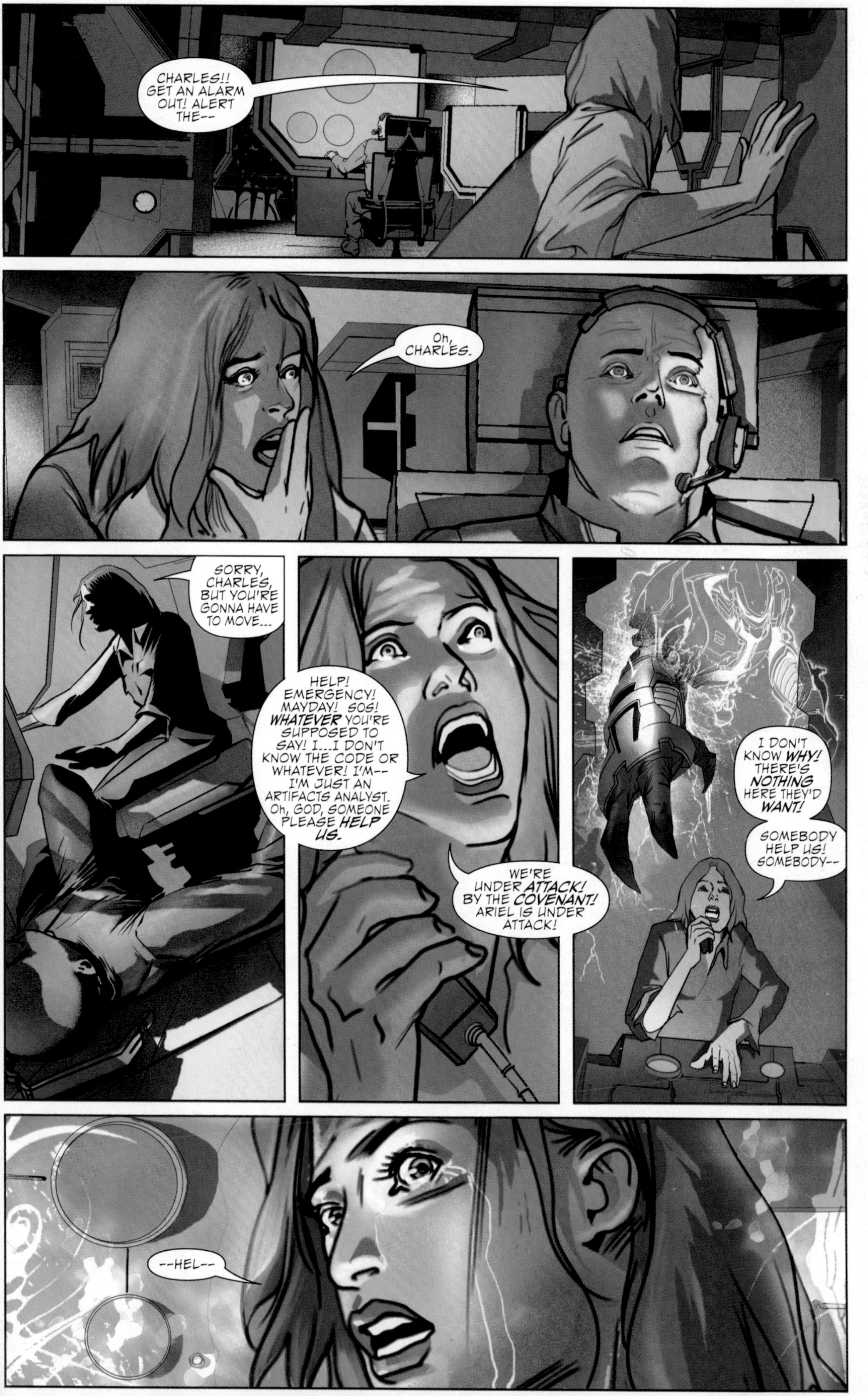
CHARLES!! GET AN ALARM OUT! ALERT THE--
Oh, CHARLES.
SORRY, CHARLES, BUT YOU'RE GONNA HAVE TO MOVE...
HELP! EMERGENCY! MAYDAY! SOS! WHATEVER YOU'RE SUPPOSED TO SAY! I...I DON'T KNOW THE CODE OR WHATEVER! I'M-- I'M JUST AN ARTIFACTS ANALYST. Oh, GOD, SOMEONE PLEASE HELP US.
WE'RE UNDER ATTACK! BY THE COVENANT! ARIEL IS UNDER ATTACK!
I DON'T KNOW WHY! THERE'S NOTHING HERE THEY'D WANT!
SOMEBODY HELP US! SOMEBODY--
--HEL--

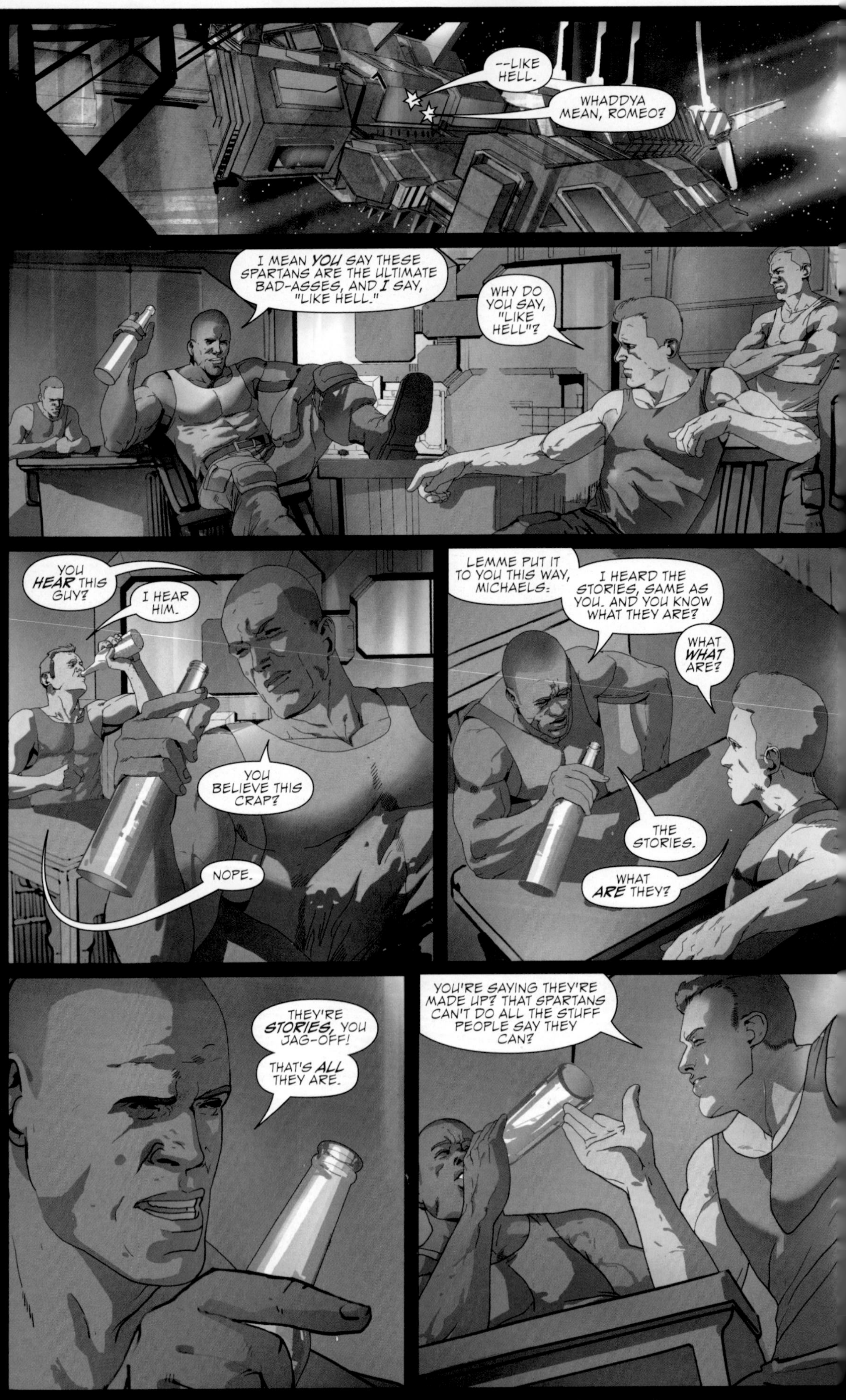
--LIKE HELL.
WHADDYA MEAN, ROMEO?
I MEAN YOU SAY THESE SPARTANS ARE THE ULTIMATE BAD-ASSES, AND I SAY, "LIKE HELL."
WHY DO YOU SAY, "LIKE HELL"?
YOU HEAR THIS GUY?
I HEAR HIM.
YOU BELIEVE THIS CRAP?
NOPE.
LEMME PUT IT TO YOU THIS WAY, MICHAELS.
I HEARD THE STORIES, SAME AS YOU. AND YOU KNOW WHAT THEY ARE?
WHAT WHAT ARE?
THE STORIES.
WHAT ARE THEY?
THEY'RE STORIES, YOU JAG-OFF!
THAT'S ALL THEY ARE.
YOU'RE SAYING THEY'RE MADE UP? THAT SPARTANS CAN'T DO ALL THE STUFF PEOPLE SAY THEY CAN?

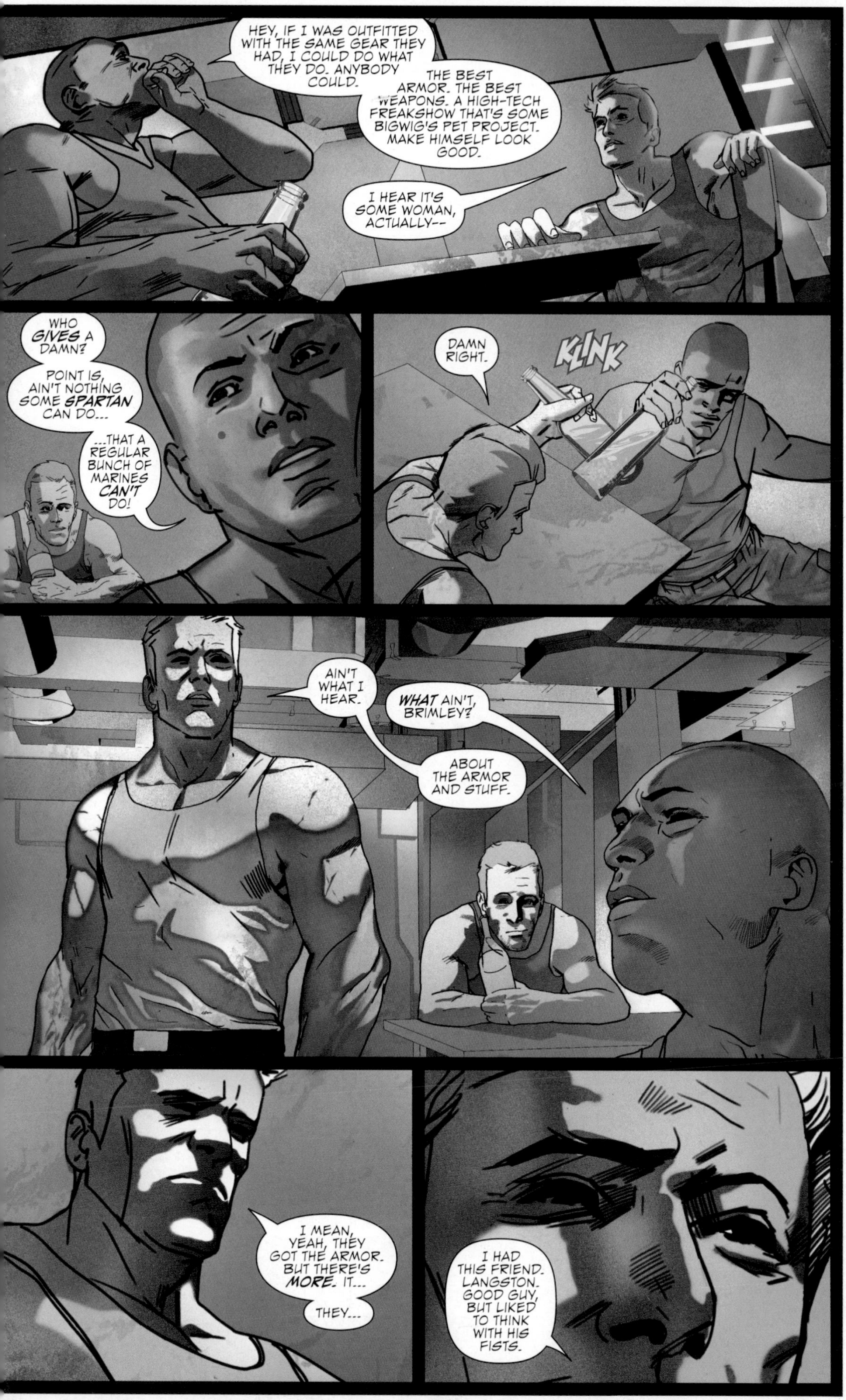
HEY, IF I WAS OUTFITTED WITH THE SAME GEAR THEY HAD, I COULD DO WHAT THEY DO. ANYBODY COULD.
THE BEST ARMOR. THE BEST WEAPONS. A HIGH-TECH FREAKSHOW THAT'S SOME BIGWIG'S PET PROJECT. MAKE HIMSELF LOOK GOOD.
I HEAR IT'S SOME WOMAN, ACTUALLY--
WHO GIVES A DAMN?
POINT IS, AIN'T NOTHING SOME SPARTAN CAN DO...
...THAT A REGULAR BUNCH OF MARINES CAN'T DO!
DAMN RIGHT.
KLINK
AIN'T WHAT I HEAR.
WHAT AIN'T, BRIMLEY?
ABOUT THE ARMOR AND STUFF.
I MEAN, YEAH, THEY GOT THE ARMOR. BUT THERE'S MORE. IT...
THEY...
I HAD THIS FRIEND. LANGSTON. GOOD GUY, BUT LIKED TO THINK WITH HIS FISTS.

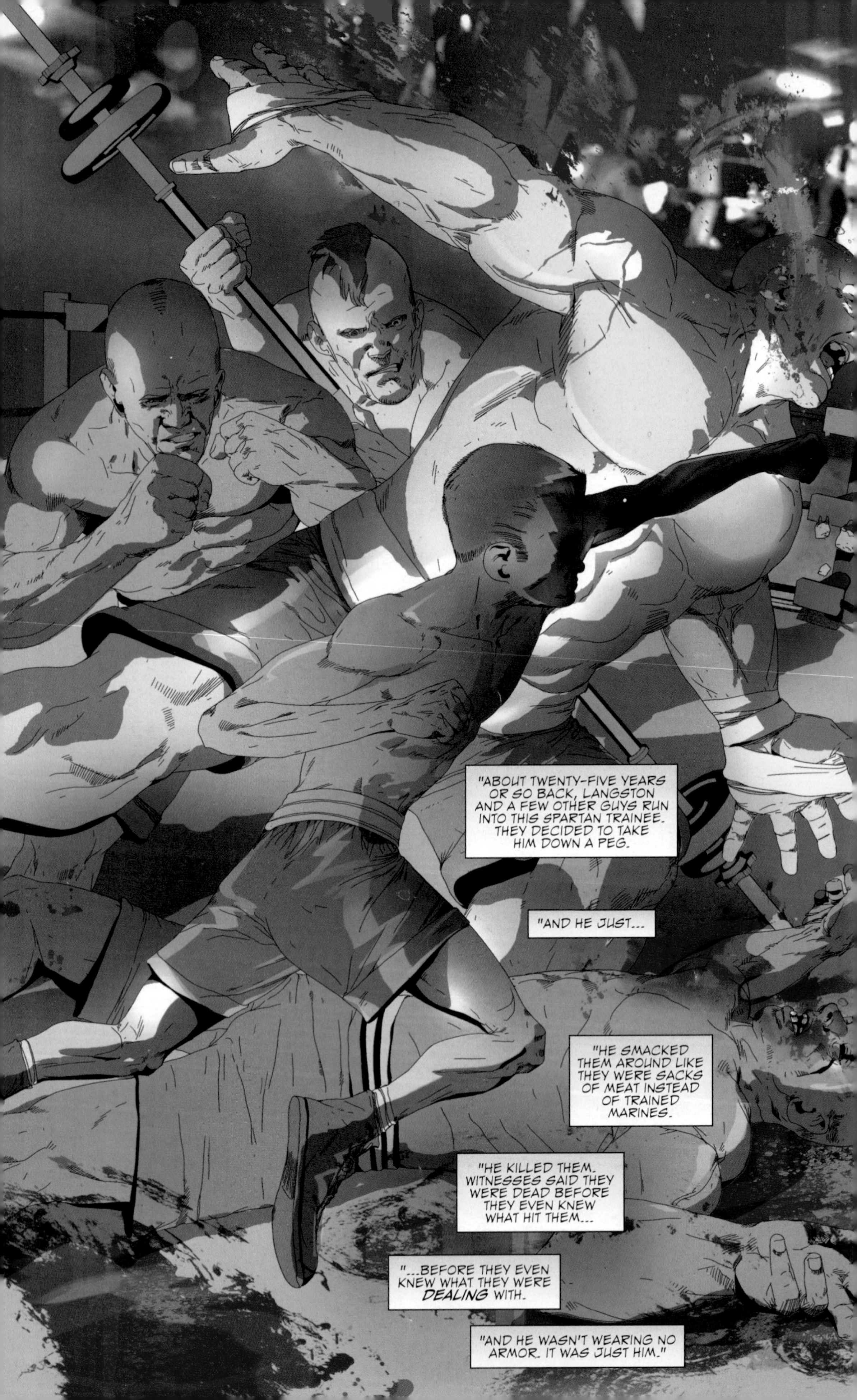
"ABOUT TWENTY-FIVE YEARS OR SO BACK, LANGSTON AND A FEW OTHER GUYS RUN INTO THIS SPARTAN TRAINEE. THEY DECIDED TO TAKE HIM DOWN A PEG.
"AND HE JUST...
"HE SMACKED THEM AROUND LIKE THEY WERE SACKS OF MEAT INSTEAD OF TRAINED MARINES.
"HE KILLED THEM. WITNESSES SAID THEY WERE DEAD BEFORE THEY EVEN KNEW WHAT HIT THEM...
"...BEFORE THEY EVEN KNEW WHAT THEY WERE *DEALING* WITH.
"AND HE WASN'T WEARING NO ARMOR. IT WAS JUST HIM."

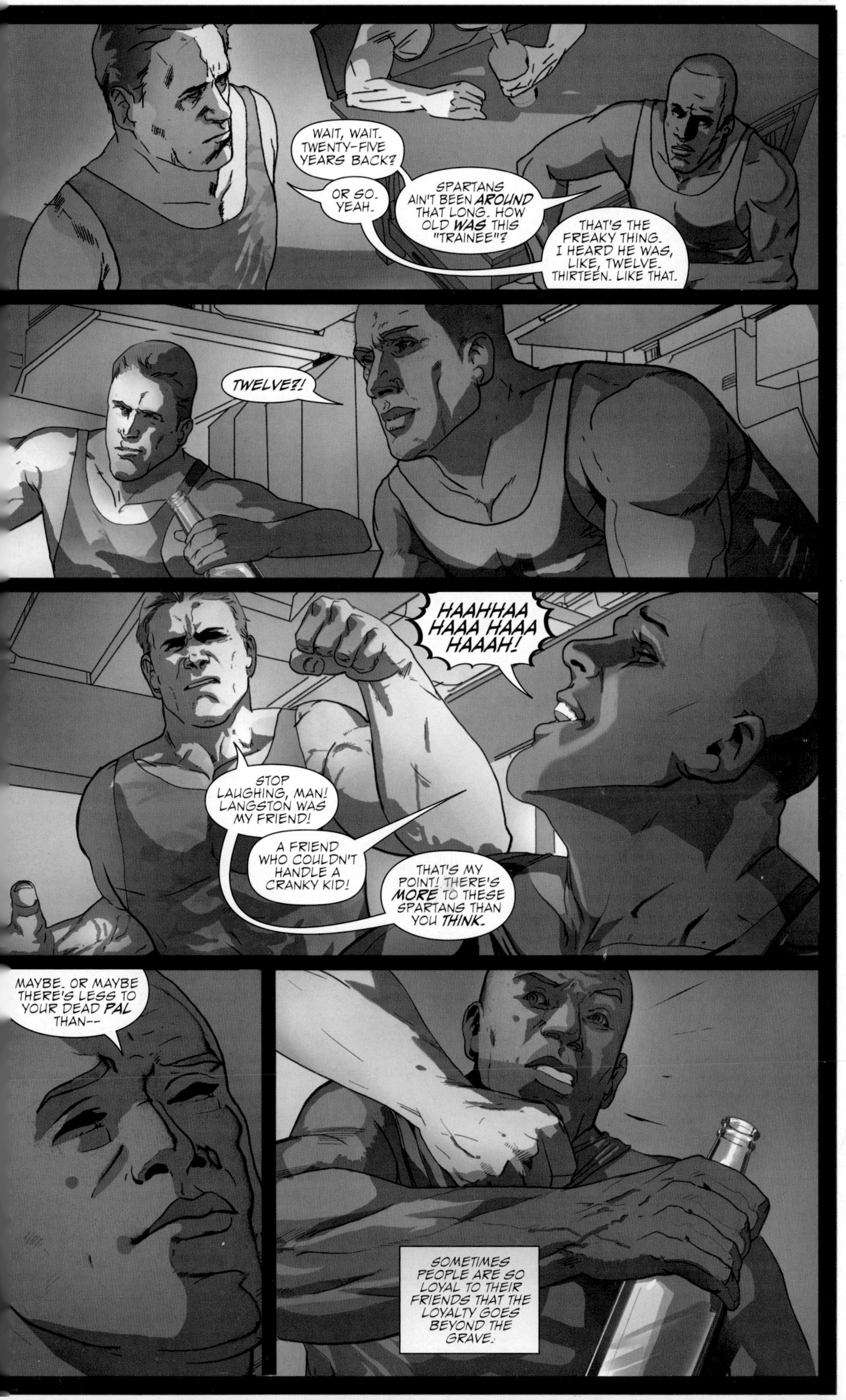
WAIT, WAIT. TWENTY-FIVE YEARS BACK?
OR SO. YEAH.
SPARTANS AIN'T BEEN AROUND THAT LONG. HOW OLD WAS THIS "TRAINEE"?
THAT'S THE FREAKY THING. I HEARD HE WAS, LIKE, TWELVE. THIRTEEN. LIKE THAT.
TWELVE?!
HAAHHAA HAAA HAAA HAAAH!
STOP LAUGHING, MAN! LANGSTON WAS MY FRIEND!
A FRIEND WHO COULDN'T HANDLE A CRANKY KID!
THAT'S MY POINT! THERE'S MORE TO THESE SPARTANS THAN YOU THINK.
MAYBE. OR MAYBE THERE'S LESS TO YOUR DEAD PAL THAN--
SOMETIMES PEOPLE ARE SO LOYAL TO THEIR FRIENDS THAT THE LOYALTY GOES BEYOND THE GRAVE.

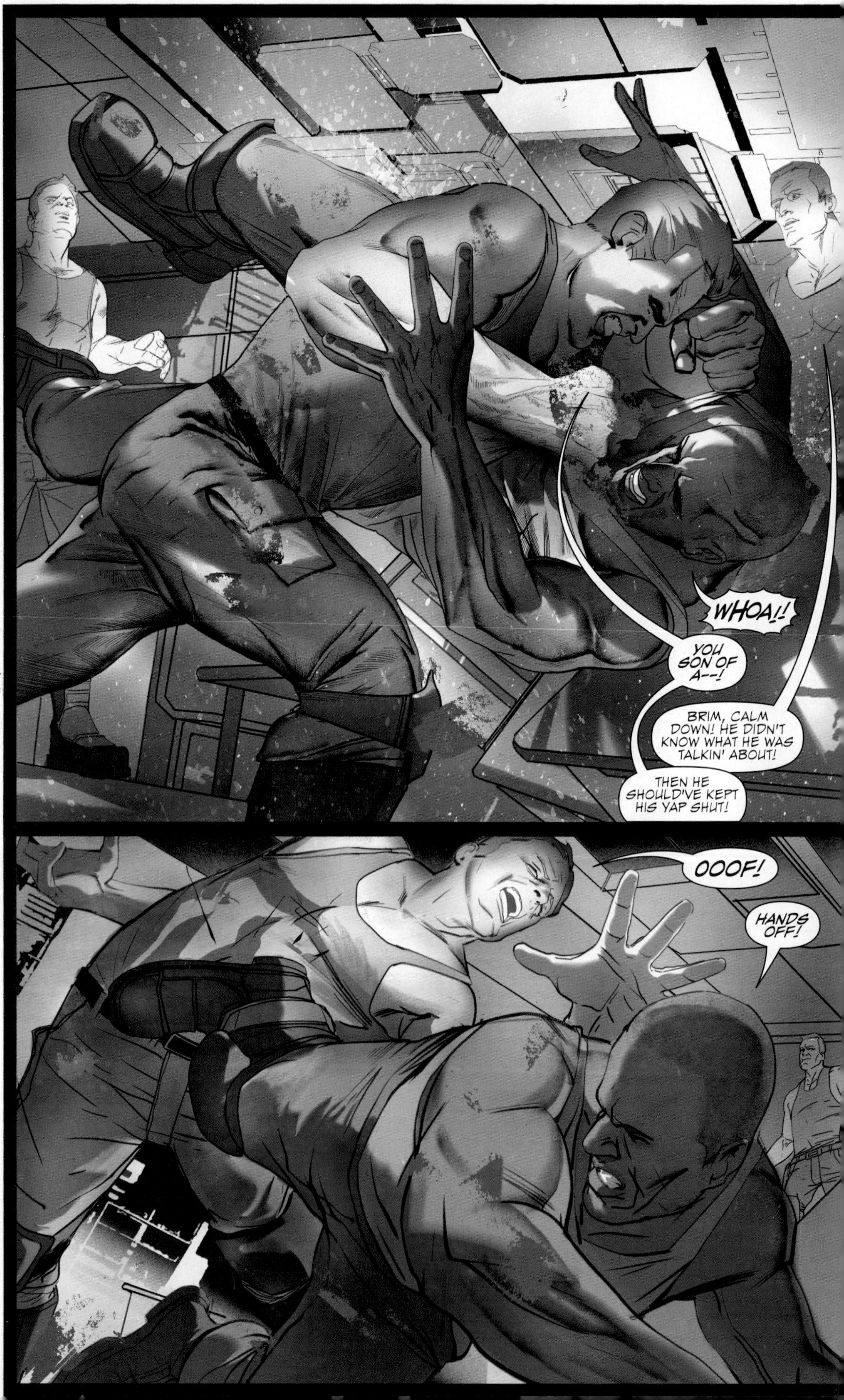
WHOA!!
YOU SON OF A--!
BRIM, CALM DOWN! HE DIDN'T KNOW WHAT HE WAS TALKIN' ABOUT!
THEN HE SHOULD'VE KEPT HIS YAP SHUT!
OOOF!
HANDS OFF!

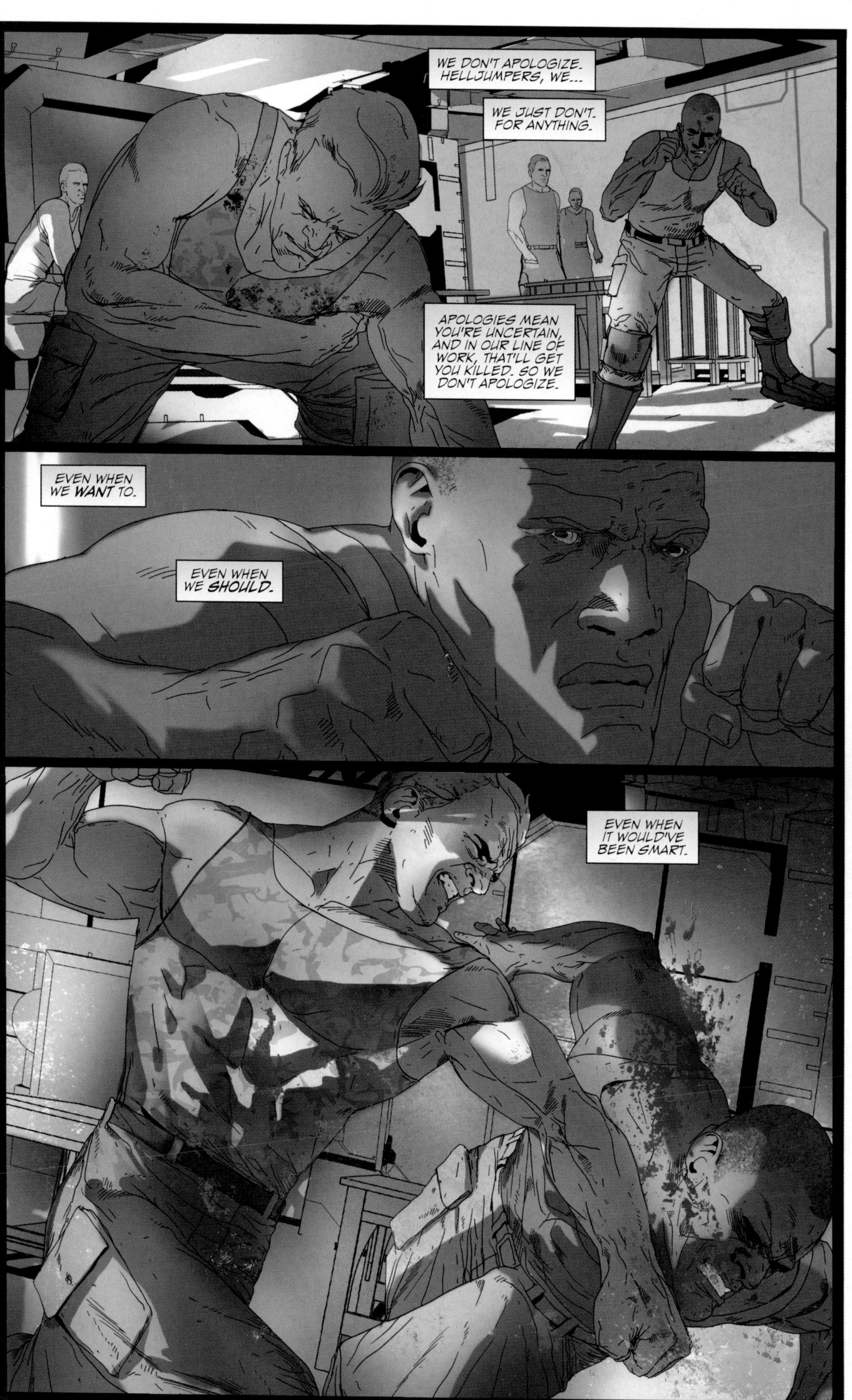
WE DON'T APOLOGIZE. HELLJUMPERS, WE...
WE JUST DON'T. FOR ANYTHING.
APOLOGIES MEAN YOU'RE UNCERTAIN, AND IN OUR LINE OF WORK, THAT'LL GET YOU KILLED. SO WE DON'T APOLOGIZE.
EVEN WHEN WE WANT TO.
EVEN WHEN WE SHOULD.
EVEN WHEN IT WOULD'VE BEEN SMART.

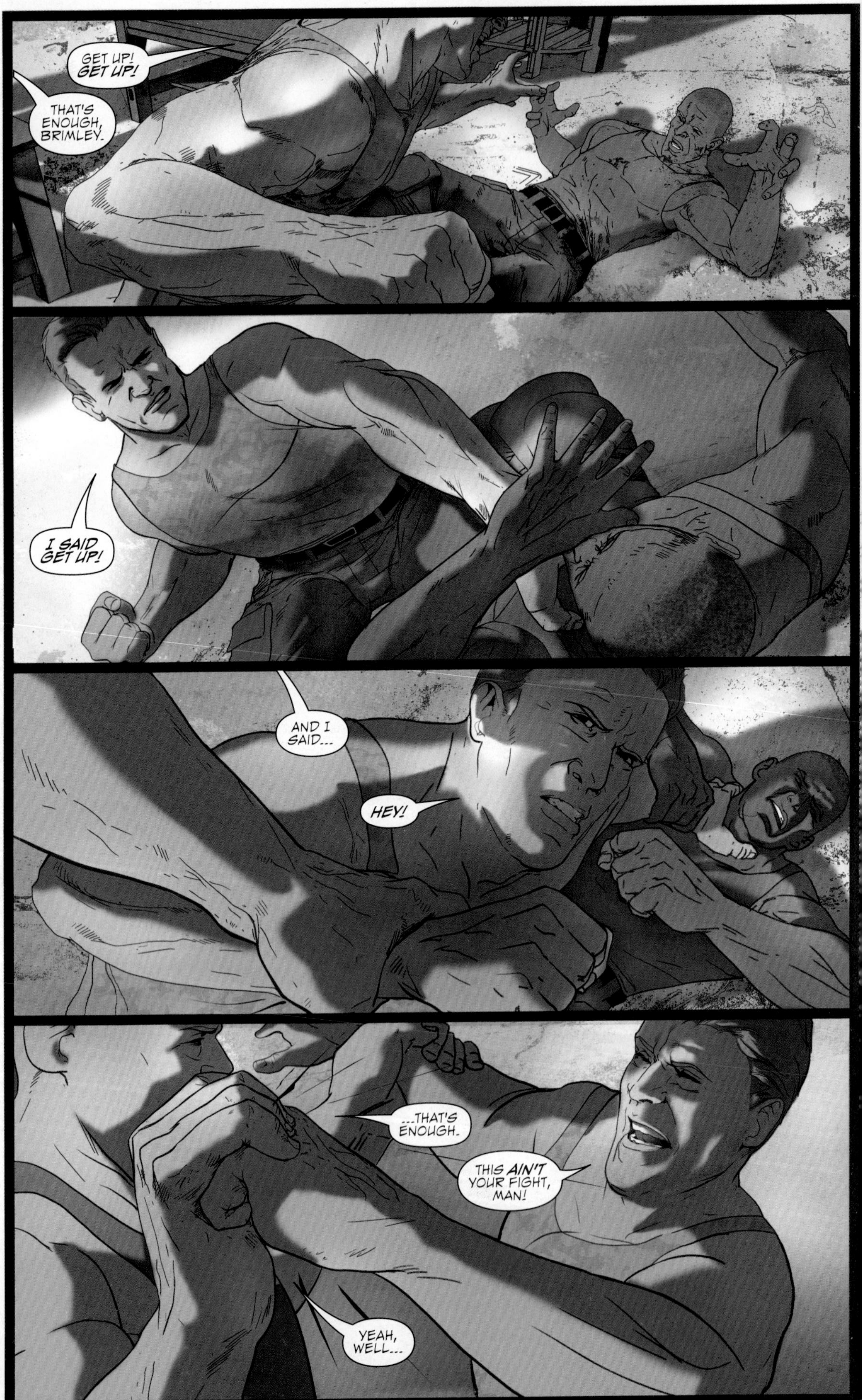

GET UP! GET UP!
THAT'S ENOUGH, BRIMLEY.
I SAID GET UP!
AND I SAID...
HEY!
...THAT'S ENOUGH.
THIS AIN'T YOUR FIGHT, MAN!
YEAH, WELL...

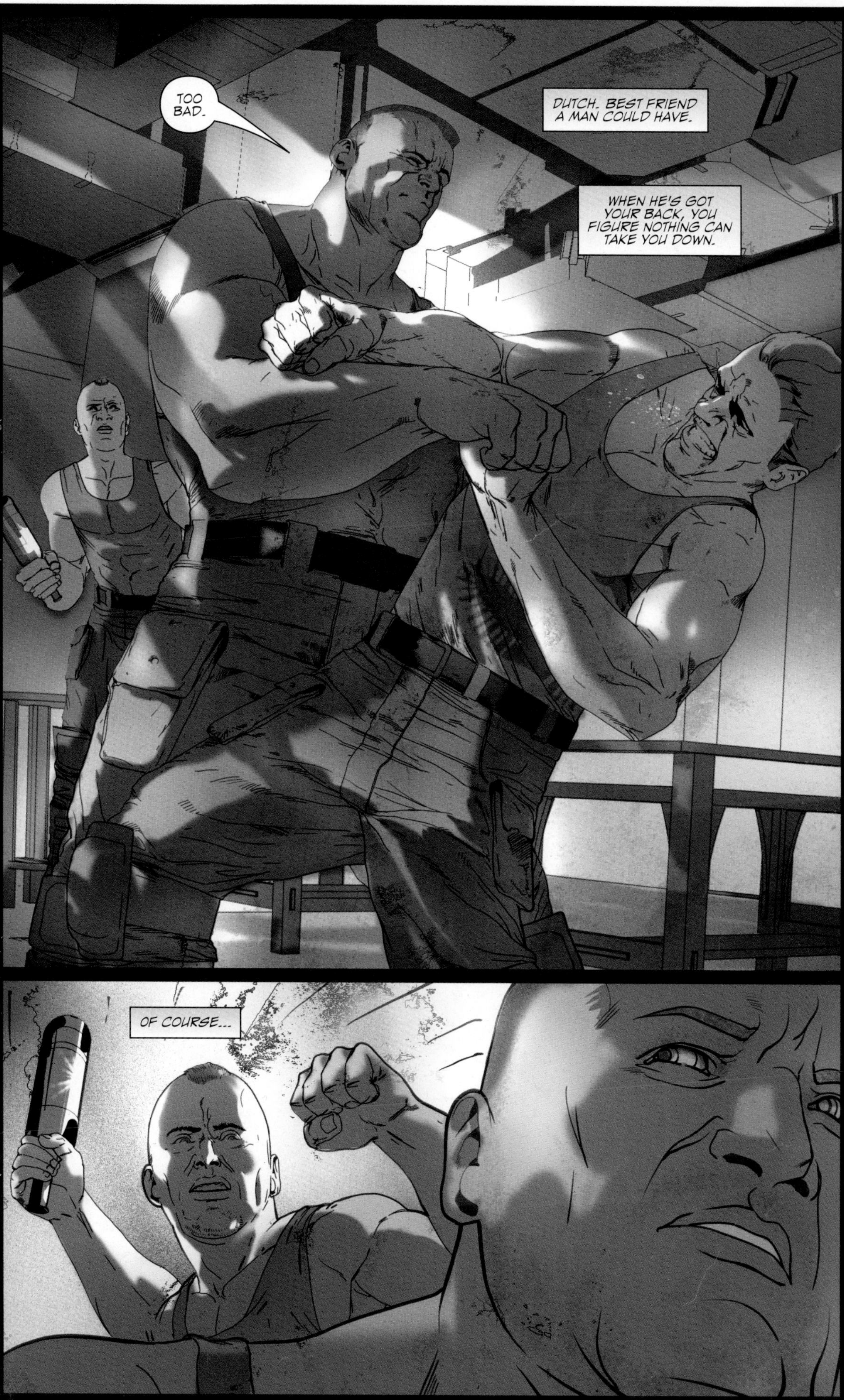
TOO BAD.
DUTCH. BEST FRIEND A MAN COULD HAVE.
WHEN HE'S GOT YOUR BACK, YOU FIGURE NOTHING CAN TAKE YOU DOWN.
OF COURSE...

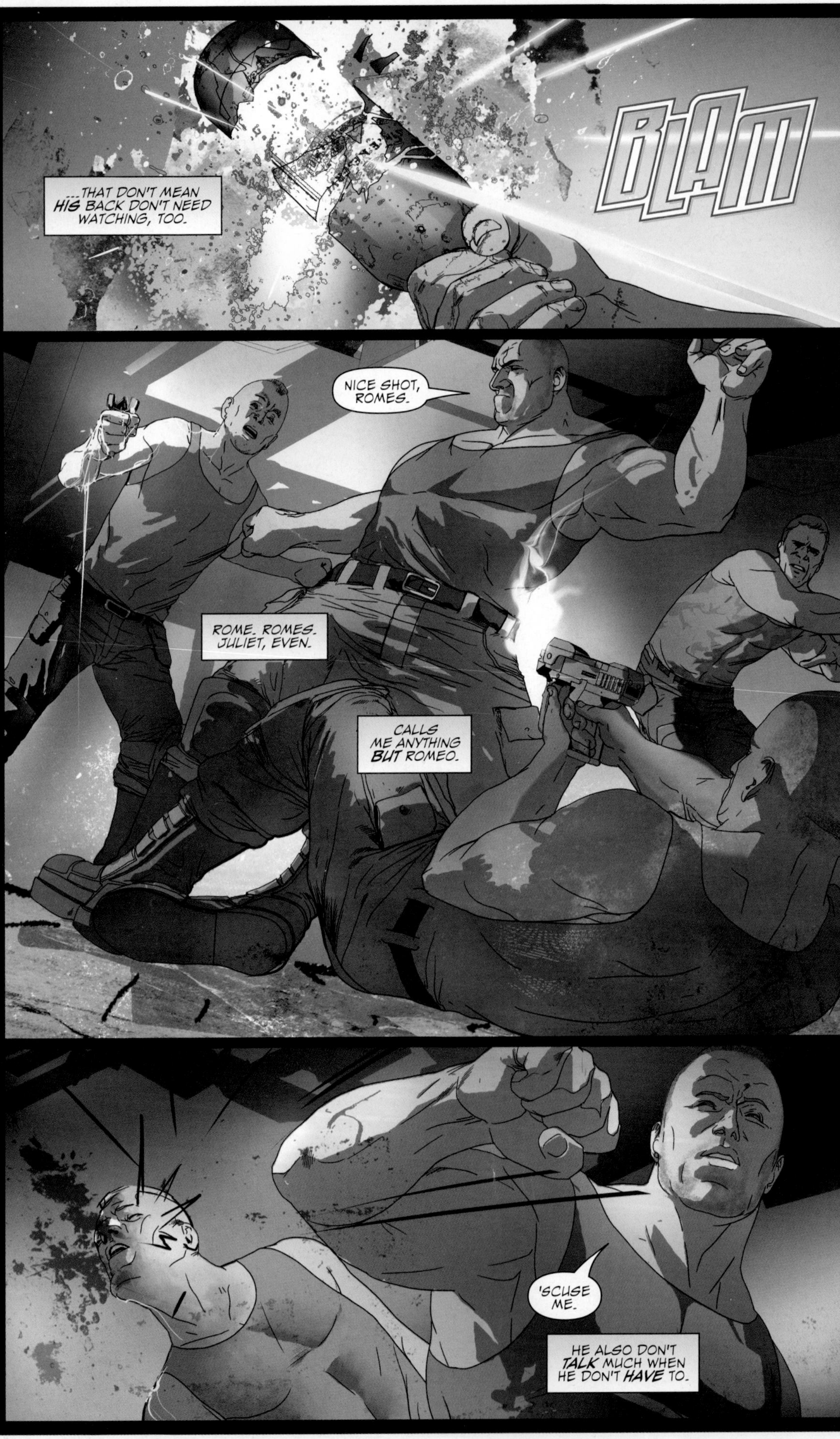
BLAM
...THAT DON'T MEAN HIS BACK DON'T NEED WATCHING, TOO.
NICE SHOT, ROMES.
ROME. ROMES. JULIET, EVEN.
CALLS ME ANYTHING BUT ROMEO.
'SCUSE ME.
HE ALSO DON'T TALK MUCH WHEN HE DON'T HAVE TO.

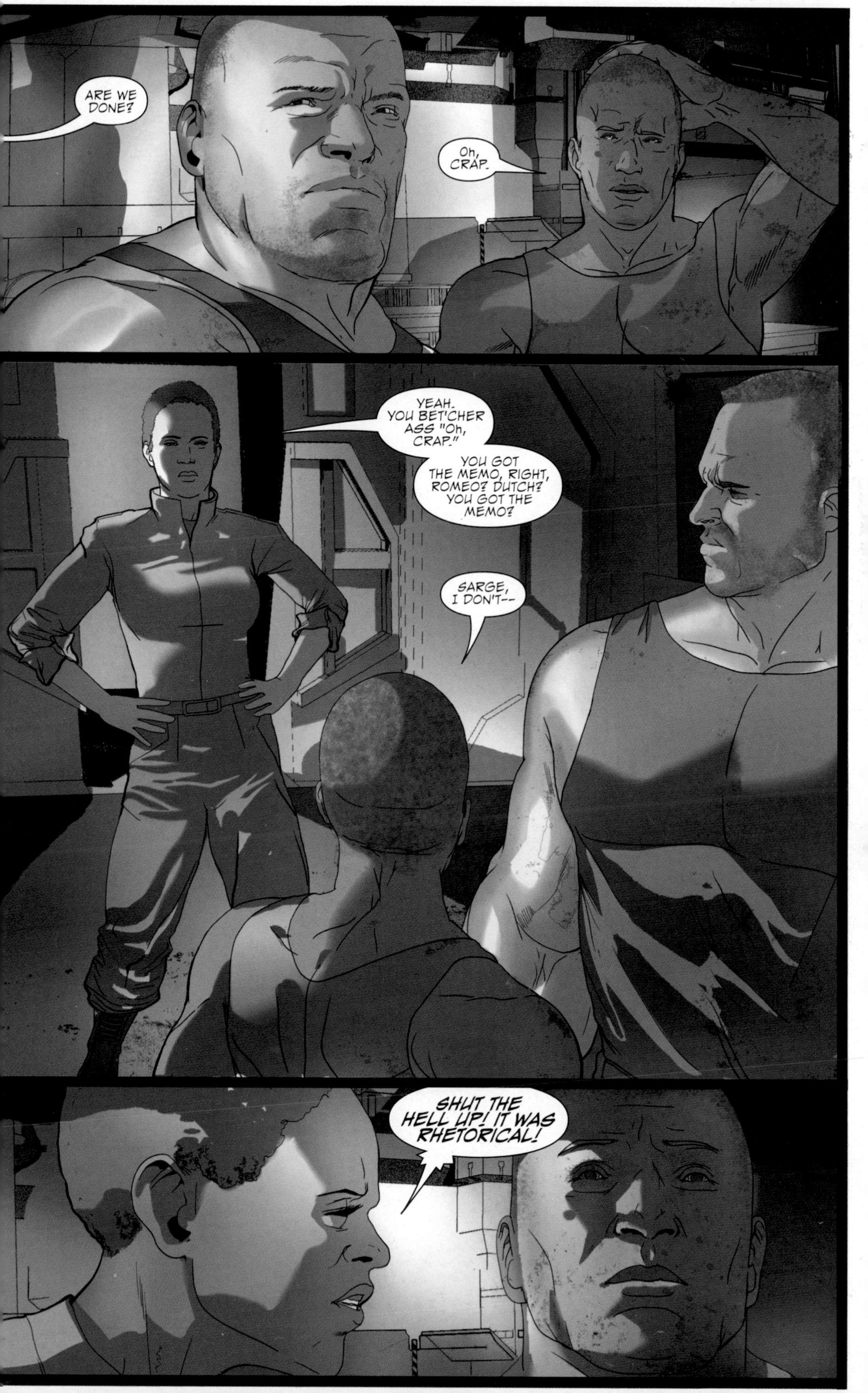
ARE WE DONE?
Oh, CRAP.
YEAH. YOU BET'CHER ASS "Oh, CRAP."
YOU GOT THE MEMO, RIGHT, ROMEO? DUTCH? YOU GOT THE MEMO?
SARGE, I DON'T--
SHUT THE HELL UP! IT WAS RHETORICAL!

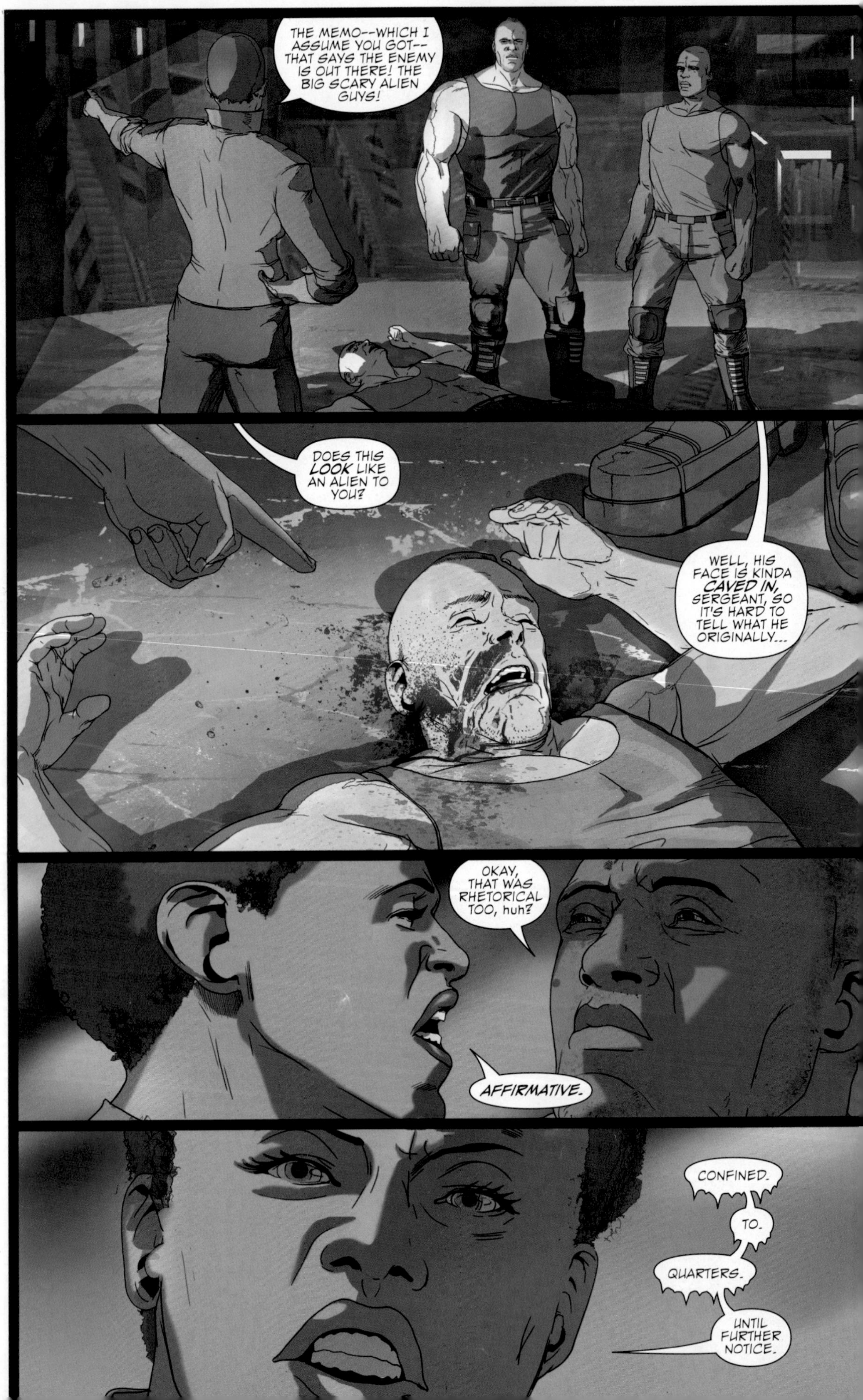
THE MEMO--WHICH I ASSUME YOU GOT--THAT SAYS THE ENEMY IS OUT THERE! THE BIG SCARY ALIEN GUYS!
DOES THIS LOOK LIKE AN ALIEN TO YOU?
WELL, HIS FACE IS KINDA CAVED IN, SERGEANT, SO IT'S HARD TO TELL WHAT HE ORIGINALLY...
OKAY, THAT WAS RHETORICAL TOO, huh?
AFFIRMATIVE.
CONFINED.
TO.
QUARTERS.
UNTIL FURTHER NOTICE.

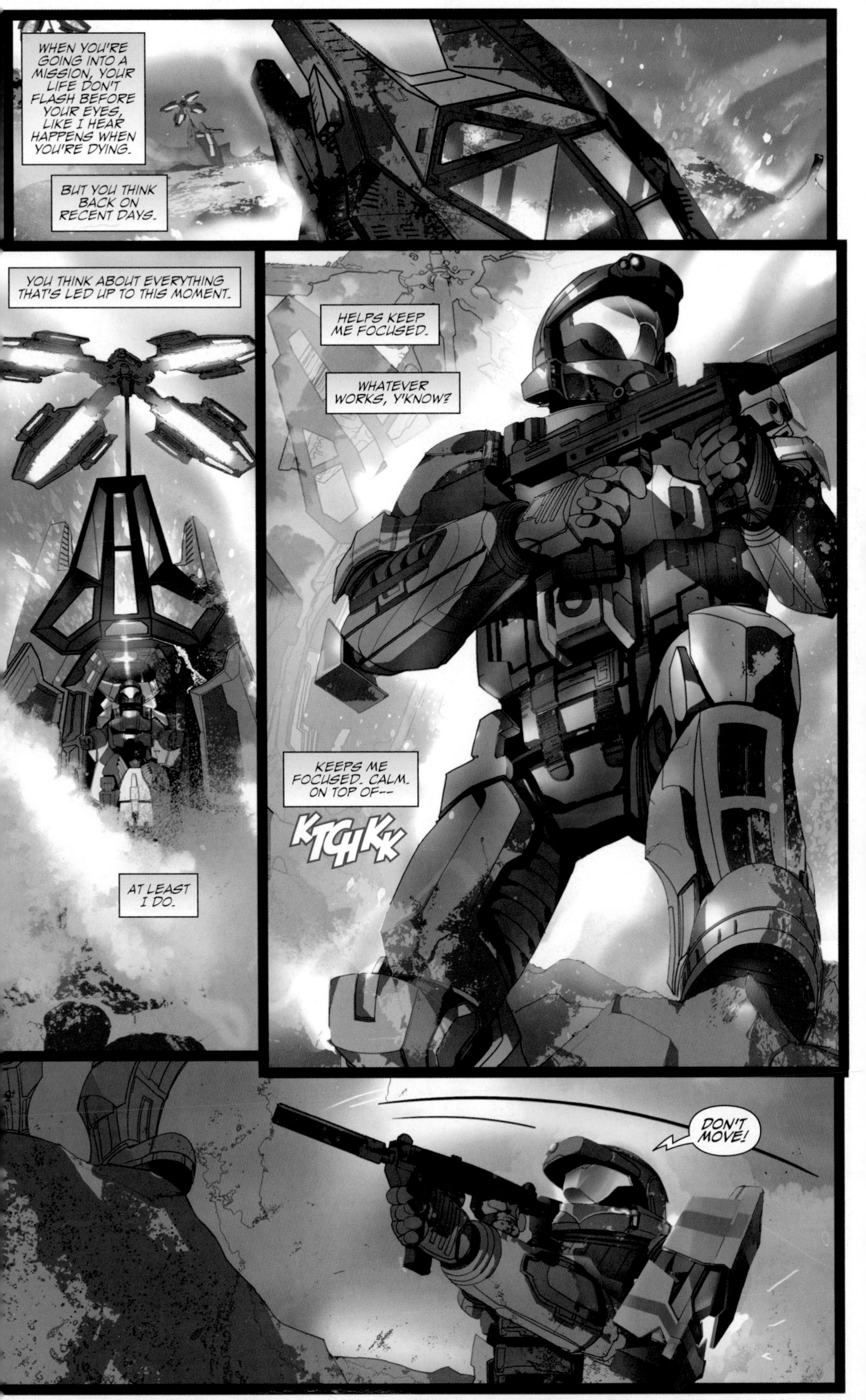
WHEN YOU'RE GOING INTO A MISSION, YOUR LIFE DON'T FLASH BEFORE YOUR EYES, LIKE I HEAR HAPPENS WHEN YOU'RE DYING.
BUT YOU THINK BACK ON RECENT DAYS.
YOU THINK ABOUT EVERYTHING THAT'S LED UP TO THIS MOMENT.
AT LEAST I DO.
HELPS KEEP ME FOCUSED.
WHATEVER WORKS, Y'KNOW?
KEEPS ME FOCUSED. CALM. ON TOP OF--
KTCHKK
DON'T MOVE!

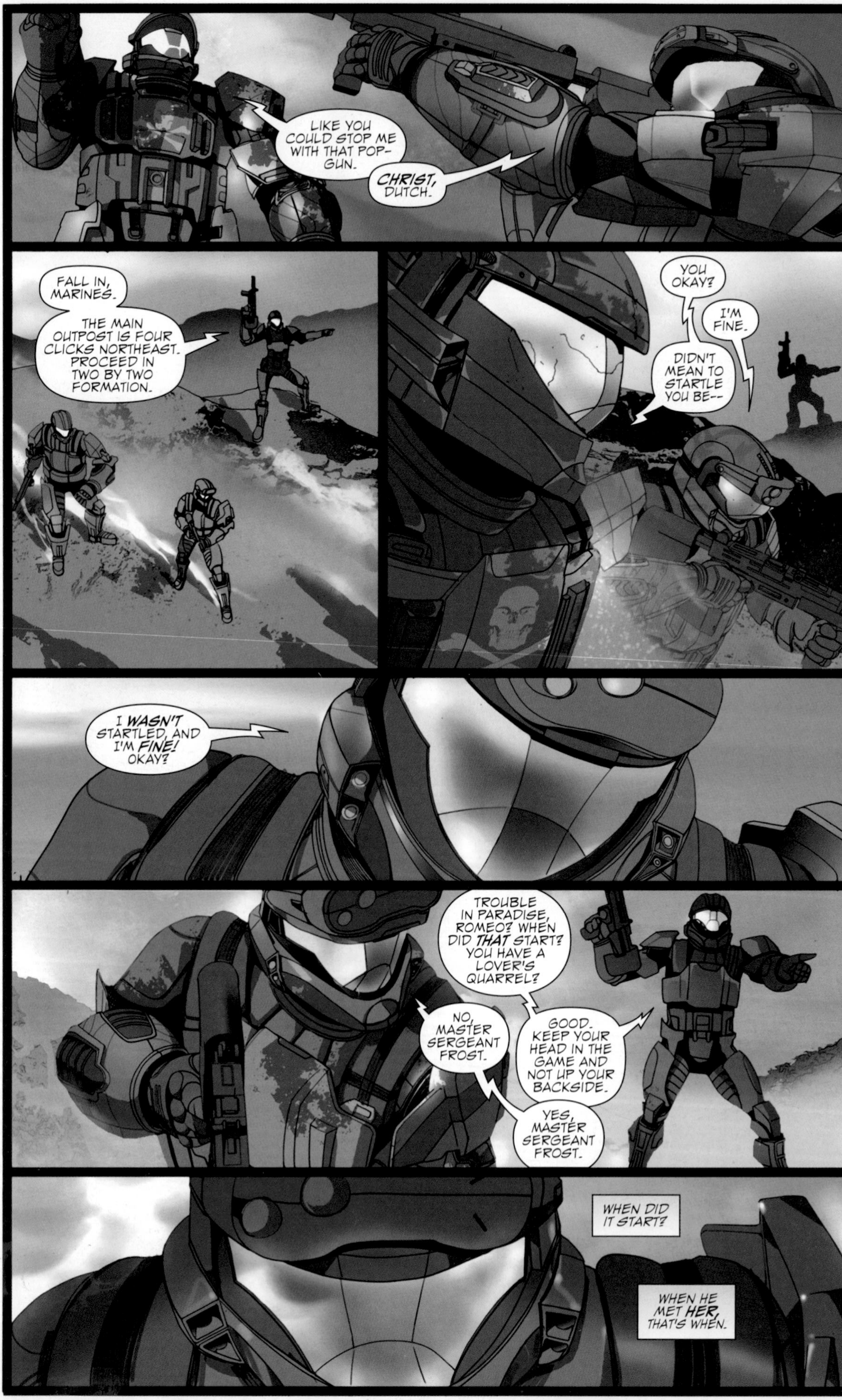
LIKE YOU COULD STOP ME WITH THAT POP-GUN.
CHRIST, DUTCH.
FALL IN, MARINES.
THE MAIN OUTPOST IS FOUR CLICKS NORTHEAST. PROCEED IN TWO BY TWO FORMATION.
YOU OKAY?
I'M FINE.
DIDN'T MEAN TO STARTLE YOU BE--
I WASN'T STARTLED, AND I'M FINE! OKAY?
TROUBLE IN PARADISE, ROMEO? WHEN DID THAT START? YOU HAVE A LOVER'S QUARREL?
NO, MASTER SERGEANT FROST.
GOOD. KEEP YOUR HEAD IN THE GAME AND NOT UP YOUR BACKSIDE.
YES, MASTER SERGEANT FROST.
WHEN DID IT START?
WHEN HE MET HER, THAT'S WHEN.

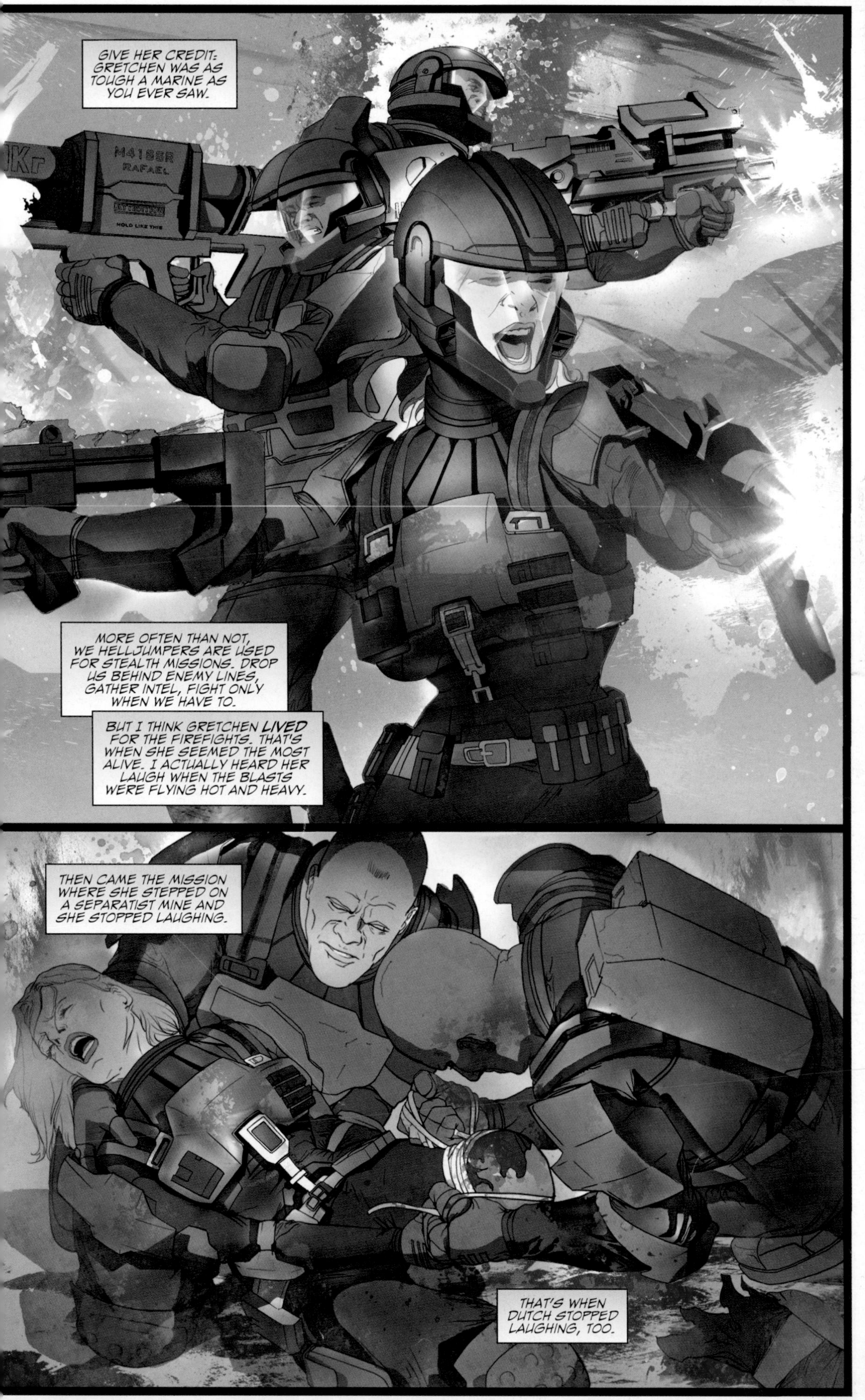
GIVE HER CREDIT: GRETCHEN WAS AS TOUGH A MARINE AS YOU EVER SAW.
MORE OFTEN THAN NOT, WE HELLJUMPERS ARE USED FOR STEALTH MISSIONS. DROP US BEHIND ENEMY LINES, GATHER INTEL, FIGHT ONLY WHEN WE HAVE TO.
BUT I THINK GRETCHEN **LIVED** FOR THE FIREFIGHTS. THAT'S WHEN SHE SEEMED THE MOST ALIVE. I ACTUALLY HEARD HER LAUGH WHEN THE BLASTS WERE FLYING HOT AND HEAVY.
THEN CAME THE MISSION WHERE SHE STEPPED ON A SEPARATIST MINE AND SHE STOPPED LAUGHING.
THAT'S WHEN DUTCH STOPPED LAUGHING, TOO.

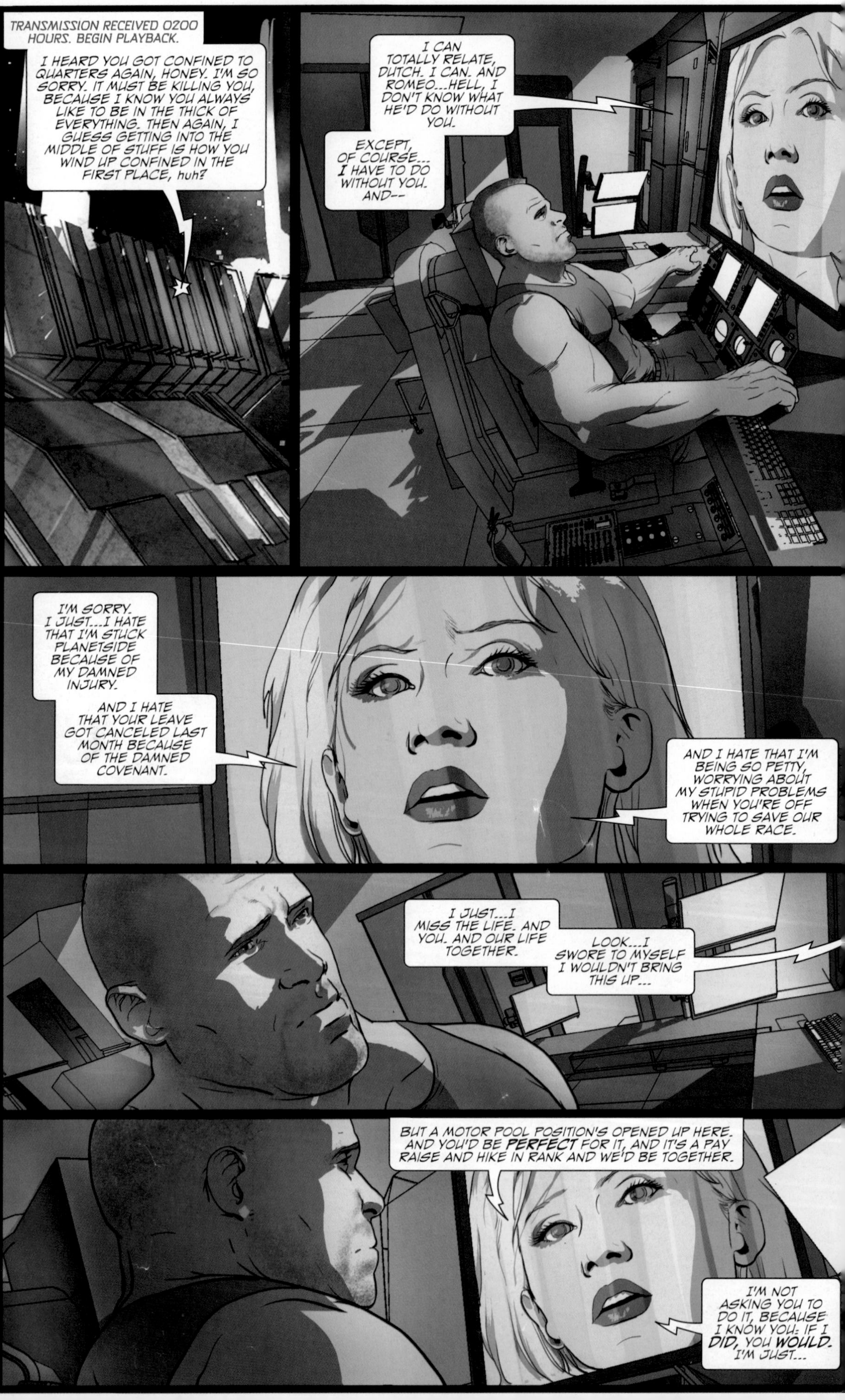
TRANSMISSION RECEIVED 0200 HOURS. BEGIN PLAYBACK.
I HEARD YOU GOT CONFINED TO QUARTERS AGAIN, HONEY. I'M SO SORRY. IT MUST BE KILLING YOU, BECAUSE I KNOW YOU ALWAYS LIKE TO BE IN THE THICK OF EVERYTHING. THEN AGAIN, I GUESS GETTING INTO THE MIDDLE OF STUFF IS HOW YOU WIND UP CONFINED IN THE FIRST PLACE, huh?
I CAN TOTALLY RELATE, DUTCH. I CAN. AND ROMEO...HELL, I DON'T KNOW WHAT HE'D DO WITHOUT YOU.
EXCEPT, OF COURSE... I HAVE TO DO WITHOUT YOU. AND--
I'M SORRY. I JUST...I HATE THAT I'M STUCK PLANETSIDE BECAUSE OF MY DAMNED INJURY.
AND I HATE THAT YOUR LEAVE GOT CANCELED LAST MONTH BECAUSE OF THE DAMNED COVENANT.
AND I HATE THAT I'M BEING SO PETTY, WORRYING ABOUT MY STUPID PROBLEMS WHEN YOU'RE OFF TRYING TO SAVE OUR WHOLE RACE.
I JUST...I MISS THE LIFE. AND YOU. AND OUR LIFE TOGETHER.
LOOK...I SWORE TO MYSELF I WOULDN'T BRING THIS UP...
BUT A MOTOR POOL POSITION'S OPENED UP HERE. AND YOU'D BE PERFECT FOR IT, AND IT'S A PAY RAISE AND HIKE IN RANK AND WE'D BE TOGETHER.
I'M NOT ASKING YOU TO DO IT, BECAUSE I KNOW YOU: IF I DID, YOU WOULD. I'M JUST...

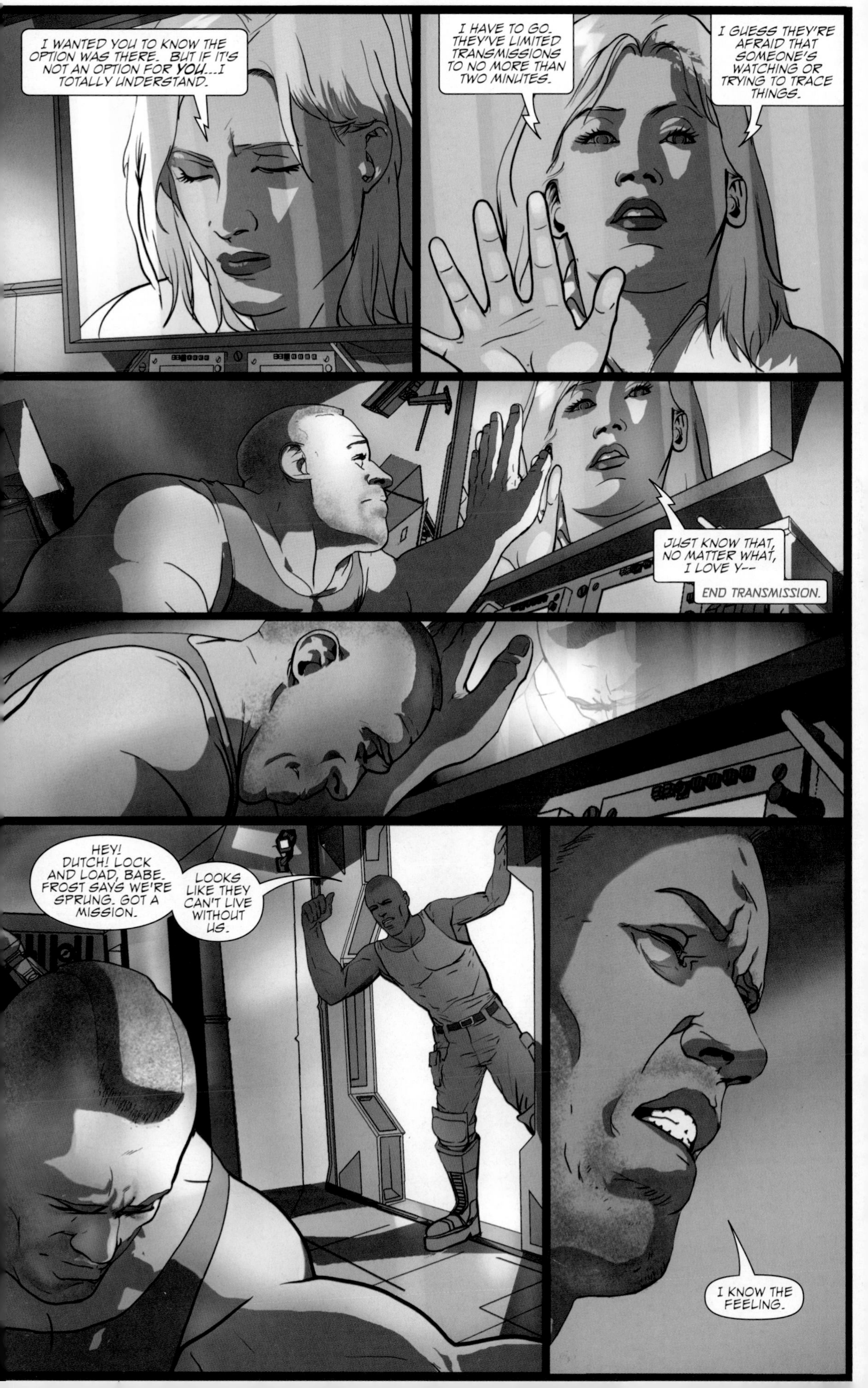
I WANTED YOU TO KNOW THE OPTION WAS THERE. BUT IF IT'S NOT AN OPTION FOR YOU...I TOTALLY UNDERSTAND.
I HAVE TO GO. THEY'VE LIMITED TRANSMISSIONS TO NO MORE THAN TWO MINUTES.
I GUESS THEY'RE AFRAID THAT SOMEONE'S WATCHING OR TRYING TO TRACE THINGS.
JUST KNOW THAT, NO MATTER WHAT, I LOVE Y--
END TRANSMISSION.
HEY! DUTCH! LOCK AND LOAD, BABE. FROST SAYS WE'RE SPRUNG. GOT A MISSION.
LOOKS LIKE THEY CAN'T LIVE WITHOUT US.
I KNOW THE FEELING.

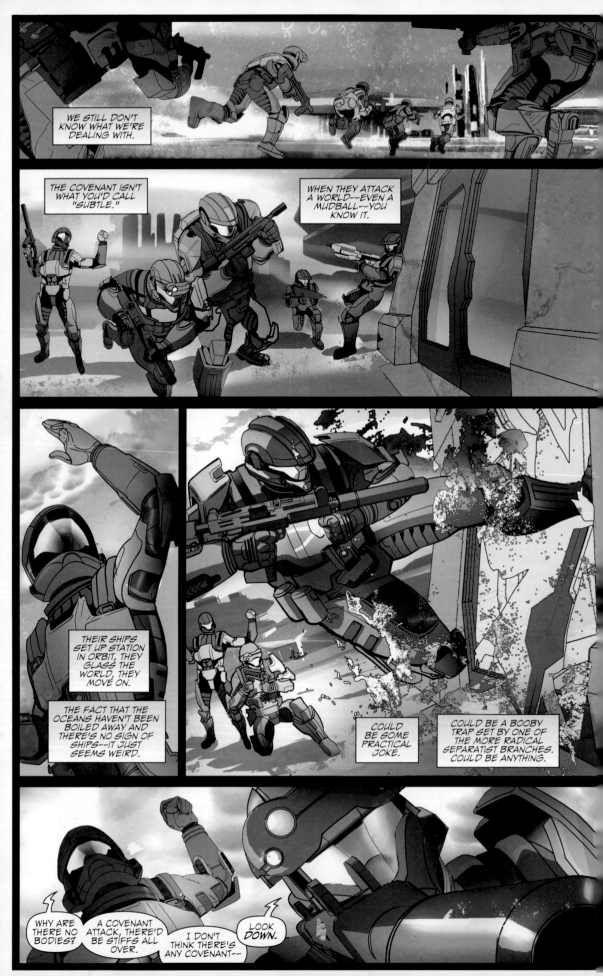

WE STILL DON'T KNOW WHAT WE'RE DEALING WITH.

THE COVENANT ISN'T WHAT YOU'D CALL "SUBTLE."

WHEN THEY ATTACK A WORLD--EVEN A MUDBALL--YOU KNOW IT.

THEIR SHIPS SET UP STATION IN ORBIT, THEY GLASS THE WORLD, THEY MOVE ON.

THE FACT THAT THE OCEANS HAVEN'T BEEN BOILED AWAY AND THERE'S NO SIGN OF SHIPS--IT JUST SEEMS WEIRD.

COULD BE SOME PRACTICAL JOKE.

COULD BE A BOOBY TRAP SET BY ONE OF THE MORE RADICAL SEPARATIST BRANCHES. COULD BE ANYTHING.

WHY ARE THERE NO BODIES?

A COVENANT ATTACK, THERE'D BE STIFFS ALL OVER.

I DON'T THINK THERE'S ANY COVENANT--

LOOK DOWN.

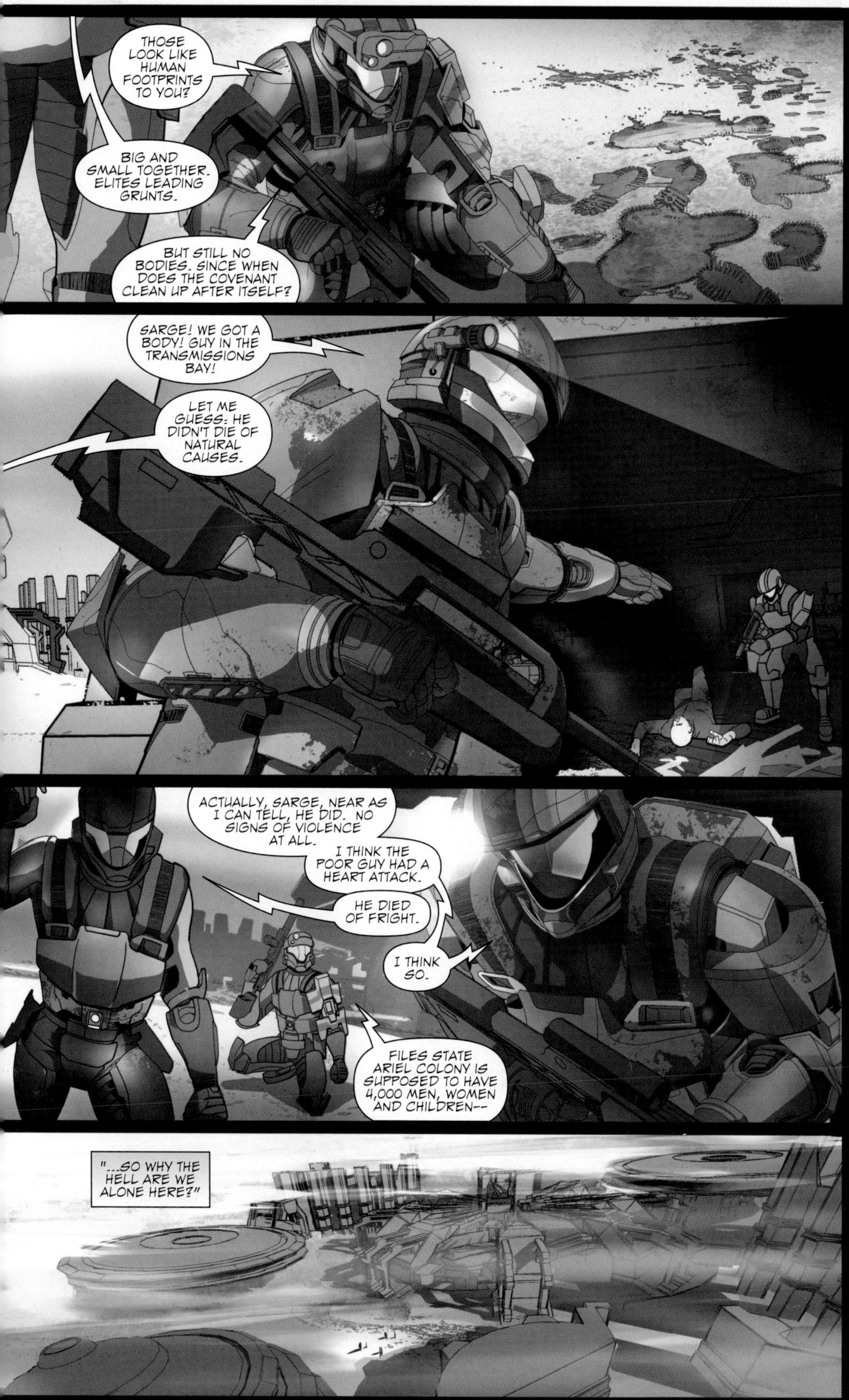
THOSE LOOK LIKE HUMAN FOOTPRINTS TO YOU?
BIG AND SMALL TOGETHER. ELITES LEADING GRUNTS.
BUT STILL NO BODIES. SINCE WHEN DOES THE COVENANT CLEAN UP AFTER ITSELF?
SARGE! WE GOT A BODY! GUY IN THE TRANSMISSIONS BAY!
LET ME GUESS: HE DIDN'T DIE OF NATURAL CAUSES.
ACTUALLY, SARGE, NEAR AS I CAN TELL, HE DID. NO SIGNS OF VIOLENCE AT ALL.
I THINK THE POOR GUY HAD A HEART ATTACK.
HE DIED OF FRIGHT.
I THINK SO.
FILES STATE ARIEL COLONY IS SUPPOSED TO HAVE 4,000 MEN, WOMEN AND CHILDREN--
"...SO WHY THE HELL ARE WE ALONE HERE?"

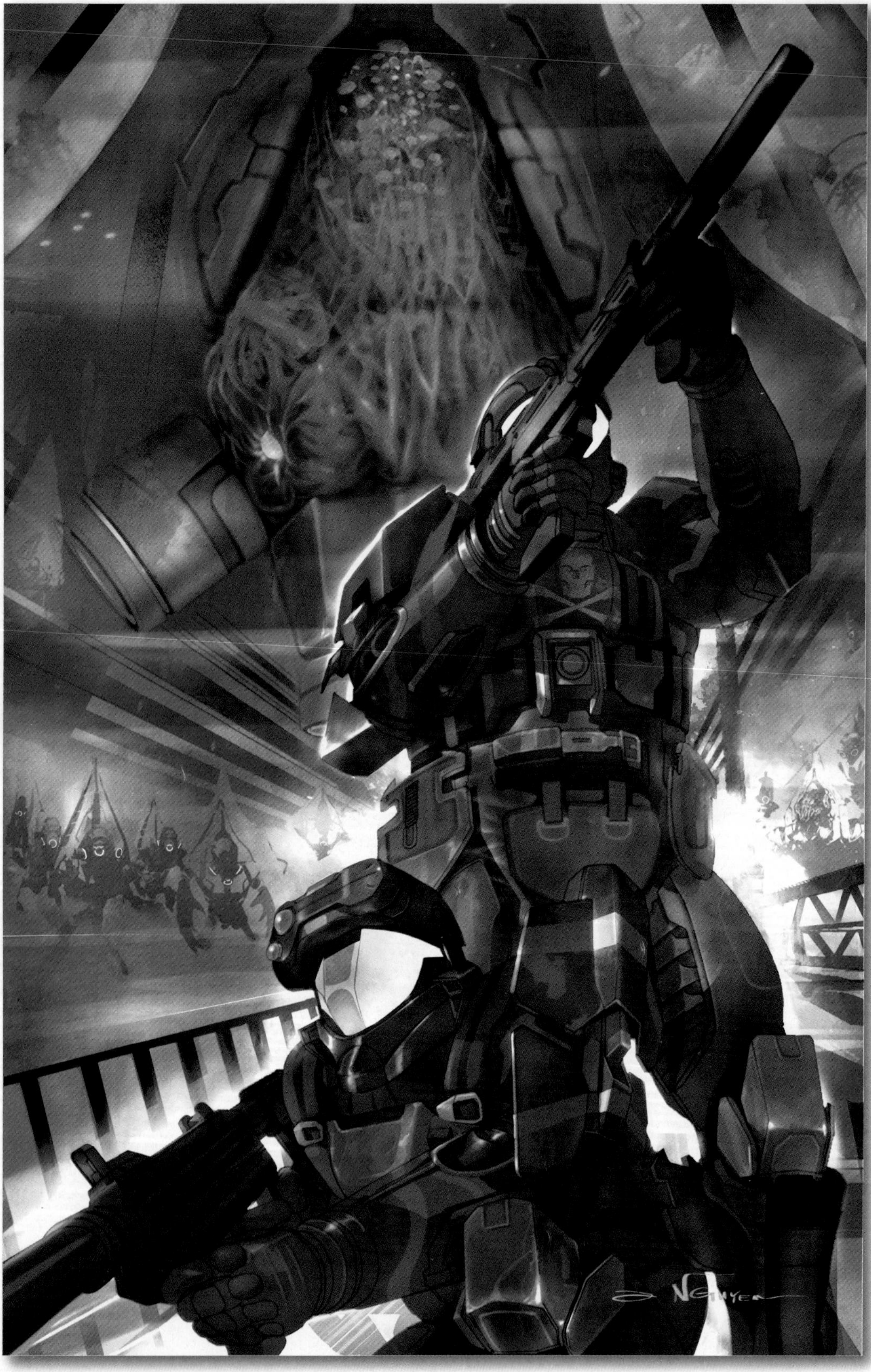

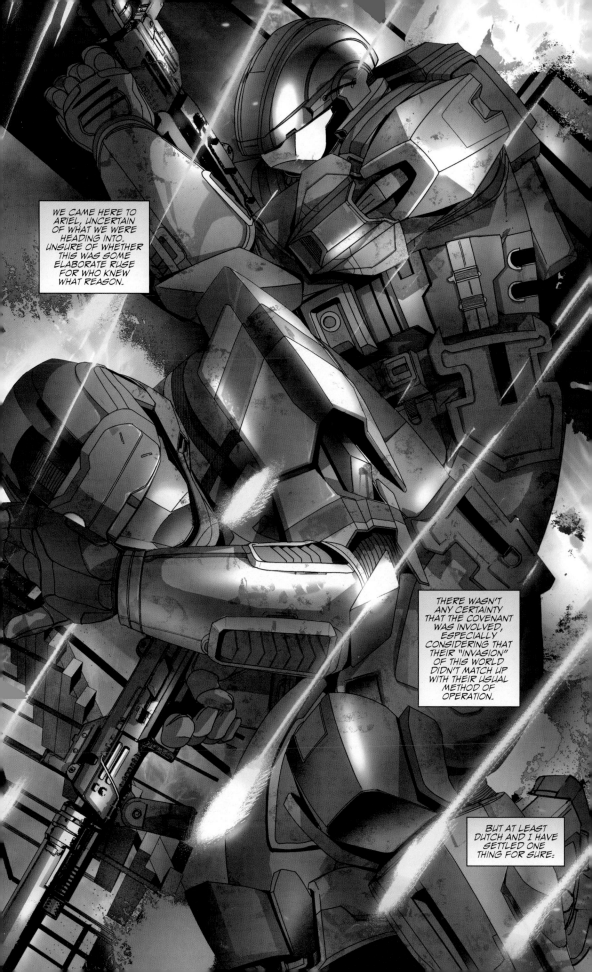

WE CAME HERE TO ARIEL, UNCERTAIN OF WHAT WE WERE HEADING INTO. UNSURE OF WHETHER THIS WAS SOME ELABORATE RUSE FOR WHO KNEW WHAT REASON.

THERE WASN'T ANY CERTAINTY THAT THE COVENANT WAS INVOLVED, ESPECIALLY CONSIDERING THAT THEIR "INVASION" OF THIS WORLD DIDN'T MATCH UP WITH THEIR USUAL METHOD OF OPERATION.

BUT AT LEAST DUTCH AND I HAVE SETTLED ONE THING FOR SURE:

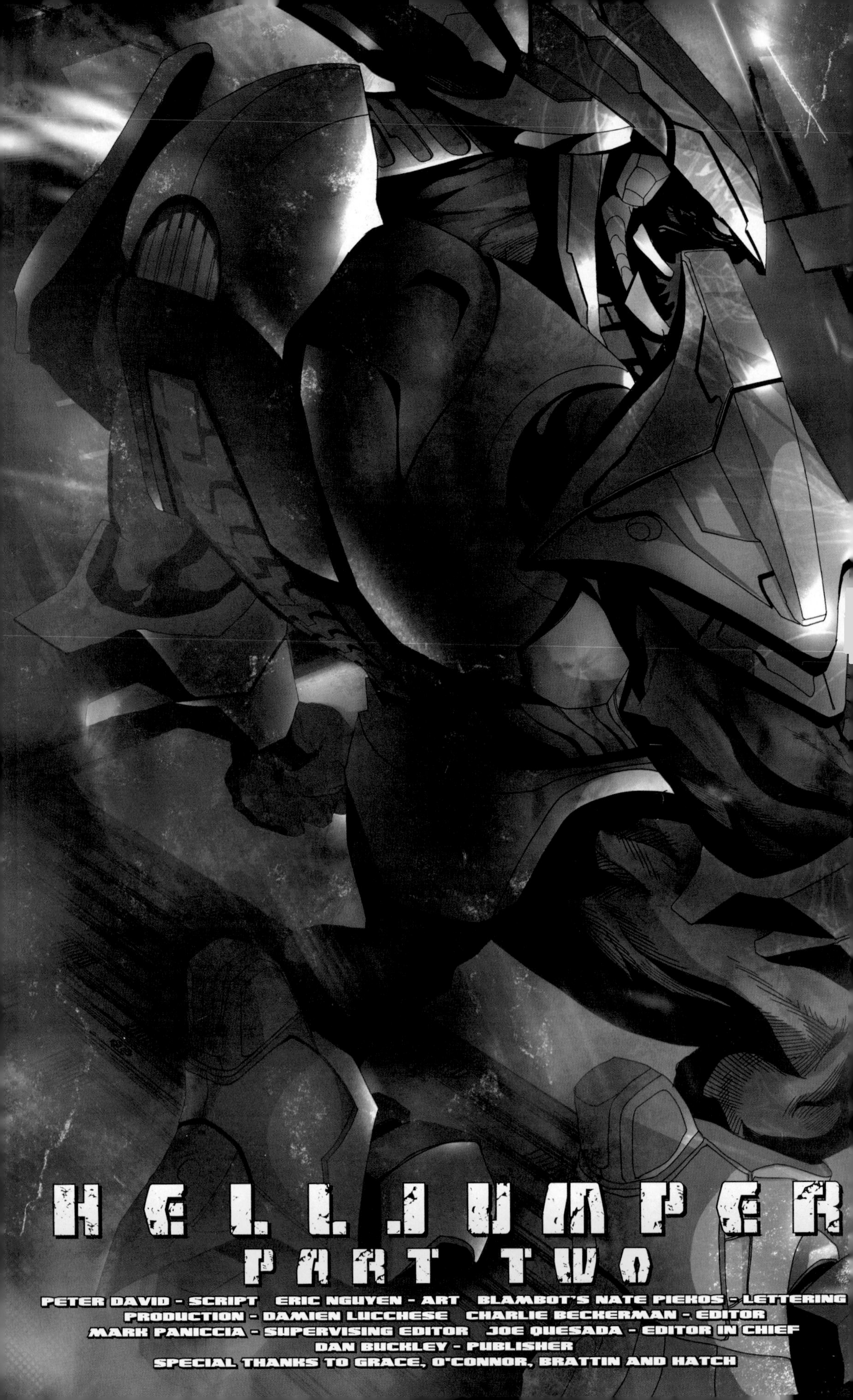
H.E.L.L.J.U.M.P.E.R
PART TWO
PETER DAVID - SCRIPT   ERIC NGUYEN - ART   BLAMBOT'S NATE PIEKOS - LETTERING
PRODUCTION - DAMIEN LUCCHESE   CHARLIE BECKERMAN - EDITOR
MARK PANICCIA - SUPERVISING EDITOR   JOE QUESADA - EDITOR IN CHIEF
DAN BUCKLEY - PUBLISHER
SPECIAL THANKS TO GRACE, O'CONNOR, BRATTIN AND HATCH

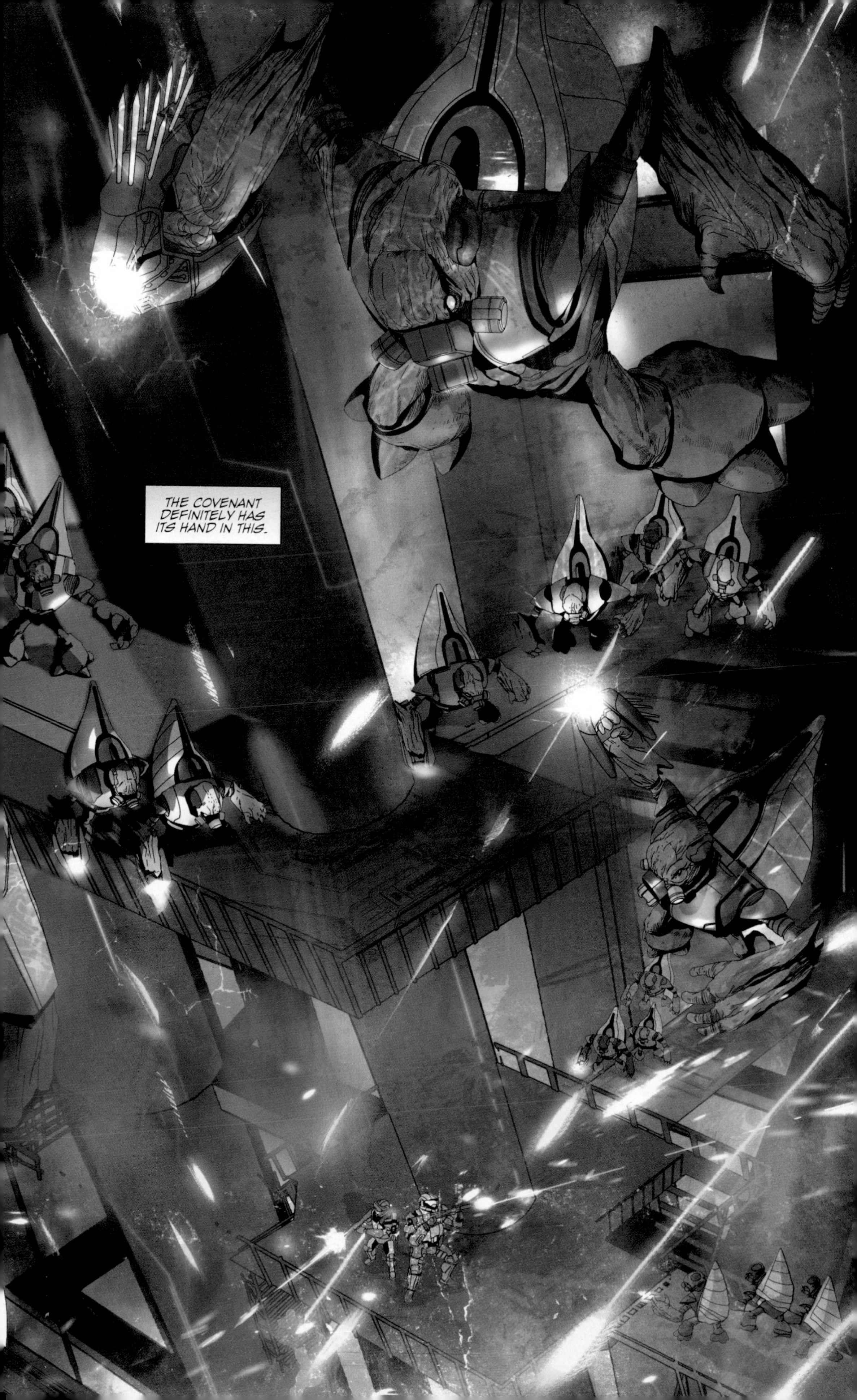
THE COVENANT DEFINITELY HAS ITS HAND IN THIS.

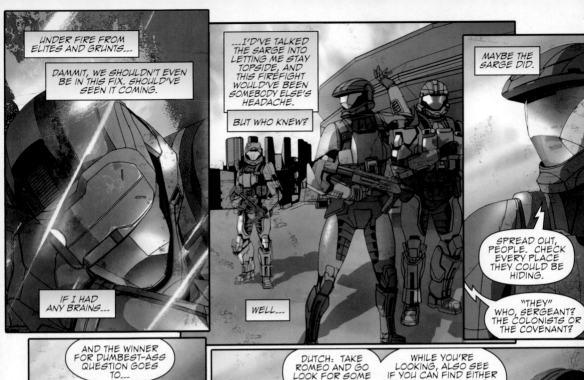

UNDER FIRE FROM ELITES AND GRUNTS...

DAMMIT, WE SHOULDN'T EVEN BE IN THIS FIX. SHOULD'VE SEEN IT COMING.

IF I HAD ANY BRAINS....

...I'D'VE TALKED THE SARGE INTO LETTING ME STAY TOPSIDE, AND THIS FIREFIGHT WOULD'VE BEEN SOMEBODY ELSE'S HEADACHE.

BUT WHO KNEW?

WELL....

MAYBE THE SARGE DID.

SPREAD OUT, PEOPLE. CHECK EVERY PLACE THEY COULD BE HIDING.

"THEY" WHO, SERGEANT? THE COLONISTS OR THE COVENANT?

AND THE WINNER FOR DUMBEST-ASS QUESTION GOES TO...

JUST LOOKING FOR CLARIFICATION, SERGEANT.

DUTCH: TAKE ROMEO AND GO LOOK FOR SOME "CLARIFICATION".

WHILE YOU'RE LOOKING, ALSO SEE IF YOU CAN FIND EITHER CIVILIANS OR HOSTILES. YOU KNOW WHICH ONES TO SHOOT, RIGHT?

SURE.

MICHAELS, WITH ME.

ROMEO, DUTCH, ENJOY YOUR TIME TOGETHER WHILE YOU CAN.

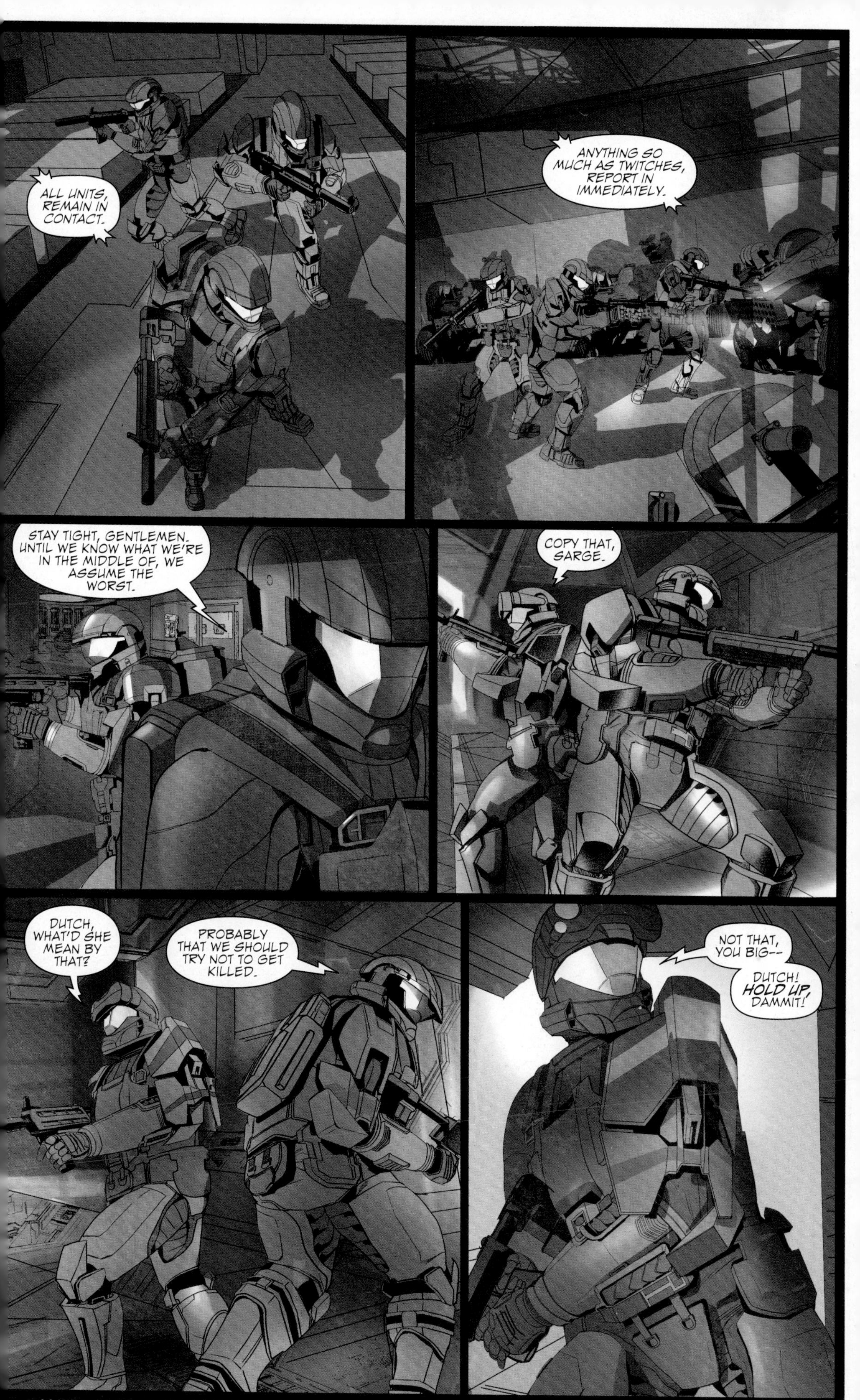
ALL UNITS, REMAIN IN CONTACT.
ANYTHING SO MUCH AS TWITCHES, REPORT IN IMMEDIATELY.
STAY TIGHT, GENTLEMEN. UNTIL WE KNOW WHAT WE'RE IN THE MIDDLE OF, WE ASSUME THE WORST.
COPY THAT, SARGE.
DUTCH, WHAT'D SHE MEAN BY THAT?
PROBABLY THAT WE SHOULD TRY NOT TO GET KILLED.
NOT THAT, YOU BIG--
DUTCH! HOLD UP, DAMMIT!

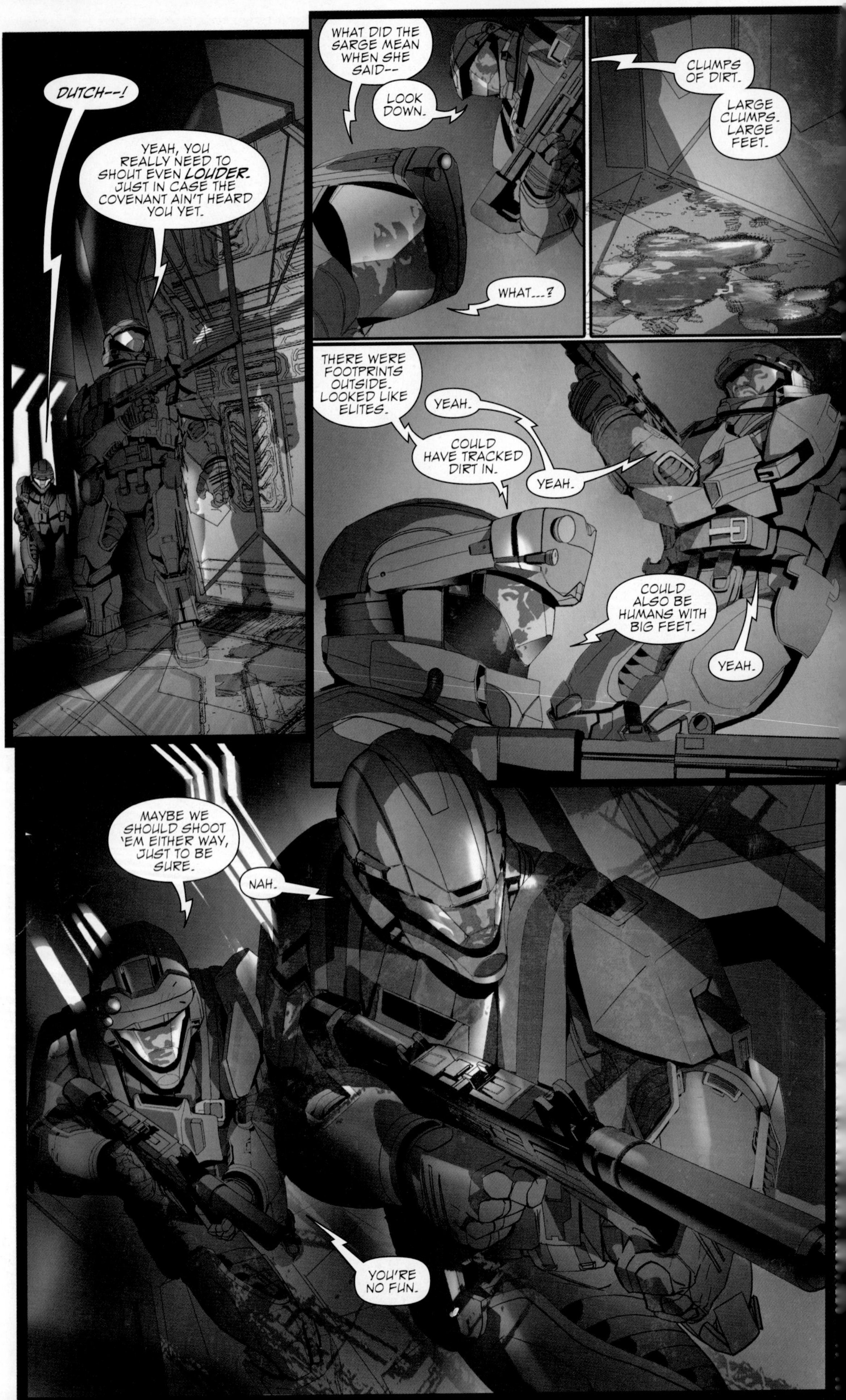
DUTCH--!
YEAH, YOU REALLY NEED TO SHOUT EVEN LOUDER. JUST IN CASE THE COVENANT AIN'T HEARD YOU YET.
WHAT DID THE SARGE MEAN WHEN SHE SAID--
LOOK DOWN.
WHAT...?
CLUMPS OF DIRT.
LARGE CLUMPS. LARGE FEET.
THERE WERE FOOTPRINTS OUTSIDE. LOOKED LIKE ELITES.
YEAH.
COULD HAVE TRACKED DIRT IN.
YEAH.
COULD ALSO BE HUMANS WITH BIG FEET.
YEAH.
MAYBE WE SHOULD SHOOT 'EM EITHER WAY, JUST TO BE SURE.
NAH.
YOU'RE NO FUN.

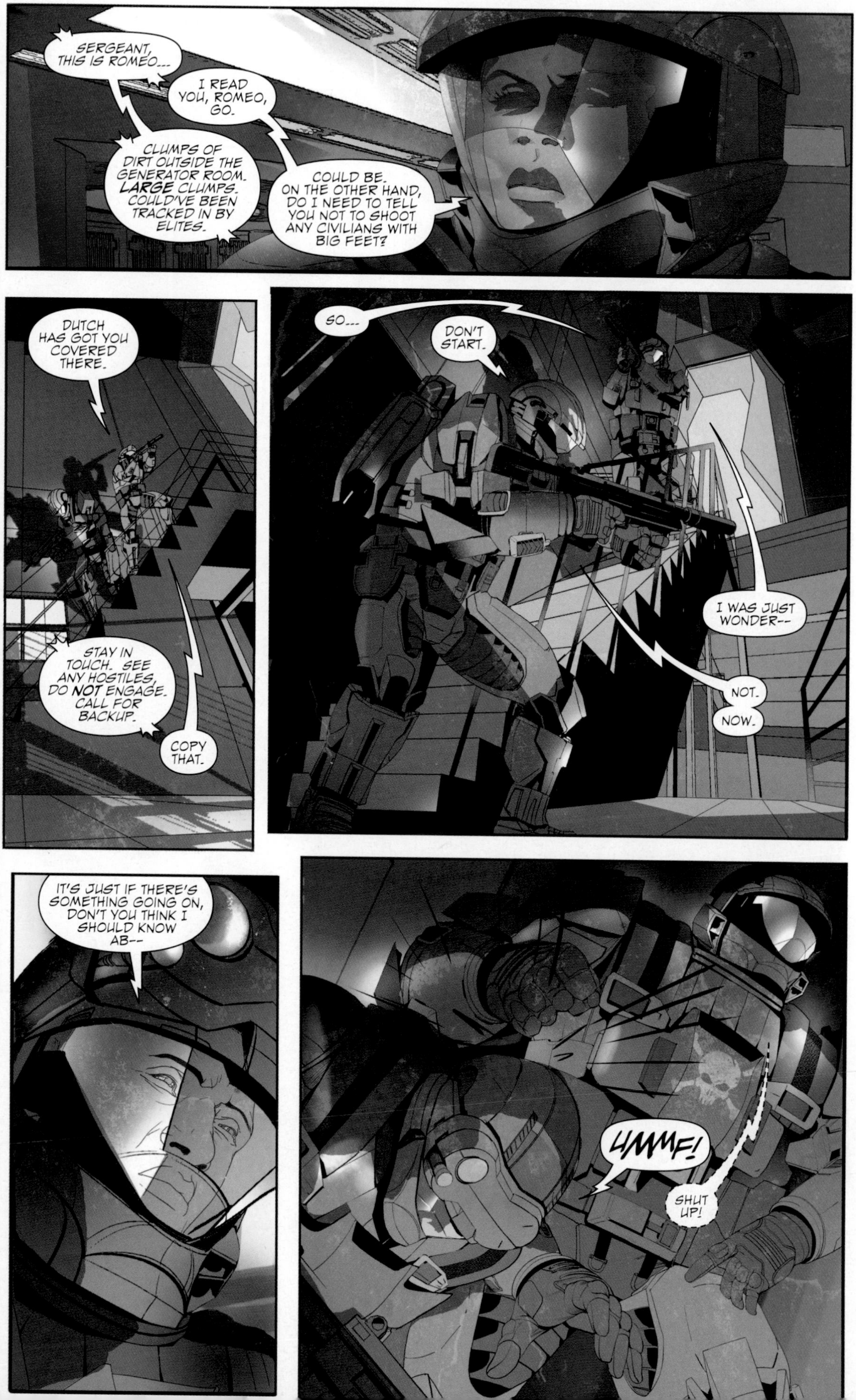
SERGEANT, THIS IS ROMEO...
I READ YOU, ROMEO, GO.
CLUMPS OF DIRT OUTSIDE THE GENERATOR ROOM. LARGE CLUMPS. COULD'VE BEEN TRACKED IN BY ELITES.
COULD BE. ON THE OTHER HAND, DO I NEED TO TELL YOU NOT TO SHOOT ANY CIVILIANS WITH BIG FEET?
DUTCH HAS GOT YOU COVERED THERE.
STAY IN TOUCH. SEE ANY HOSTILES, DO NOT ENGAGE. CALL FOR BACKUP.
COPY THAT.
SO...
DON'T START.
I WAS JUST WONDER--
NOT.
NOW.
IT'S JUST IF THERE'S SOMETHING GOING ON, DON'T YOU THINK I SHOULD KNOW AB--
UMMF!
SHUT UP!

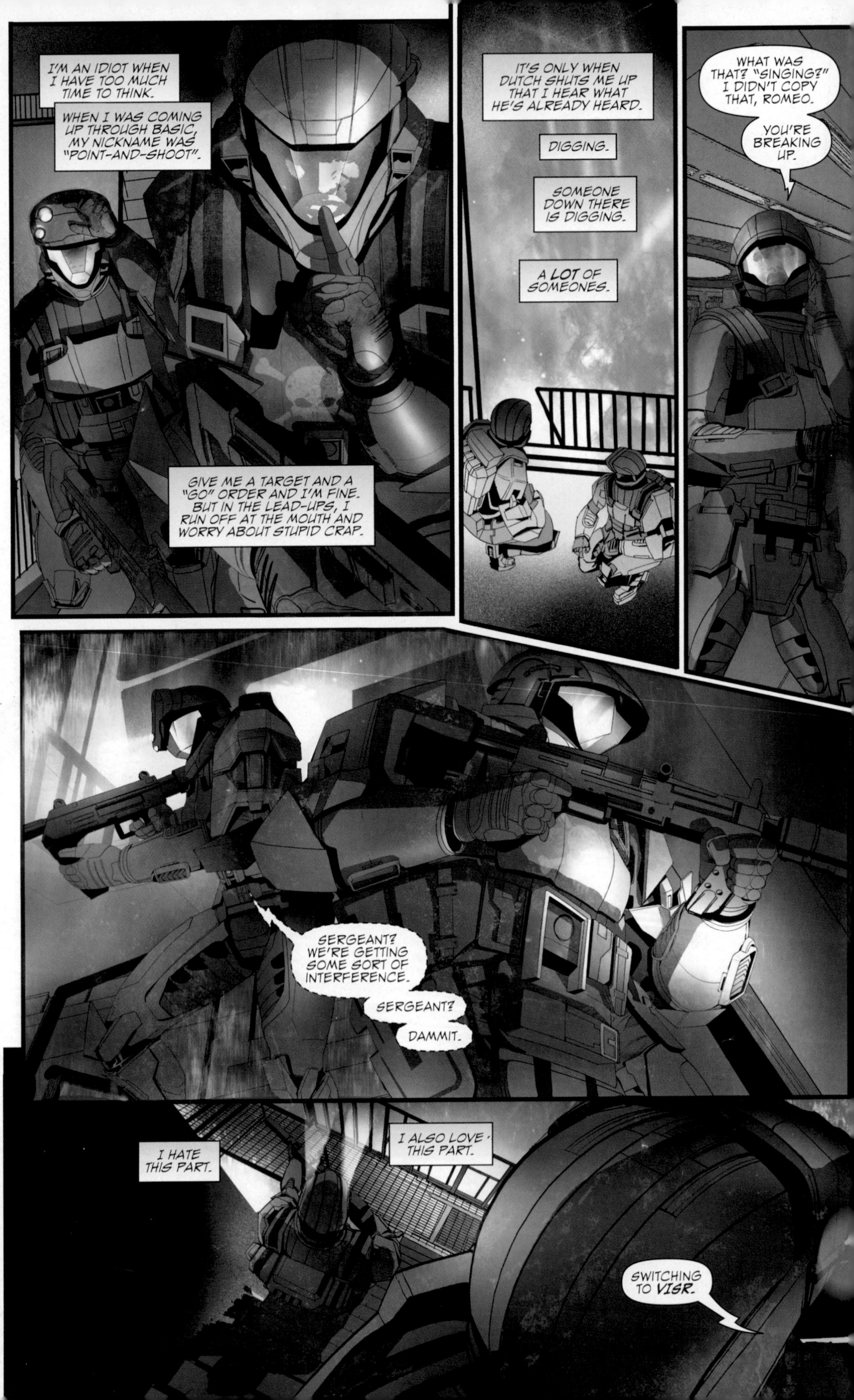
I'M AN IDIOT WHEN I HAVE TOO MUCH TIME TO THINK.
WHEN I WAS COMING UP THROUGH BASIC, MY NICKNAME WAS "POINT-AND-SHOOT".
GIVE ME A TARGET AND A "GO" ORDER AND I'M FINE. BUT IN THE LEAD-UPS, I RUN OFF AT THE MOUTH AND WORRY ABOUT STUPID CRAP.
IT'S ONLY WHEN DUTCH SHUTS ME UP THAT I HEAR WHAT HE'S ALREADY HEARD.
DIGGING.
SOMEONE DOWN THERE IS DIGGING.
A LOT OF SOMEONES.
WHAT WAS THAT? "SINGING?" I DIDN'T COPY THAT, ROMEO.
YOU'RE BREAKING UP.
SERGEANT? WE'RE GETTING SOME SORT OF INTERFERENCE.
SERGEANT?
DAMMIT.
I HATE THIS PART.
I ALSO LOVE THIS PART.
SWITCHING TO VISR.

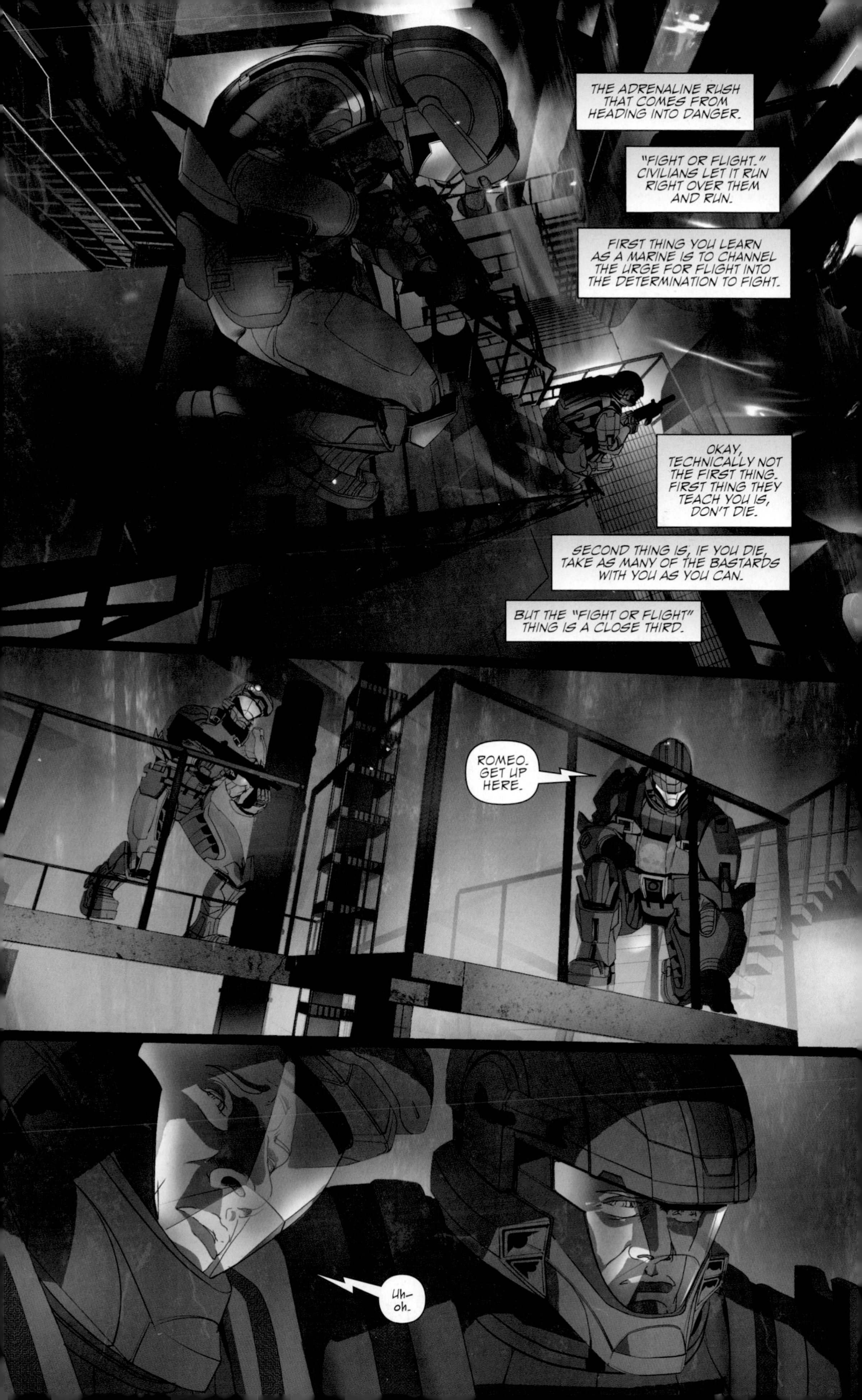
THE ADRENALINE RUSH THAT COMES FROM HEADING INTO DANGER.
"FIGHT OR FLIGHT." CIVILIANS LET IT RUN RIGHT OVER THEM AND RUN.
FIRST THING YOU LEARN AS A MARINE IS TO CHANNEL THE URGE FOR FLIGHT INTO THE DETERMINATION TO FIGHT.
OKAY, TECHNICALLY NOT THE FIRST THING. FIRST THING THEY TEACH YOU IS, DON'T DIE.
SECOND THING IS, IF YOU DIE, TAKE AS MANY OF THE BASTARDS WITH YOU AS YOU CAN.
BUT THE "FIGHT OR FLIGHT" THING IS A CLOSE THIRD.
ROMEO. GET UP HERE.
Uh-oh.

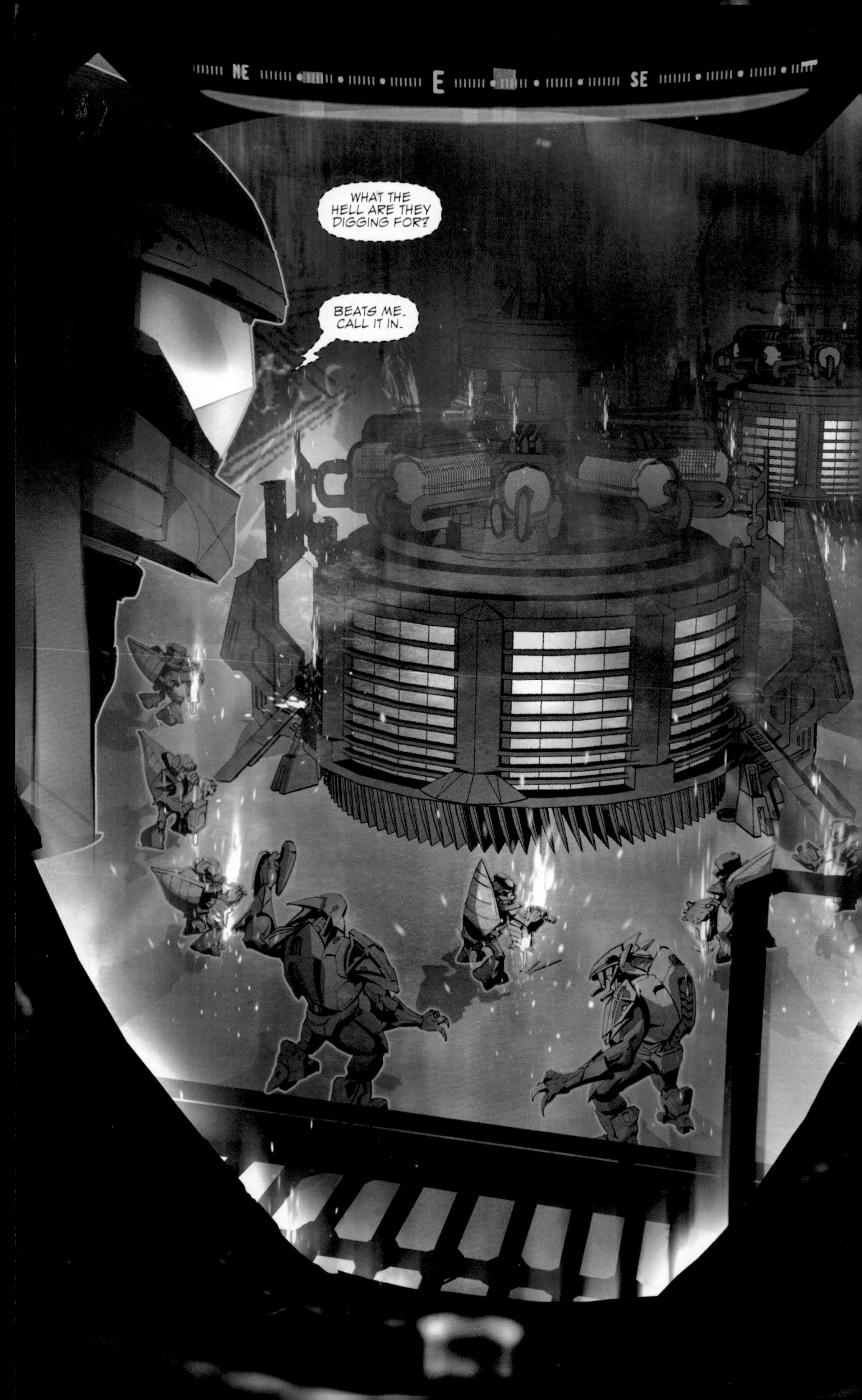
NE
E
SE
WHAT THE HELL ARE THEY DIGGING FOR?
BEATS ME. CALL IT IN.

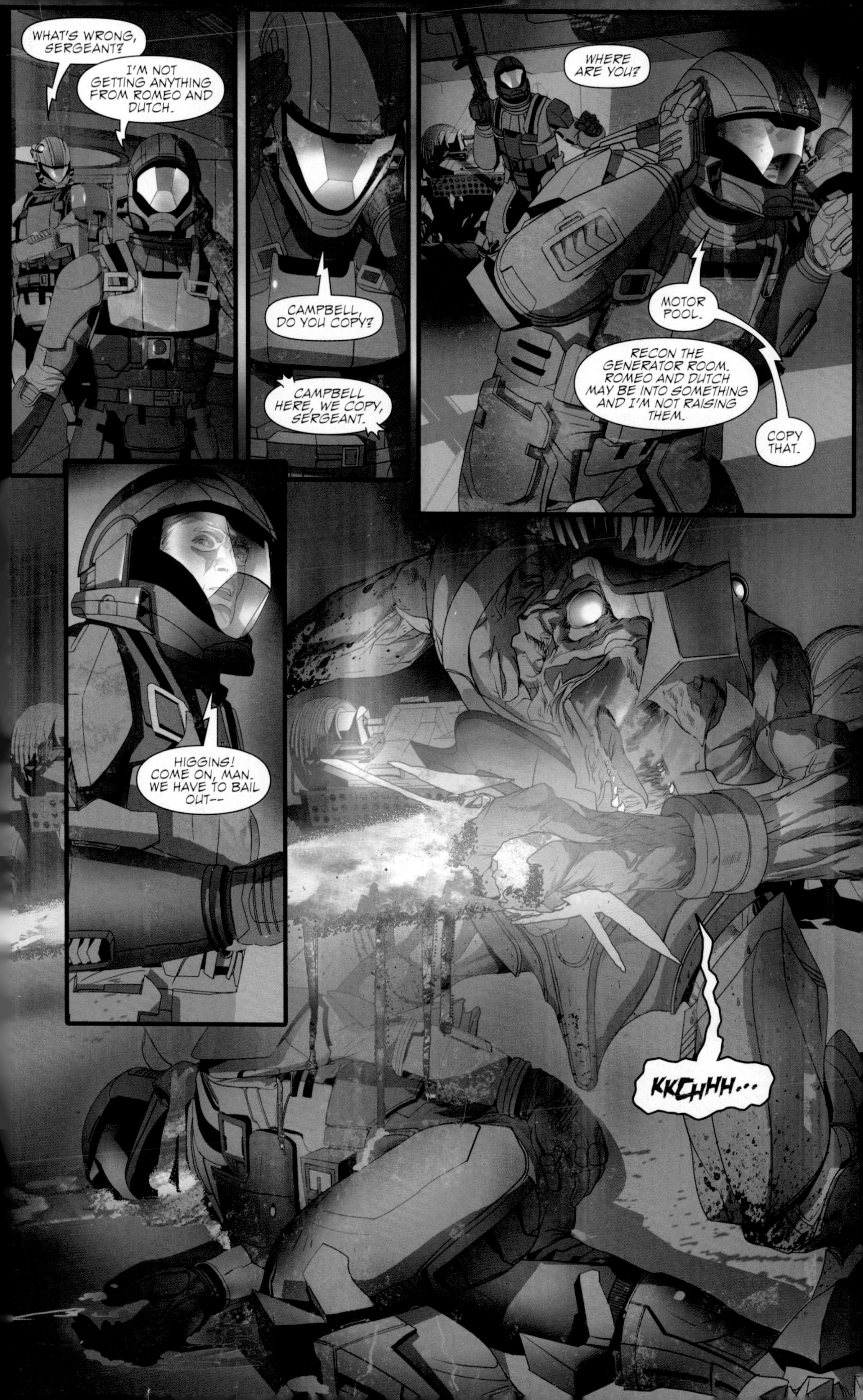
WHAT'S WRONG, SERGEANT?
I'M NOT GETTING ANYTHING FROM ROMEO AND DUTCH.
CAMPBELL, DO YOU COPY?
CAMPBELL HERE, WE COPY, SERGEANT.
WHERE ARE YOU?
MOTOR POOL.
RECON THE GENERATOR ROOM. ROMEO AND DUTCH MAY BE INTO SOMETHING AND I'M NOT RAISING THEM.
COPY THAT.
HIGGINS! COME ON, MAN. WE HAVE TO BAIL OUT--
KKCHHH...

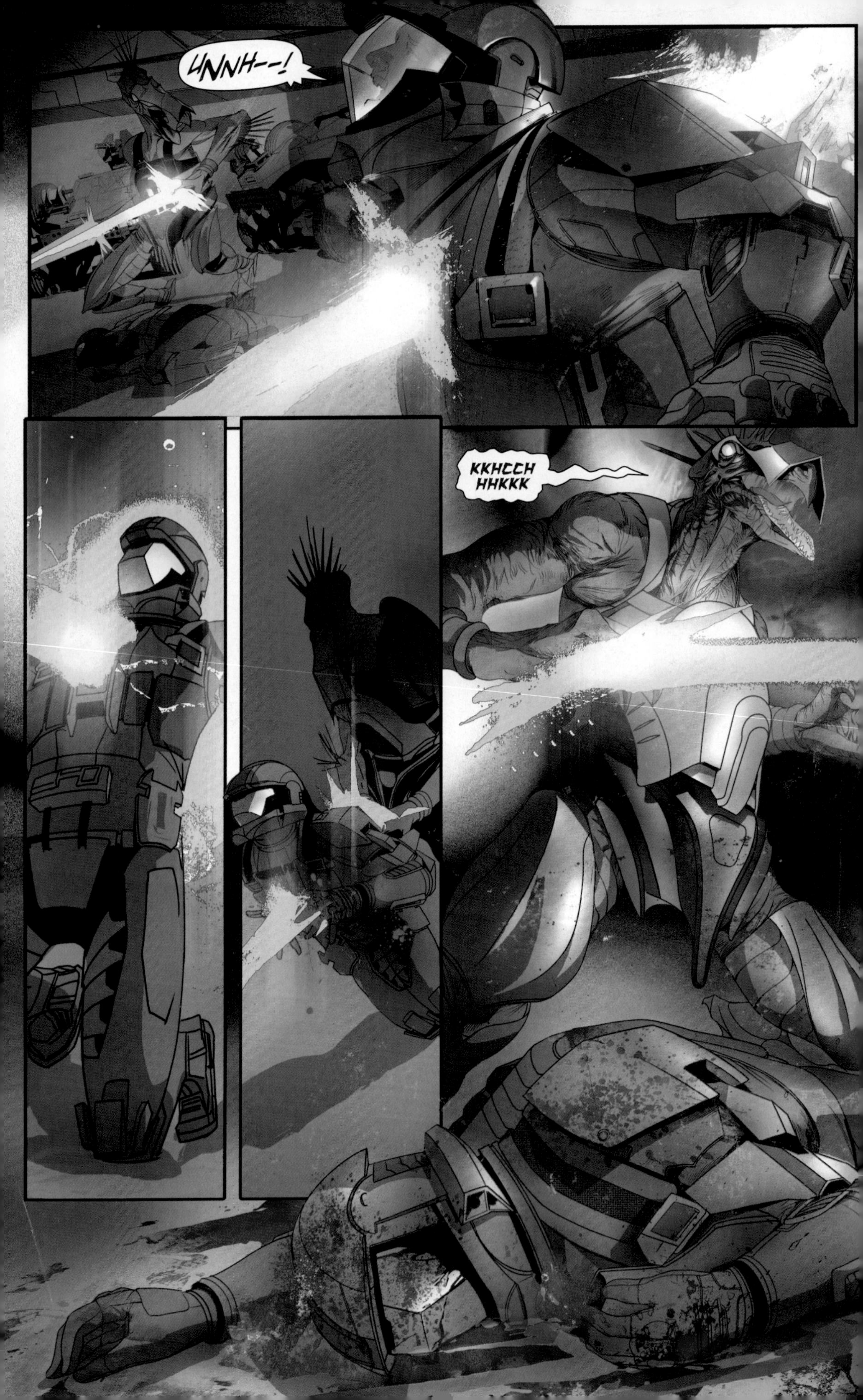
UNNH--!
KKHCCH HHKKK

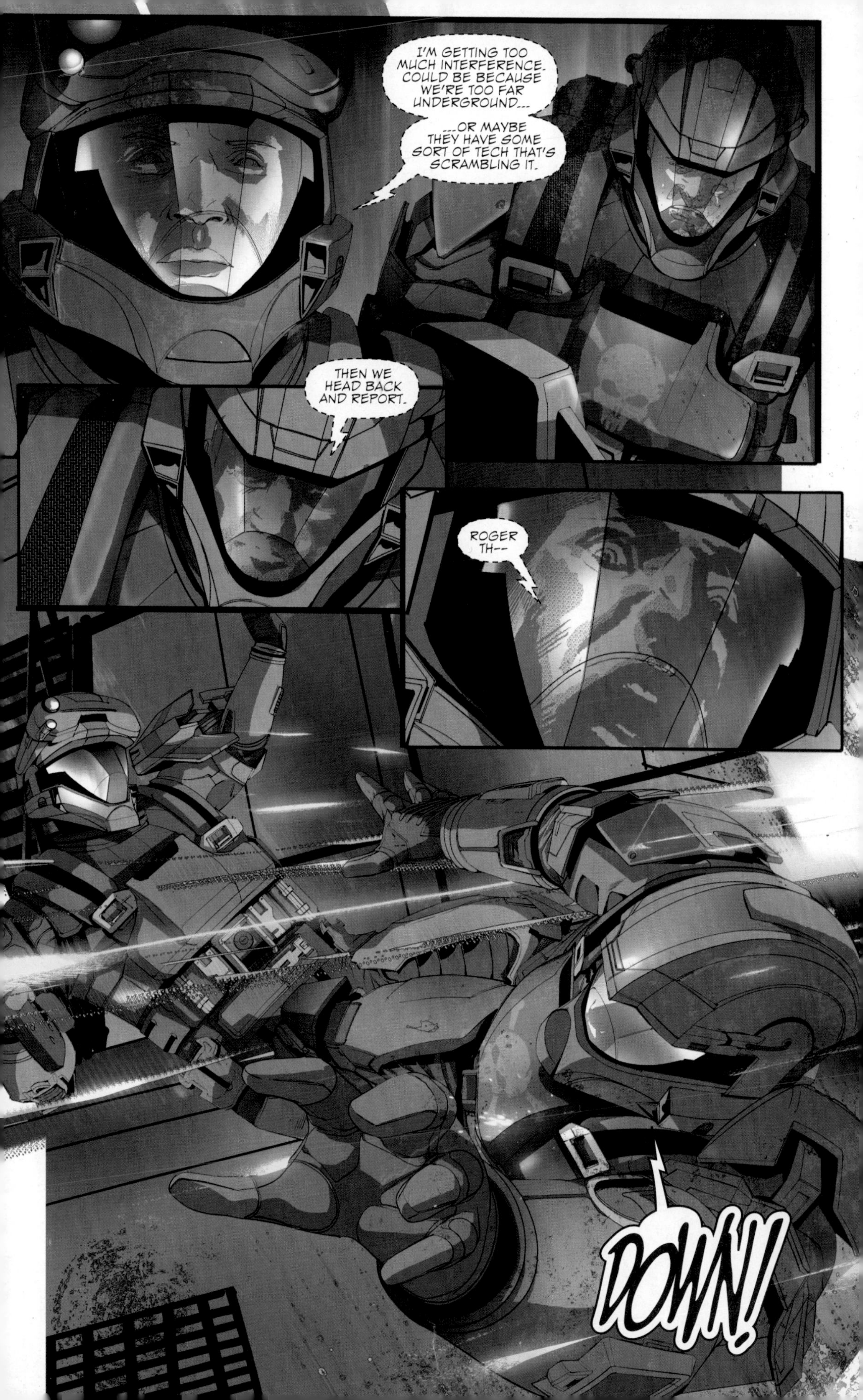
I'M GETTING TOO MUCH INTERFERENCE. COULD BE BECAUSE WE'RE TOO FAR UNDERGROUND...
...OR MAYBE THEY HAVE SOME SORT OF TECH THAT'S SCRAMBLING IT.
THEN WE HEAD BACK AND REPORT.
ROGER TH--
DOWN!

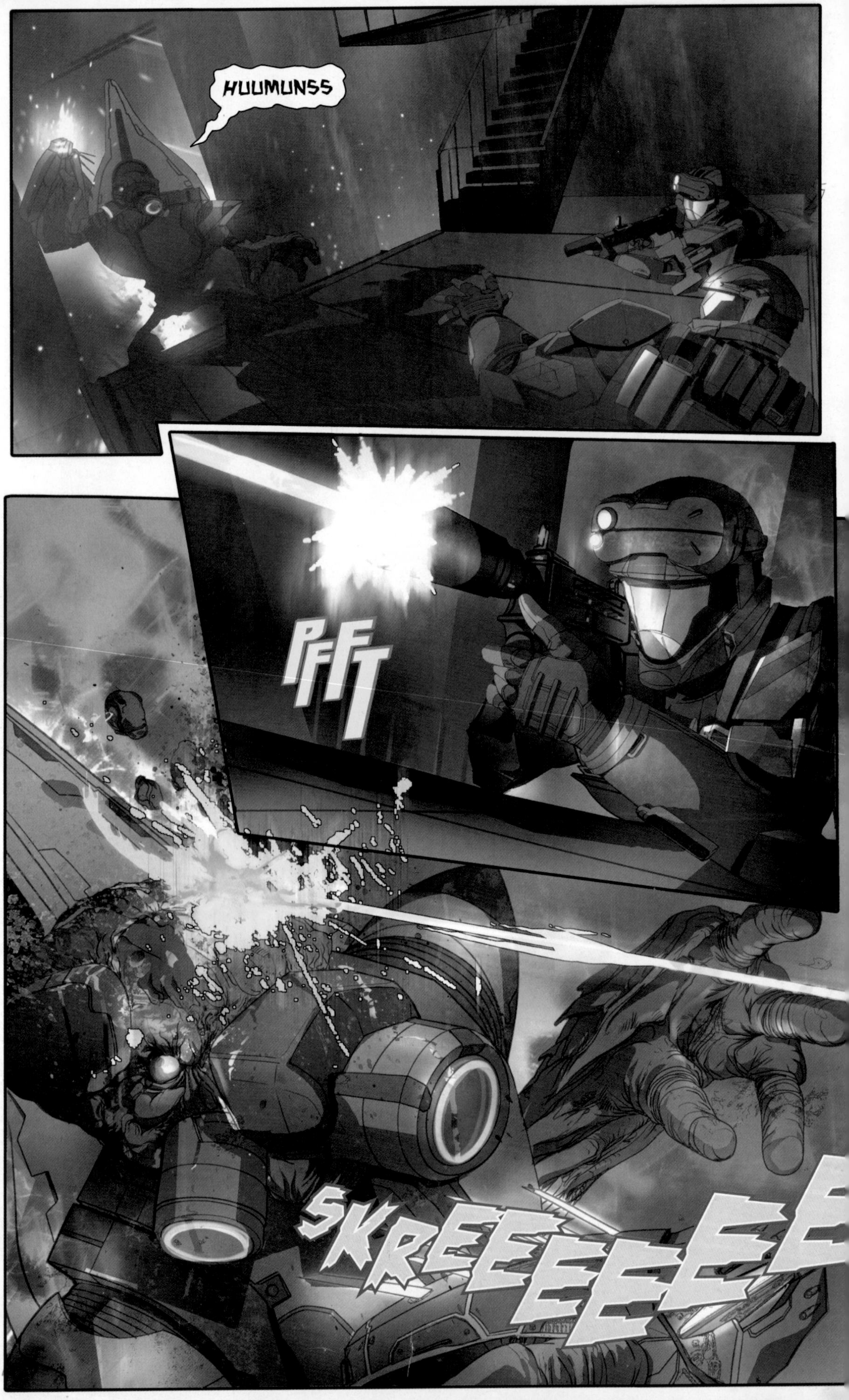
HUUMUNSS
PFFT
SKREEEEEEE

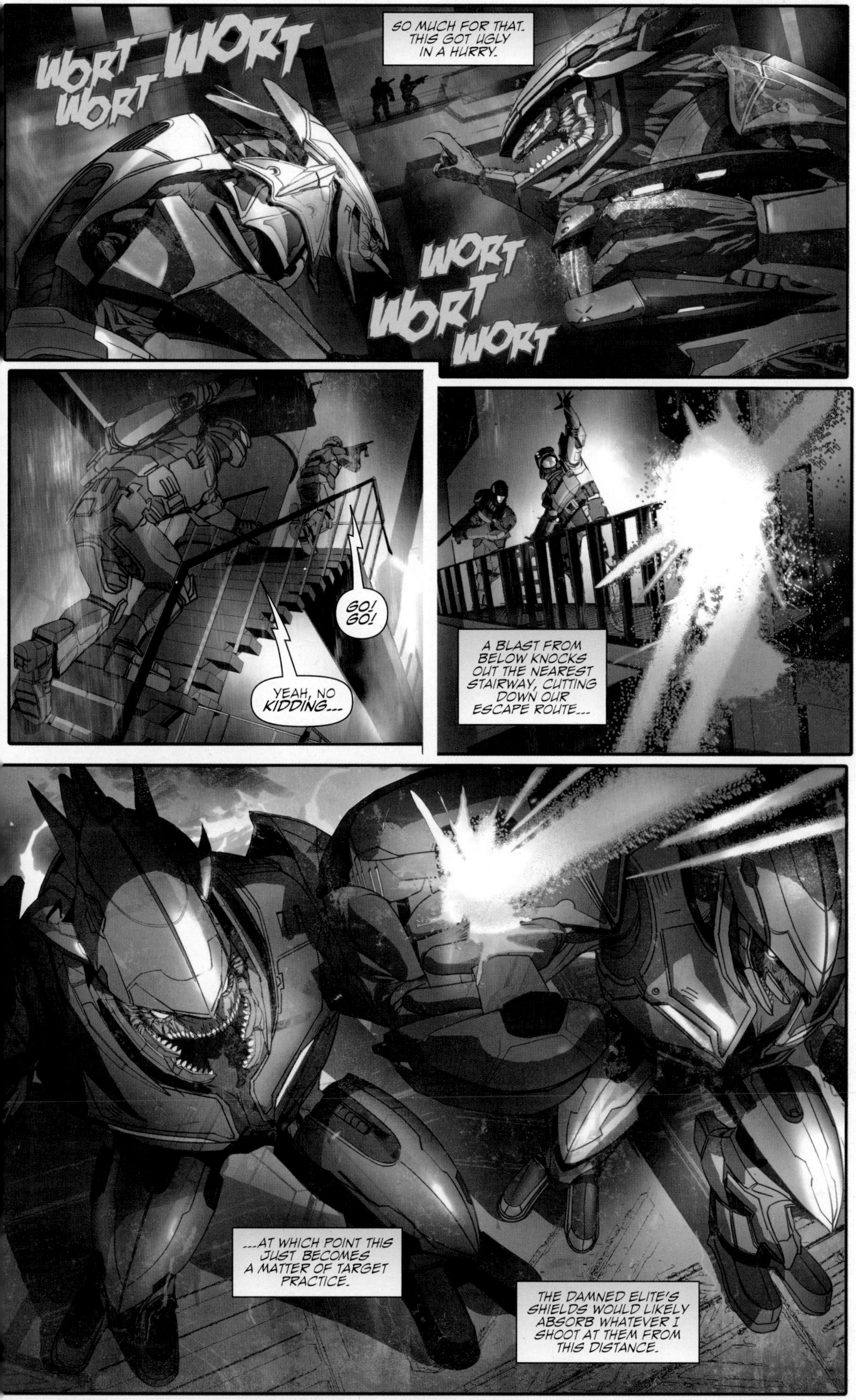
WORT WORT WORT
WORT
SO MUCH FOR THAT. THIS GOT UGLY IN A HURRY.
WORT WORT WORT
GO! GO!
YEAH, NO KIDDING...
A BLAST FROM BELOW KNOCKS OUT THE NEAREST STAIRWAY, CUTTING DOWN OUR ESCAPE ROUTE...
...AT WHICH POINT THIS JUST BECOMES A MATTER OF TARGET PRACTICE.
THE DAMNED ELITE'S SHIELDS WOULD LIKELY ABSORB WHATEVER I SHOOT AT THEM FROM THIS DISTANCE.

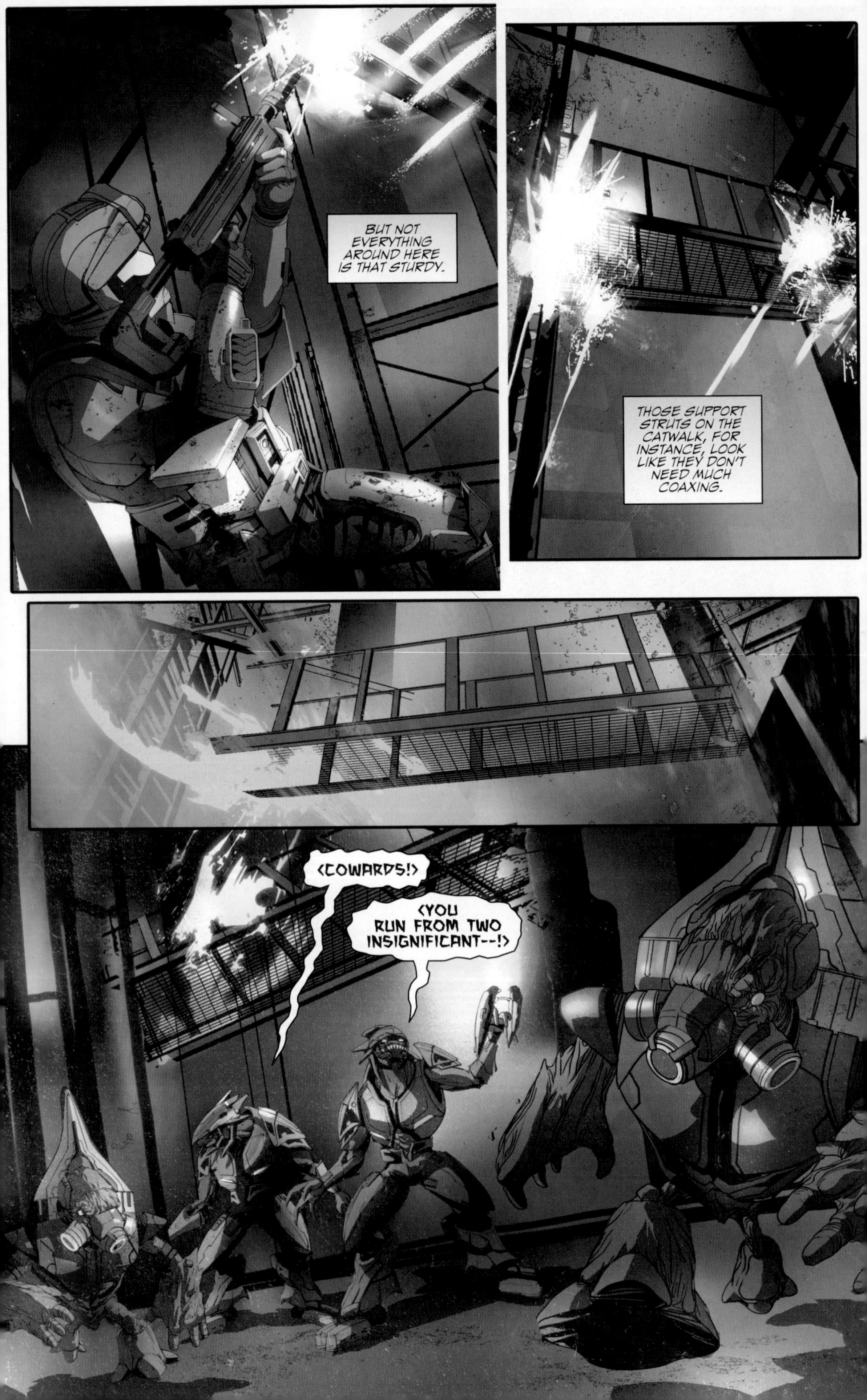
BUT NOT EVERYTHING AROUND HERE IS THAT STURDY.
THOSE SUPPORT STRUTS ON THE CATWALK, FOR INSTANCE, LOOK LIKE THEY DON'T NEED MUCH COAXING.
<COWARDS!>
<YOU RUN FROM TWO INSIGNIFICANT--!>

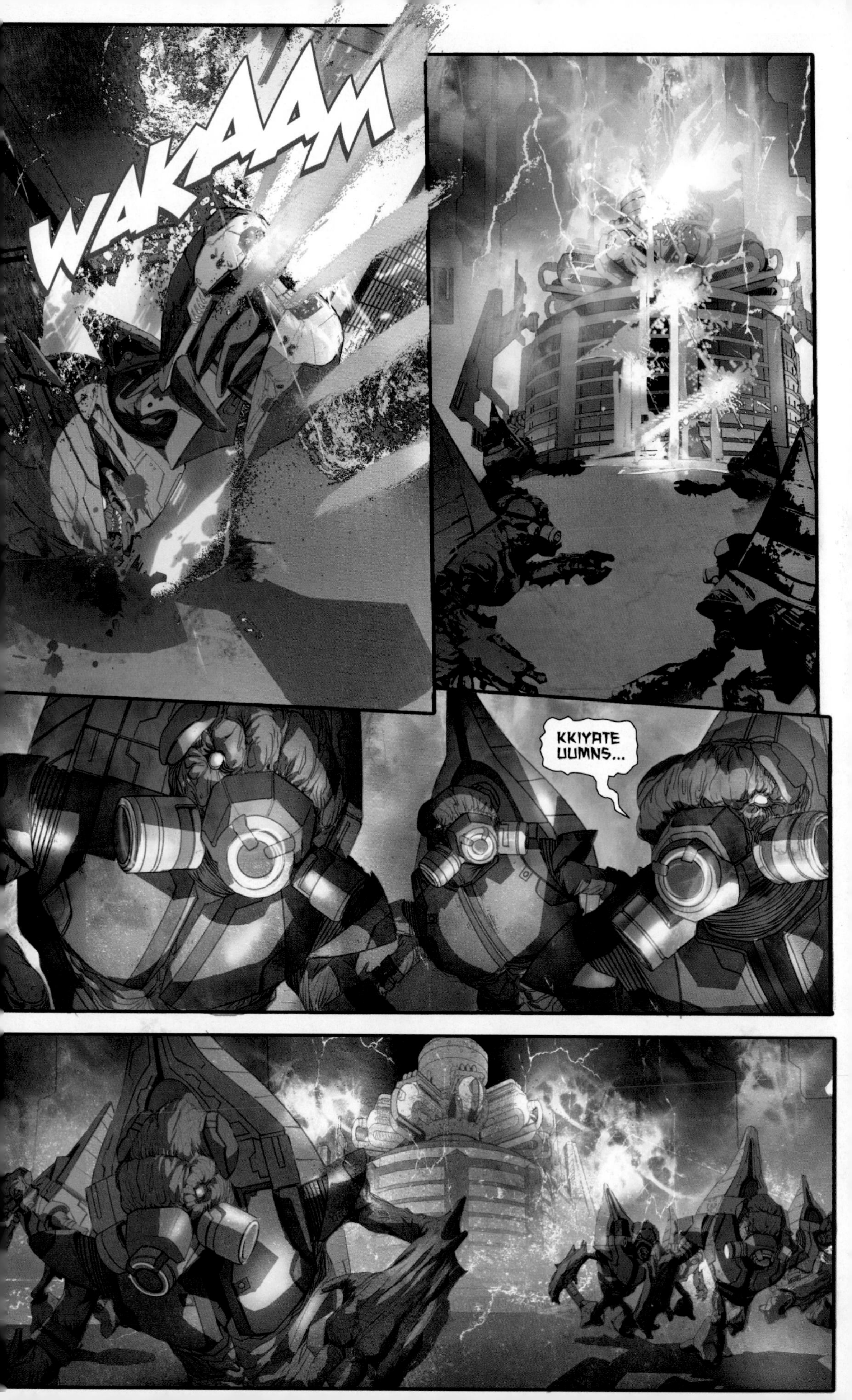
WAKAAM
KKIYATE UUMNS...

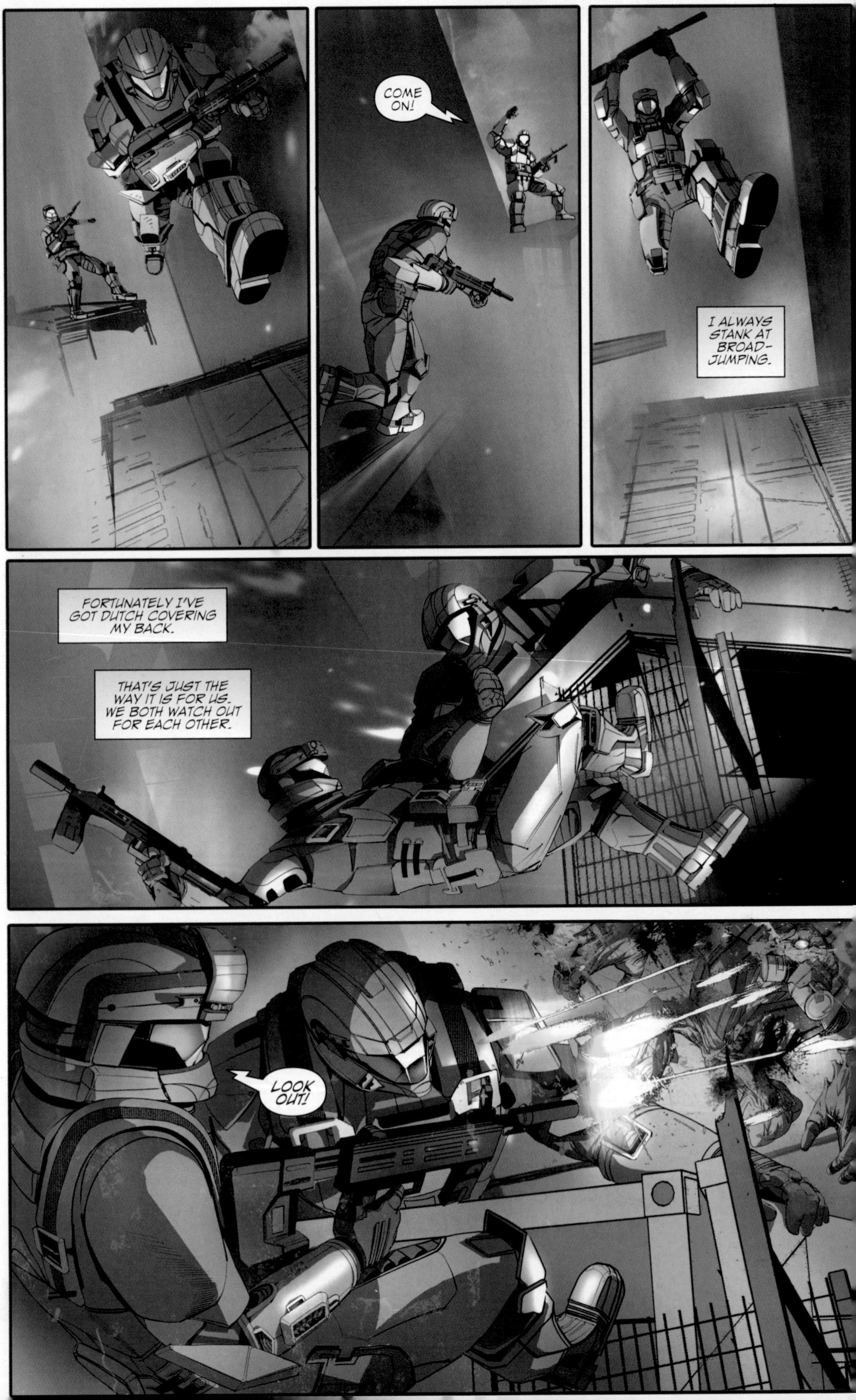
COME ON!
I ALWAYS STANK AT BROAD-JUMPING.
FORTUNATELY I'VE GOT DUTCH COVERING MY BACK.
THAT'S JUST THE WAY IT IS FOR US. WE BOTH WATCH OUT FOR EACH OTHER.
LOOK OUT!

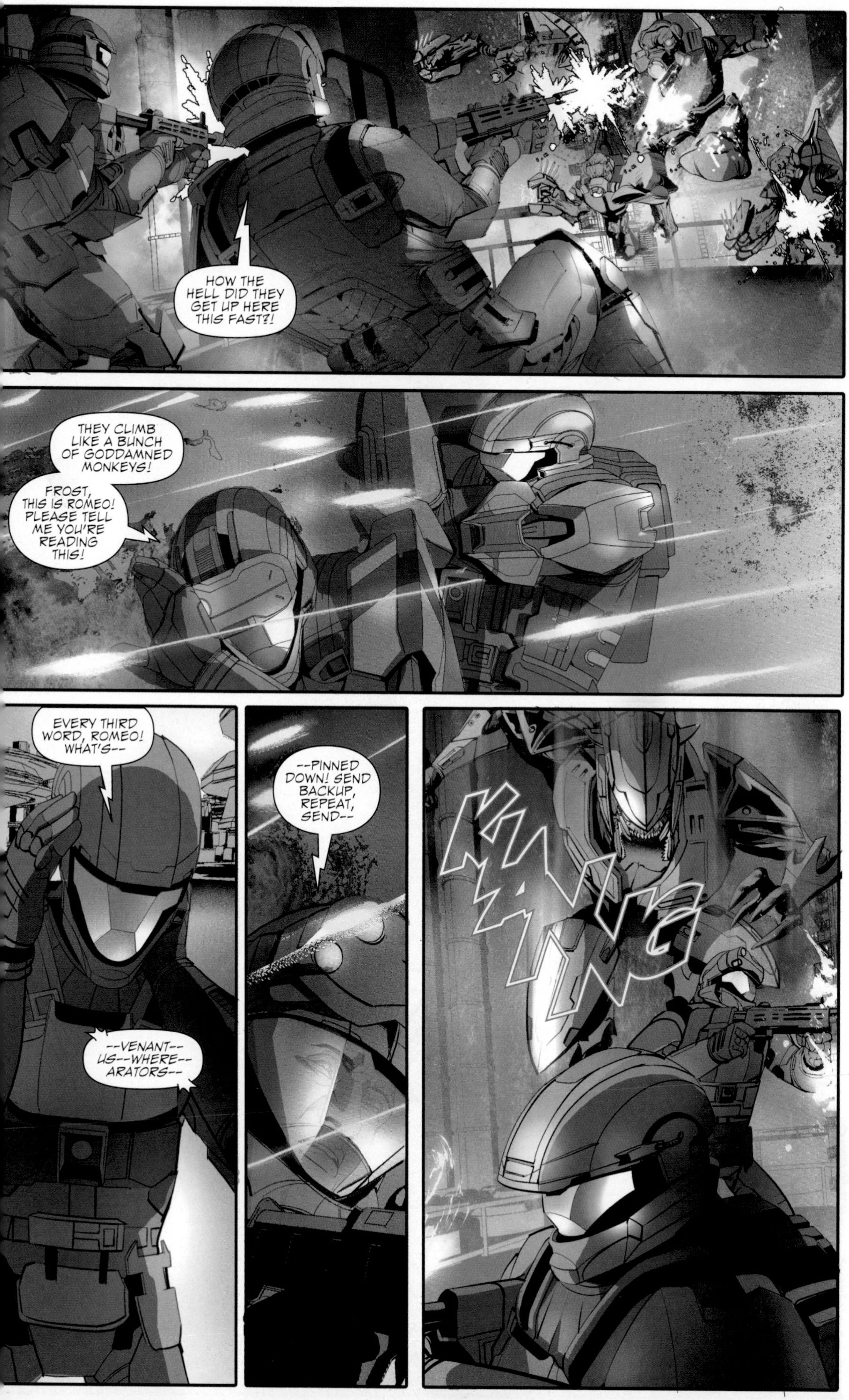
HOW THE HELL DID THEY GET UP HERE THIS FAST?!
THEY CLIMB LIKE A BUNCH OF GODDAMNED MONKEYS!
FROST, THIS IS ROMEO! PLEASE TELL ME YOU'RE READING THIS!
EVERY THIRD WORD, ROMEO! WHAT'S--
--VENANT-- US--WHERE-- ARATORS--
--PINNED DOWN! SEND BACKUP, REPEAT, SEND--
KRANNNG

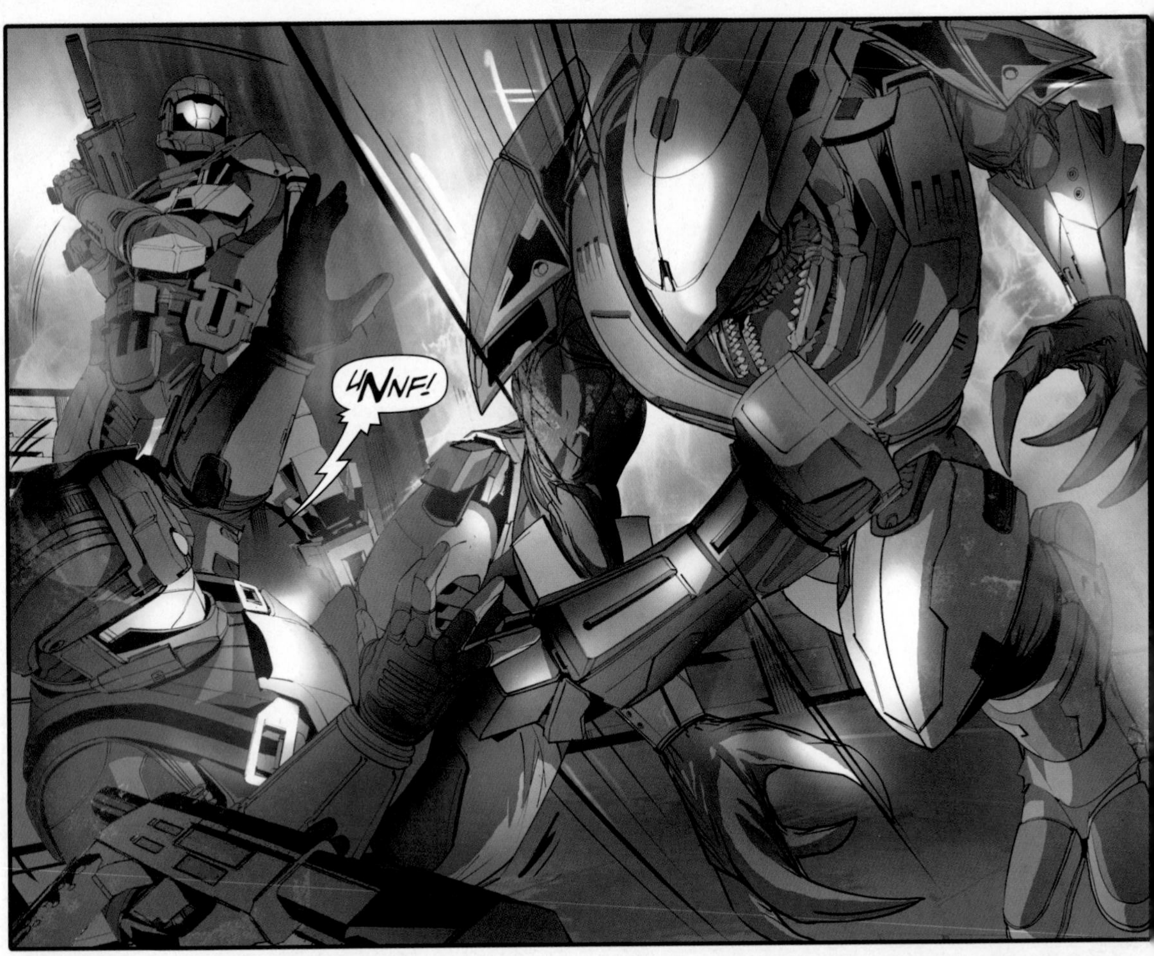
UNNF!

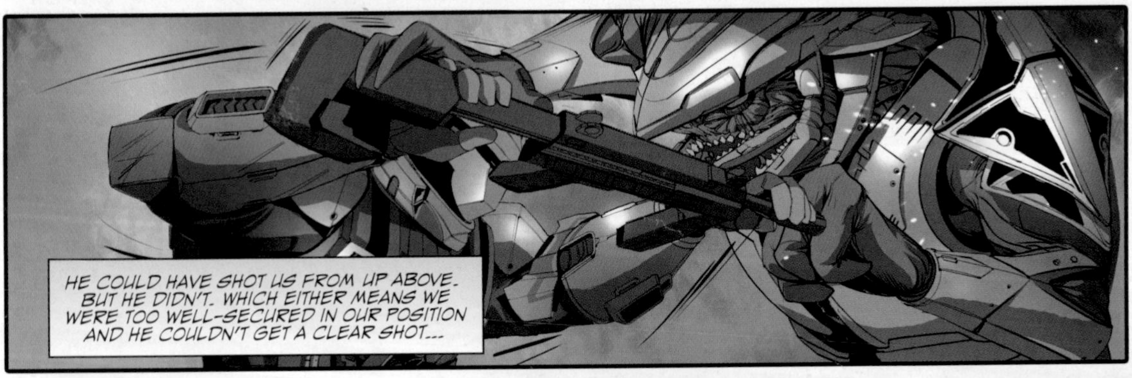
HE COULD HAVE SHOT US FROM UP ABOVE. BUT HE DIDN'T. WHICH EITHER MEANS WE WERE TOO WELL-SECURED IN OUR POSITION AND HE COULDN'T GET A CLEAR SHOT...

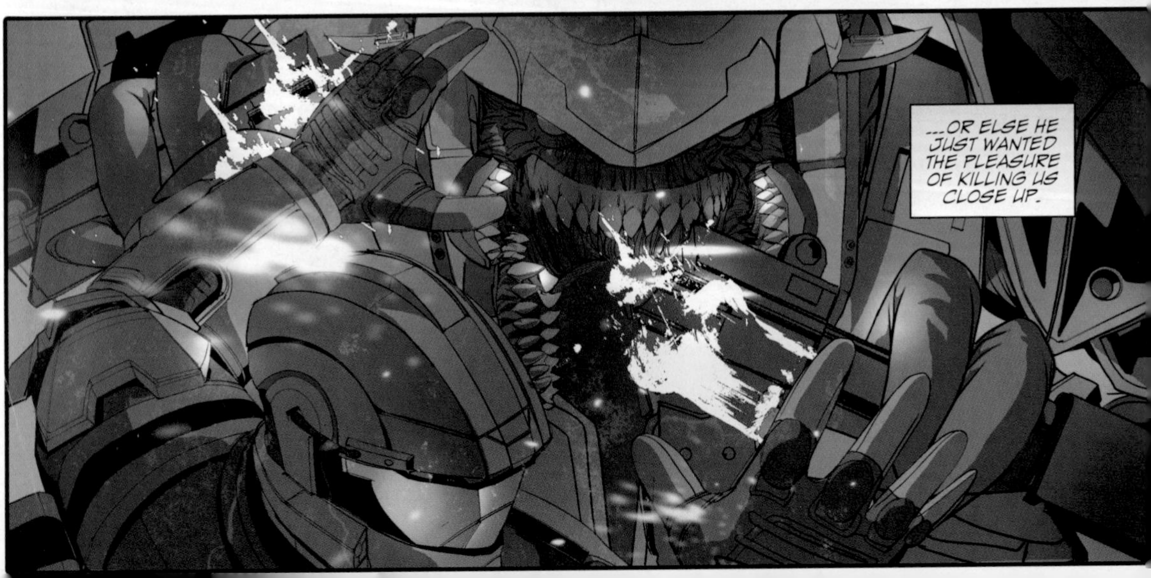
...OR ELSE HE JUST WANTED THE PLEASURE OF KILLING US CLOSE UP.

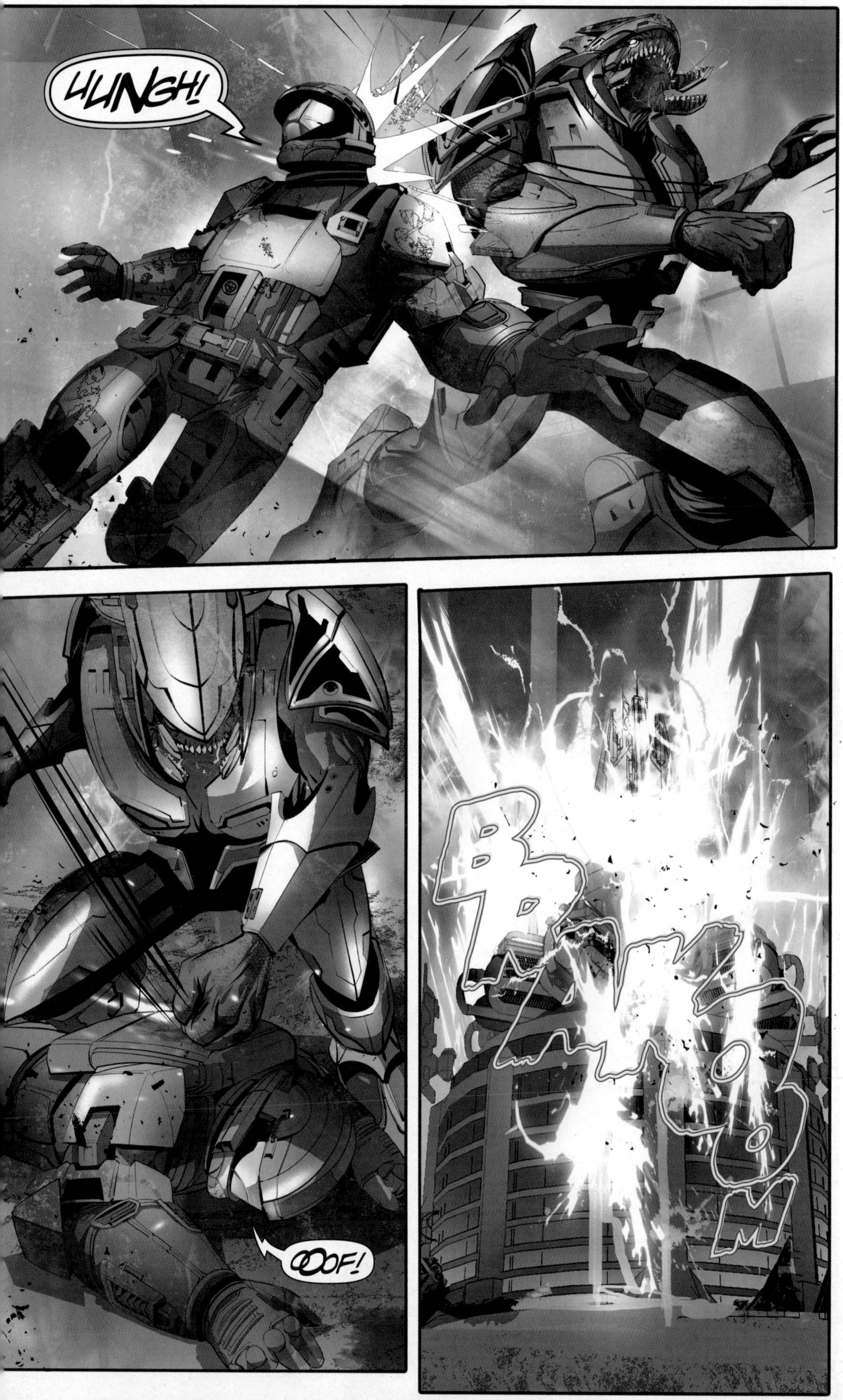
UUNGH!
OOOF!
BRAKOOOM

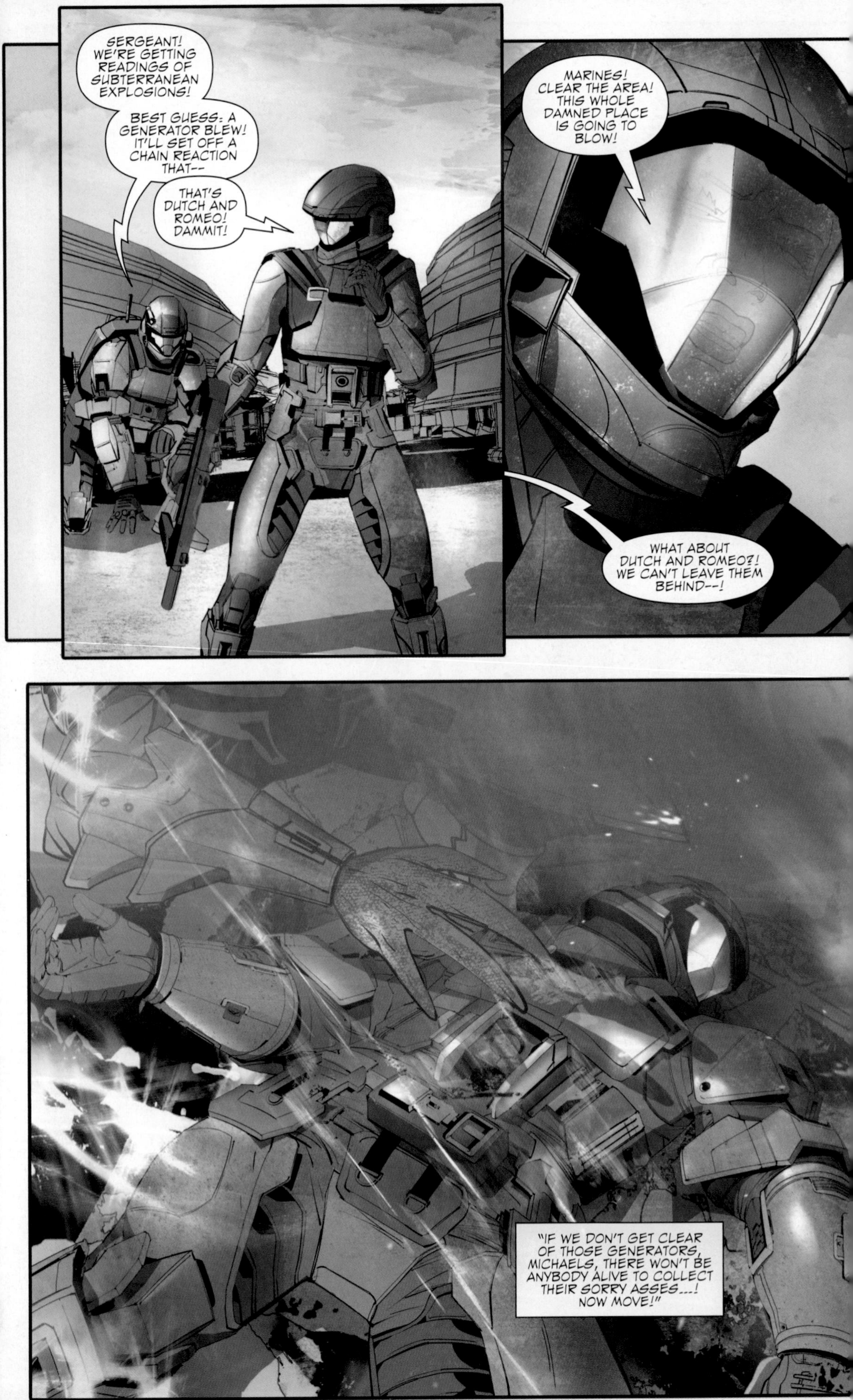
SERGEANT! WE'RE GETTING READINGS OF SUBTERRANEAN EXPLOSIONS!
BEST GUESS: A GENERATOR BLEW! IT'LL SET OFF A CHAIN REACTION THAT--
THAT'S DUTCH AND ROMEO! DAMMIT!
MARINES! CLEAR THE AREA! THIS WHOLE DAMNED PLACE IS GOING TO BLOW!
WHAT ABOUT DUTCH AND ROMEO?! WE CAN'T LEAVE THEM BEHIND--!
"IF WE DON'T GET CLEAR OF THOSE GENERATORS, MICHAELS, THERE WON'T BE ANYBODY ALIVE TO COLLECT THEIR SORRY ASSES...! NOW MOVE!"

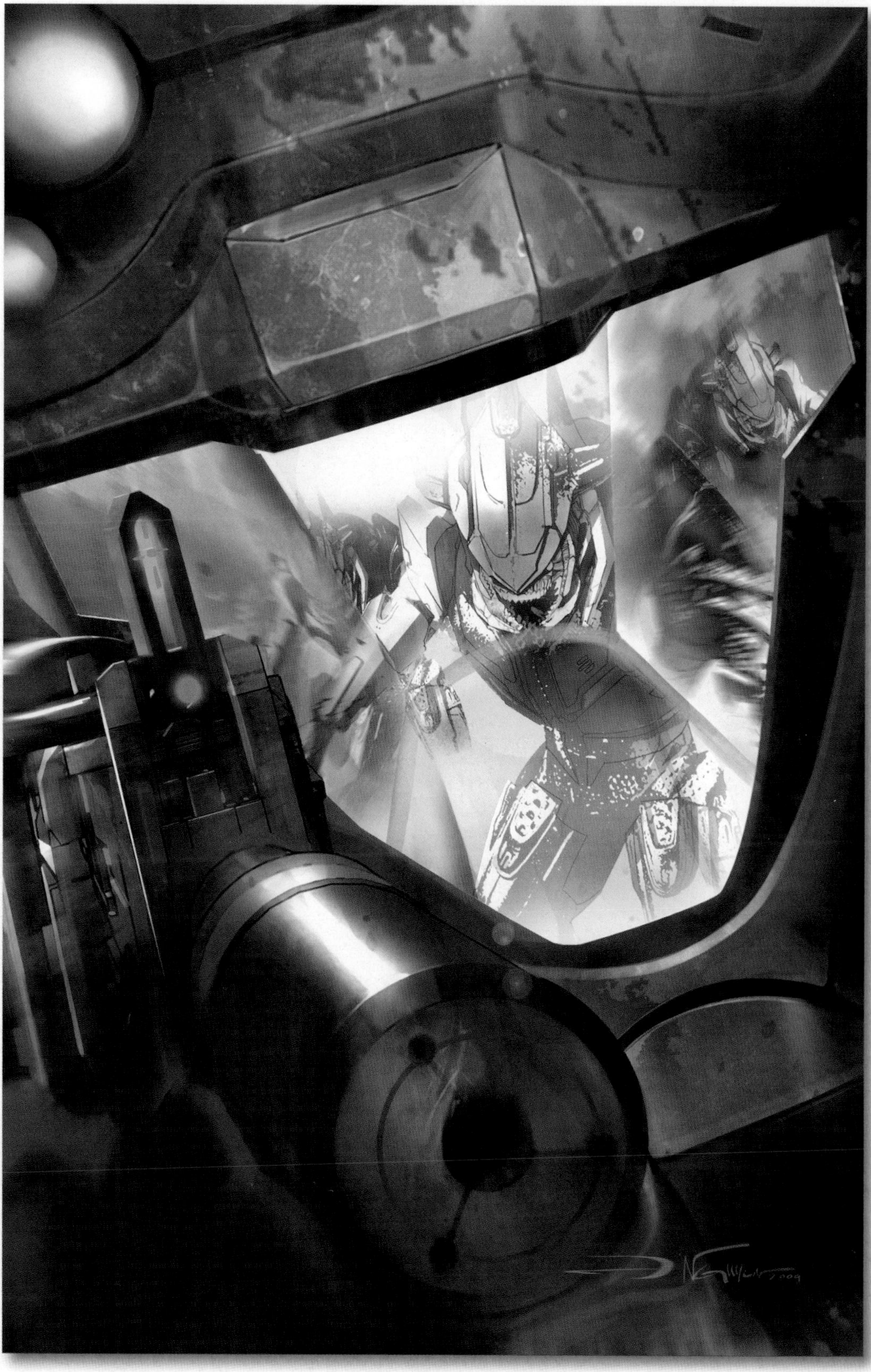

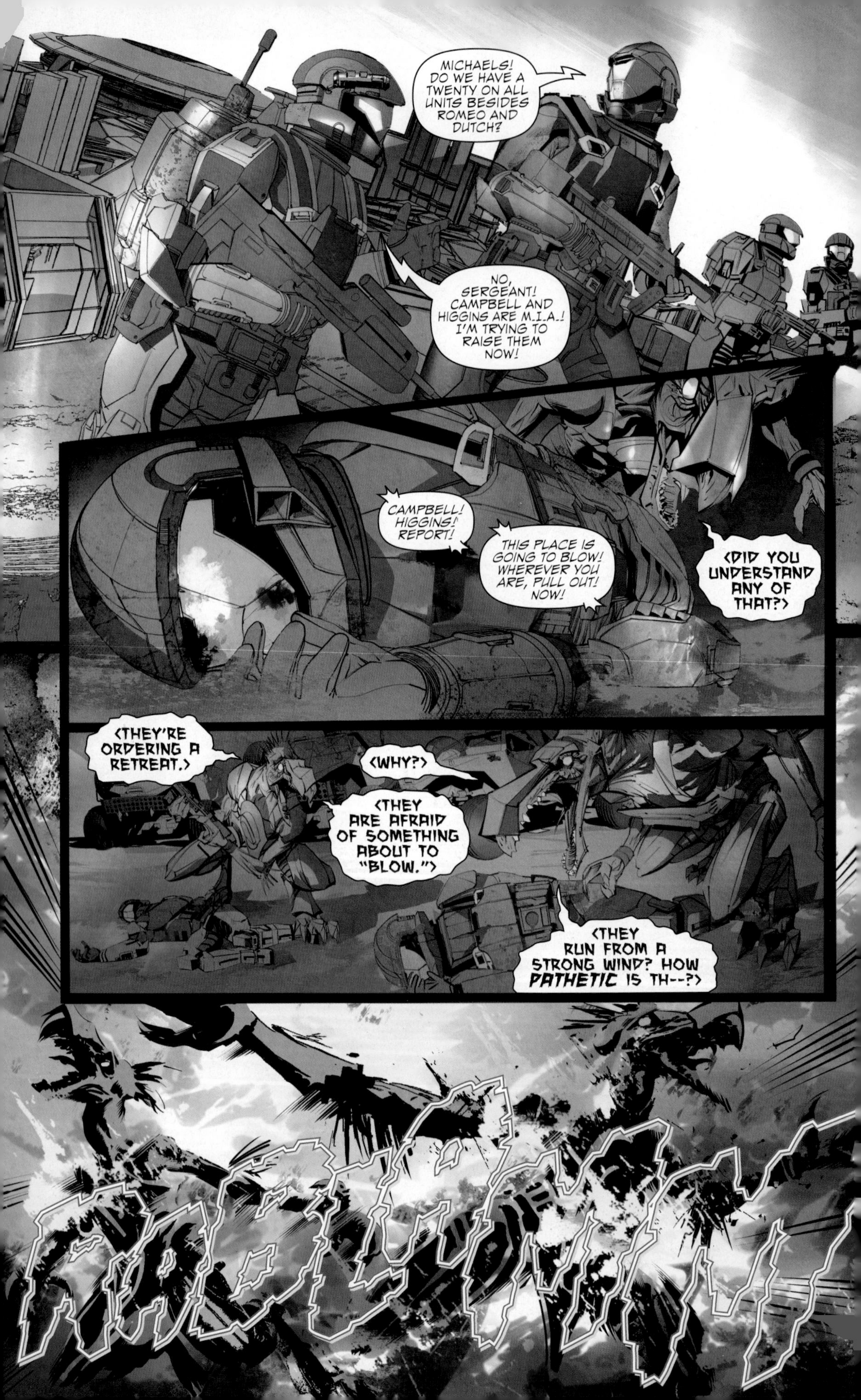
MICHAELS! DO WE HAVE A TWENTY ON ALL UNITS BESIDES ROMEO AND DUTCH?
NO, SERGEANT! CAMPBELL AND HIGGINS ARE M.I.A.! I'M TRYING TO RAISE THEM NOW!
CAMPBELL! HIGGINS! REPORT!
THIS PLACE IS GOING TO BLOW! WHEREVER YOU ARE, PULL OUT! NOW!
<DID YOU UNDERSTAND ANY OF THAT?>
<THEY'RE ORDERING A RETREAT.>
<WHY?>
<THEY ARE AFRAID OF SOMETHING ABOUT TO "BLOW.">
<THEY RUN FROM A STRONG WIND? HOW PATHETIC IS TH--?>

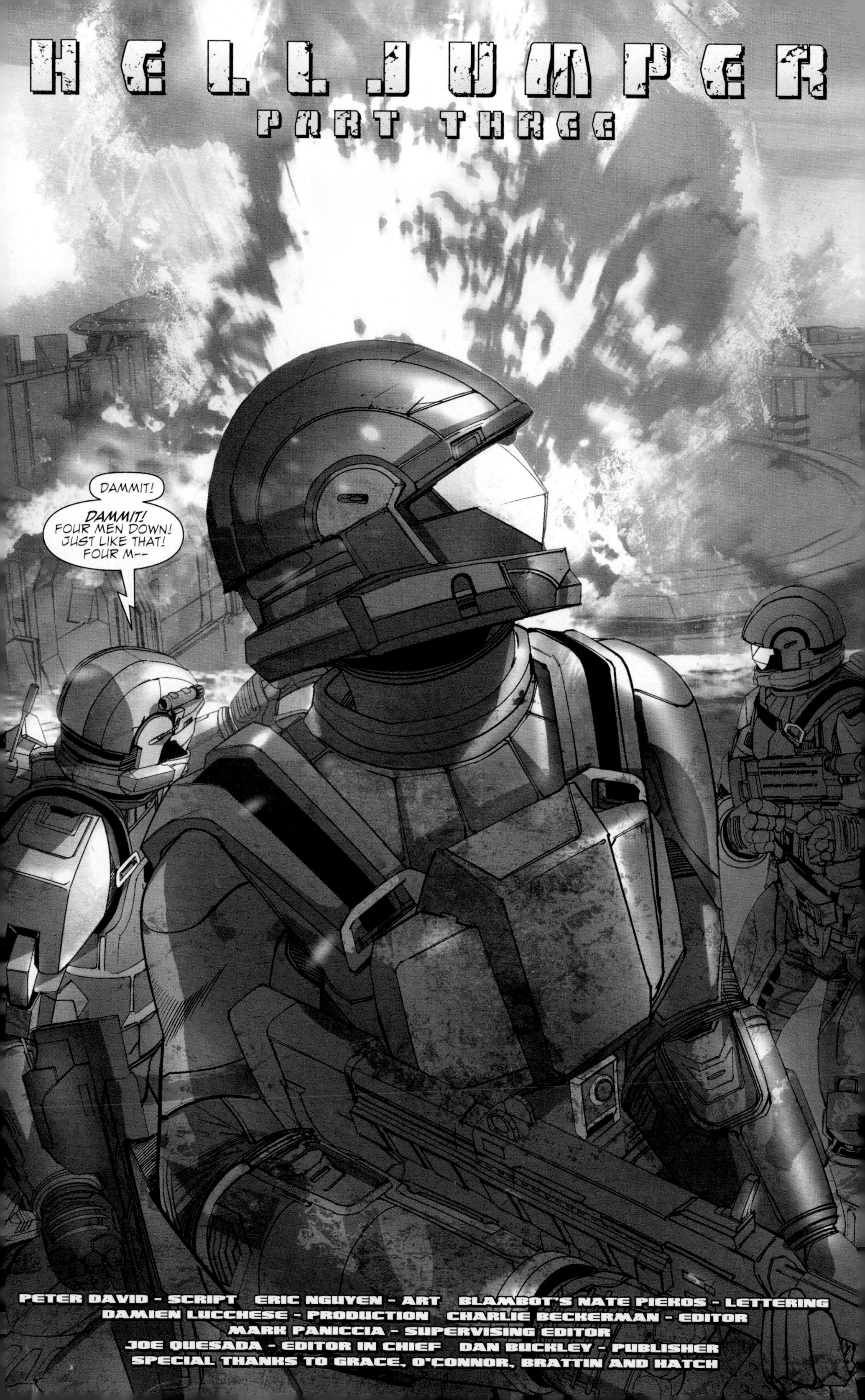
HELLJUMPER
PART THREE
DAMMIT!
DAMMIT! FOUR MEN DOWN! JUST LIKE THAT! FOUR M--
PETER DAVID - SCRIPT ERIC NGUYEN - ART BLAMBOT'S NATE PIEKOS - LETTERING
DAMIEN LUCCHESE - PRODUCTION CHARLIE BECKERMAN - EDITOR
MARK PANICCIA - SUPERVISING EDITOR
JOE QUESADA - EDITOR IN CHIEF DAN BUCKLEY - PUBLISHER
SPECIAL THANKS TO GRACE, O'CONNOR, BRATTIN AND HATCH

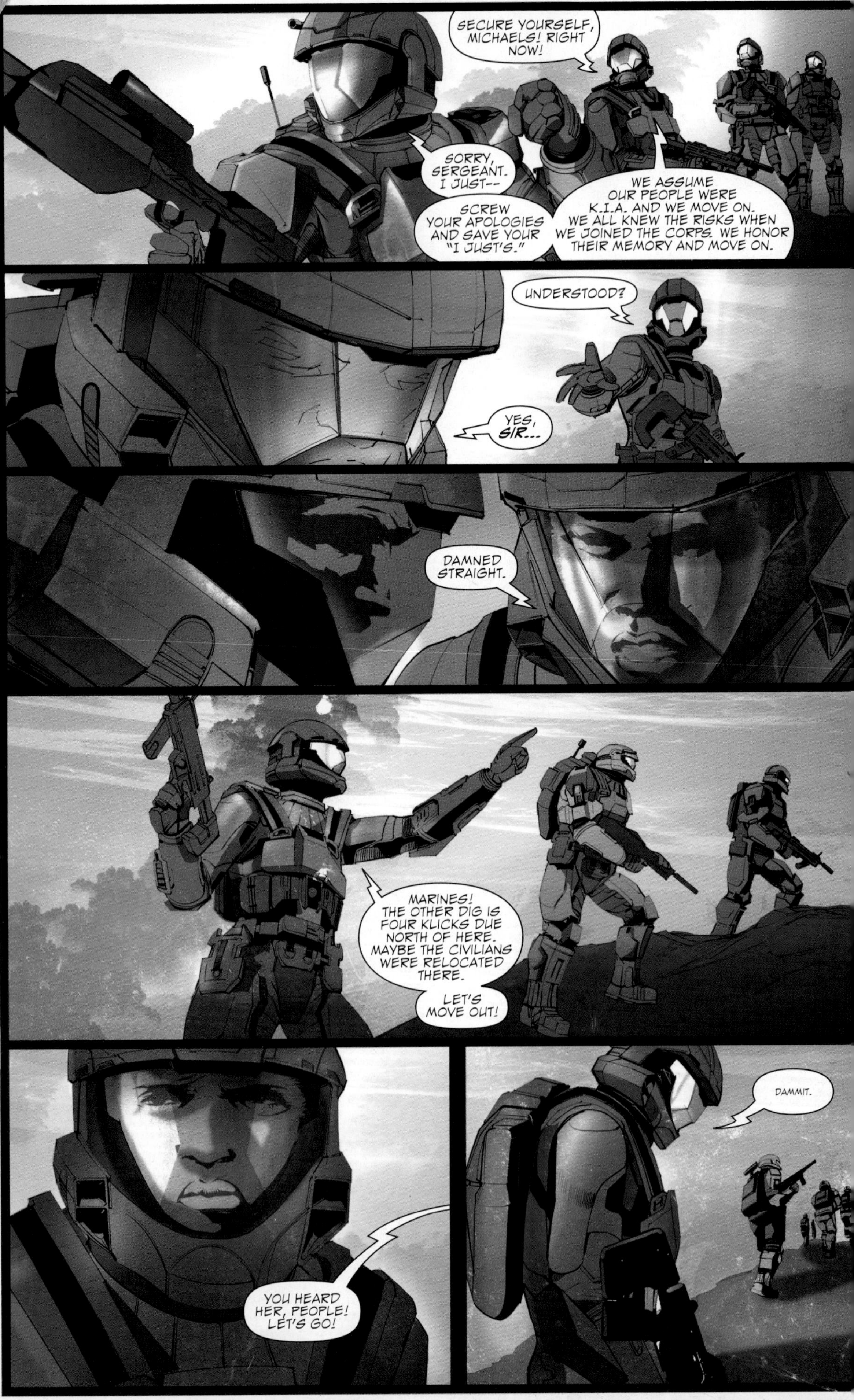
SECURE YOURSELF, MICHAELS! RIGHT NOW!
SORRY, SERGEANT. I JUST--
SCREW YOUR APOLOGIES AND SAVE YOUR "I JUST'S."
WE ASSUME OUR PEOPLE WERE K.I.A. AND WE MOVE ON. WE ALL KNEW THE RISKS WHEN WE JOINED THE CORPS. WE HONOR THEIR MEMORY AND MOVE ON.
UNDERSTOOD?
YES, SIR...
DAMNED STRAIGHT.
MARINES! THE OTHER DIG IS FOUR KLICKS DUE NORTH OF HERE. MAYBE THE CIVILIANS WERE RELOCATED THERE.
LET'S MOVE OUT!
YOU HEARD HER, PEOPLE! LET'S GO!
DAMMIT.

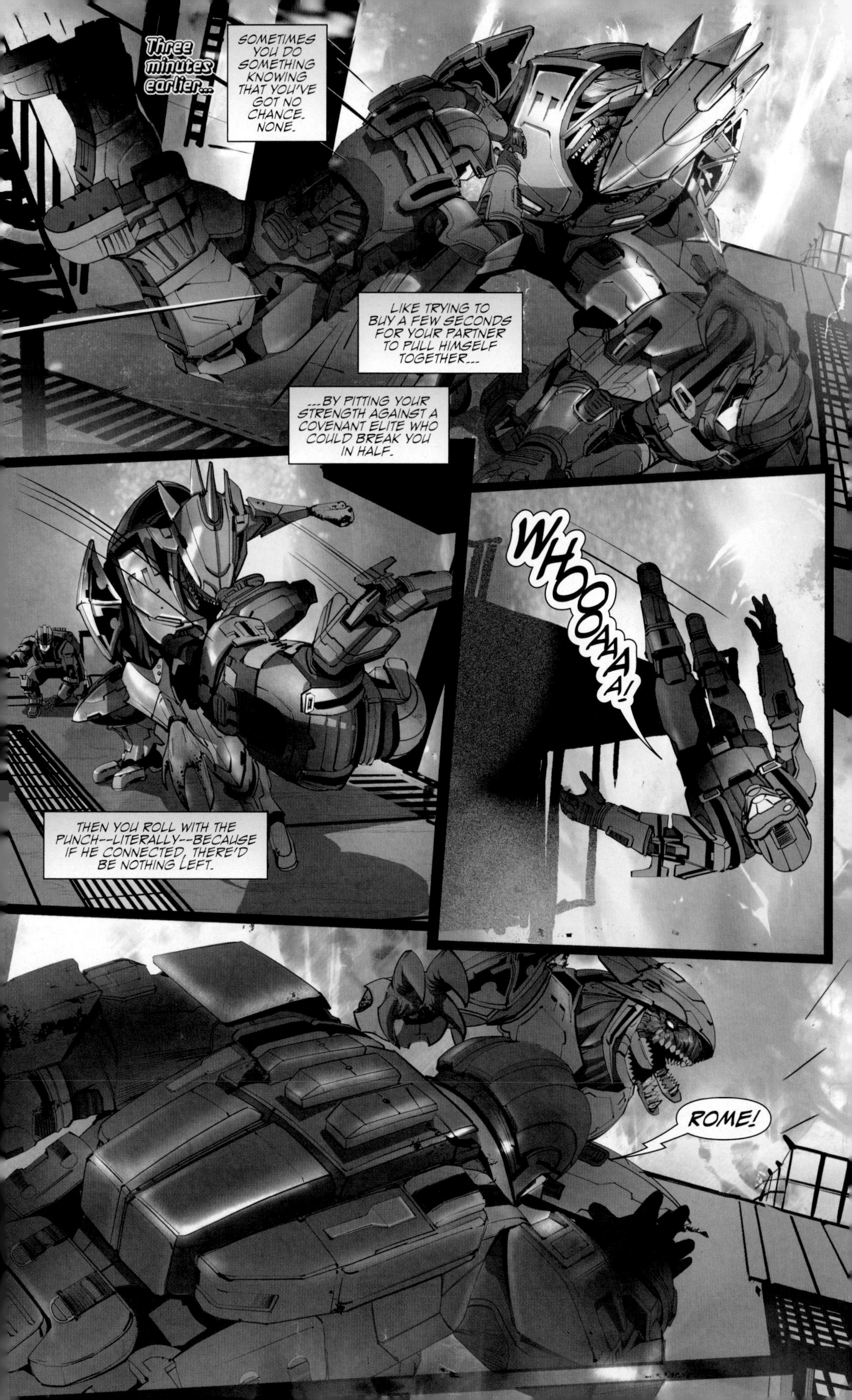
Three minutes earlier...
SOMETIMES YOU DO SOMETHING KNOWING THAT YOU'VE GOT NO CHANCE. NONE.
LIKE TRYING TO BUY A FEW SECONDS FOR YOUR PARTNER TO PULL HIMSELF TOGETHER...
...BY PITTING YOUR STRENGTH AGAINST A COVENANT ELITE WHO COULD BREAK YOU IN HALF.
THEN YOU ROLL WITH THE PUNCH--LITERALLY--BECAUSE IF HE CONNECTED, THERE'D BE NOTHING LEFT.
WHOOAAAA!
ROME!

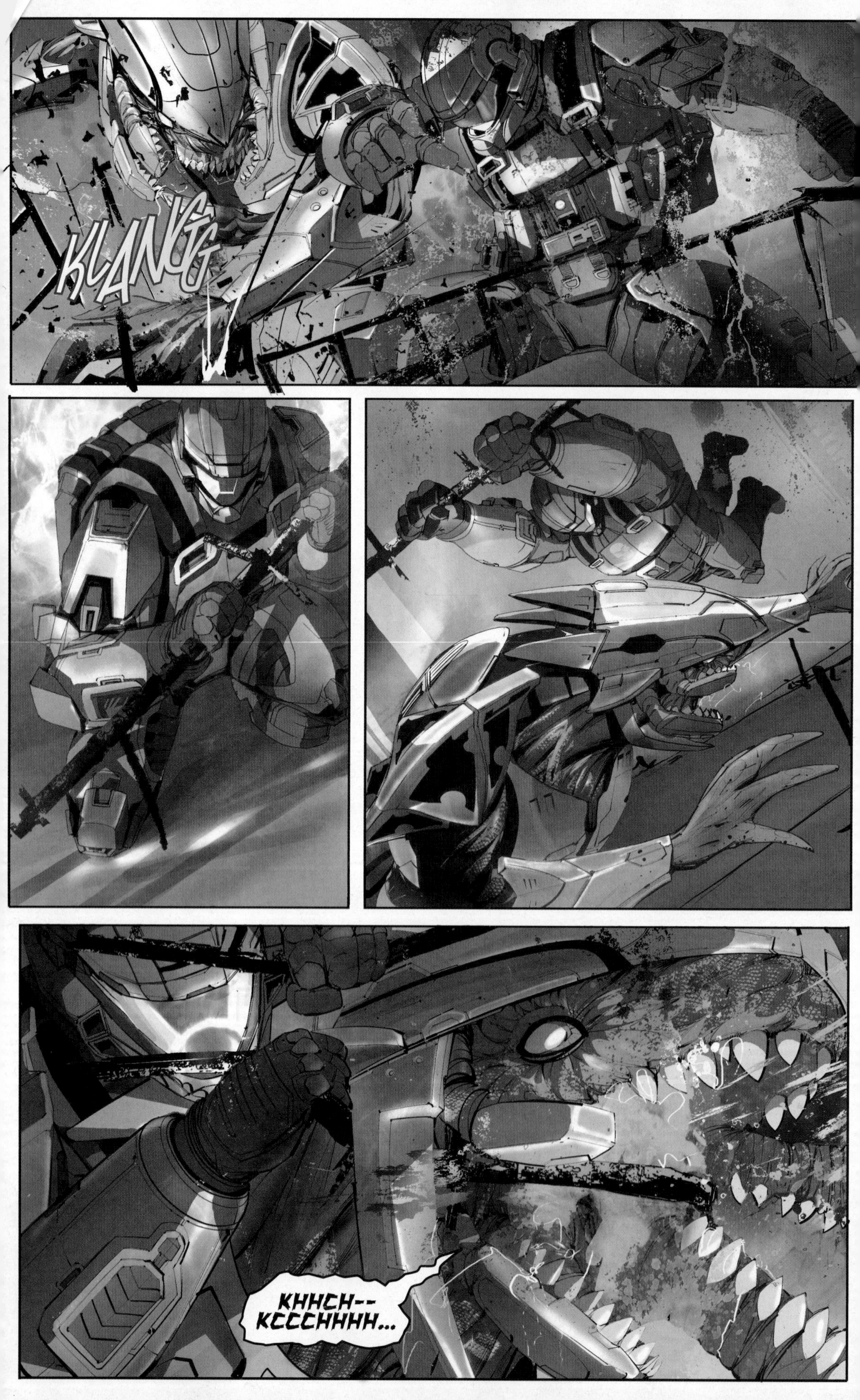
KLANGG
KHHCH--
KCCCHHHH...

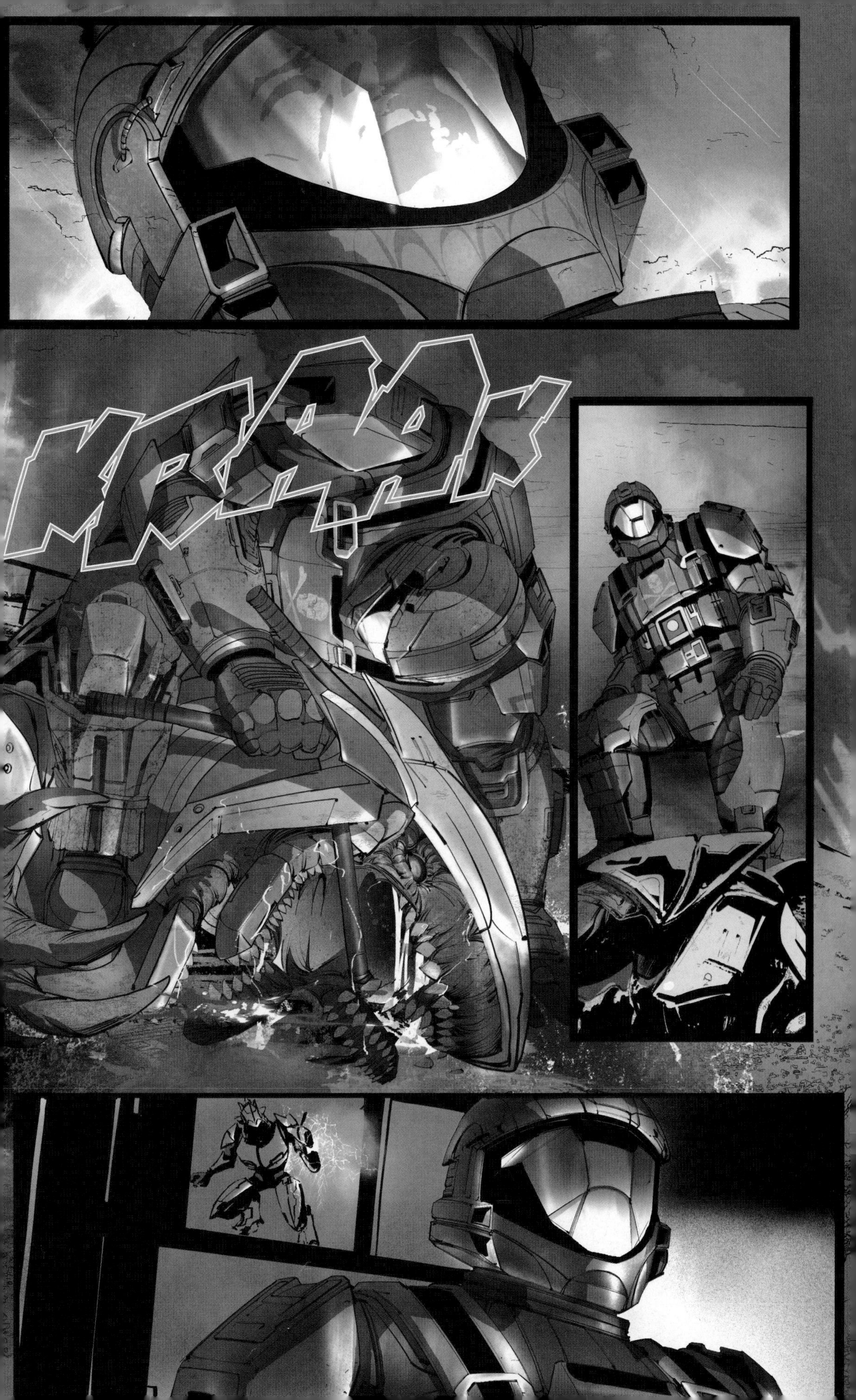
KRAAK

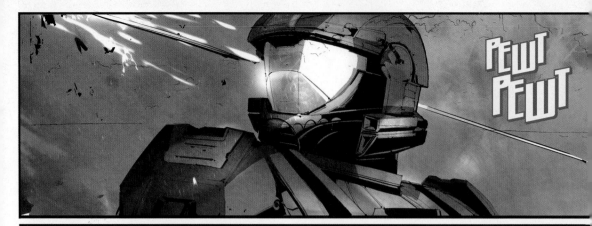

PEWT
PEWT

KRASH

FOUND MY GUN.

A LITTLE HELP HERE?

JEEZ.

WHAT, YOU DIDN'T THINK I WAS *DEAD*, DID'JA?

FRIENDS DON'T BUG OUT ON FRIENDS. NOT *EVEN* IF THEY'RE DEAD.

SHUT UP.

IS THAT ANY WAY TO--?

Uh-oh.

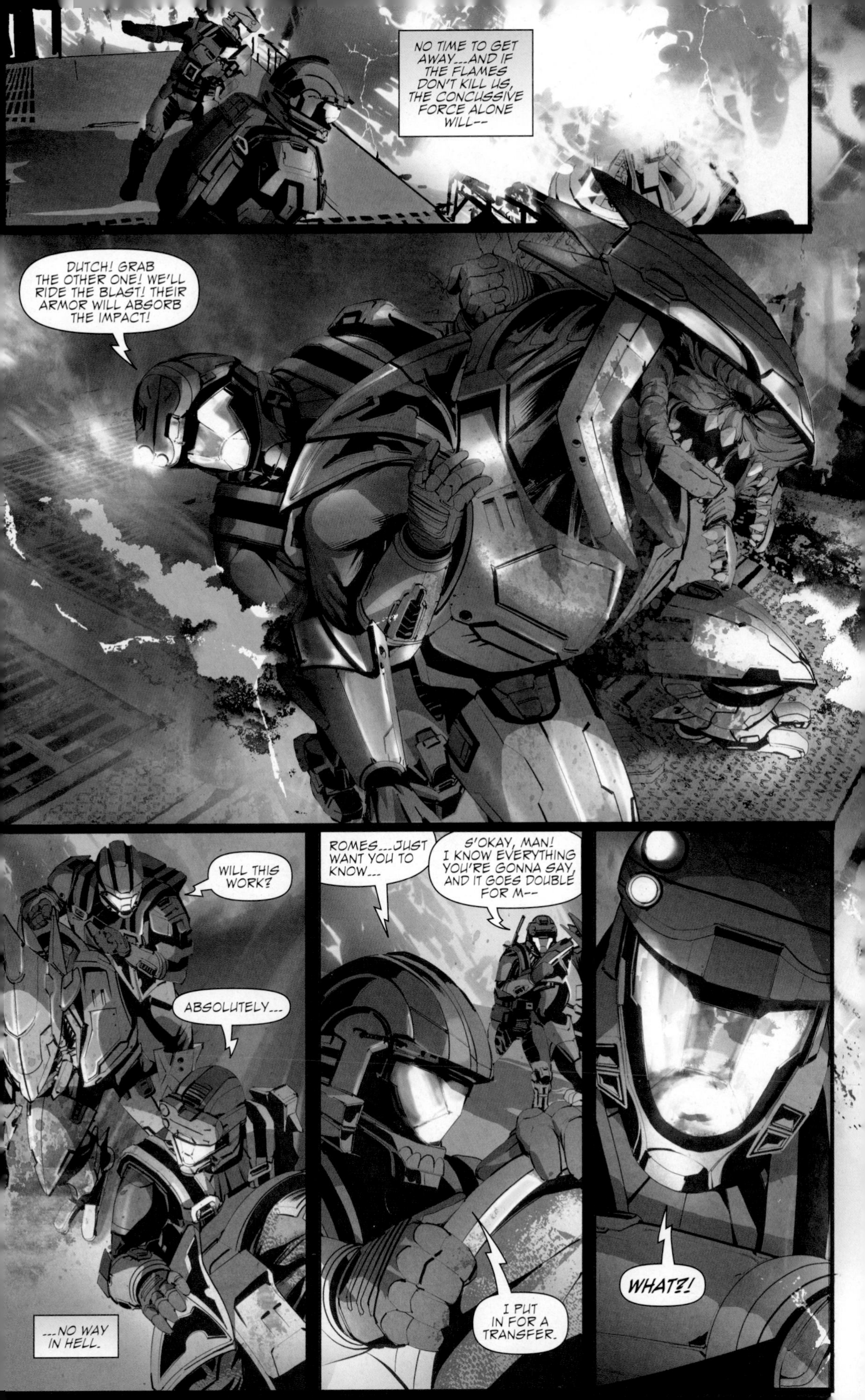
NO TIME TO GET AWAY...AND IF THE FLAMES DON'T KILL US, THE CONCUSSIVE FORCE ALONE WILL--
DUTCH! GRAB THE OTHER ONE! WE'LL RIDE THE BLAST! THEIR ARMOR WILL ABSORB THE IMPACT!
WILL THIS WORK?
ABSOLUTELY...
...NO WAY IN HELL.
ROMES...JUST WANT YOU TO KNOW...
S'OKAY, MAN! I KNOW EVERYTHING YOU'RE GONNA SAY, AND IT GOES DOUBLE FOR M--
I PUT IN FOR A TRANSFER.
WHAT?!

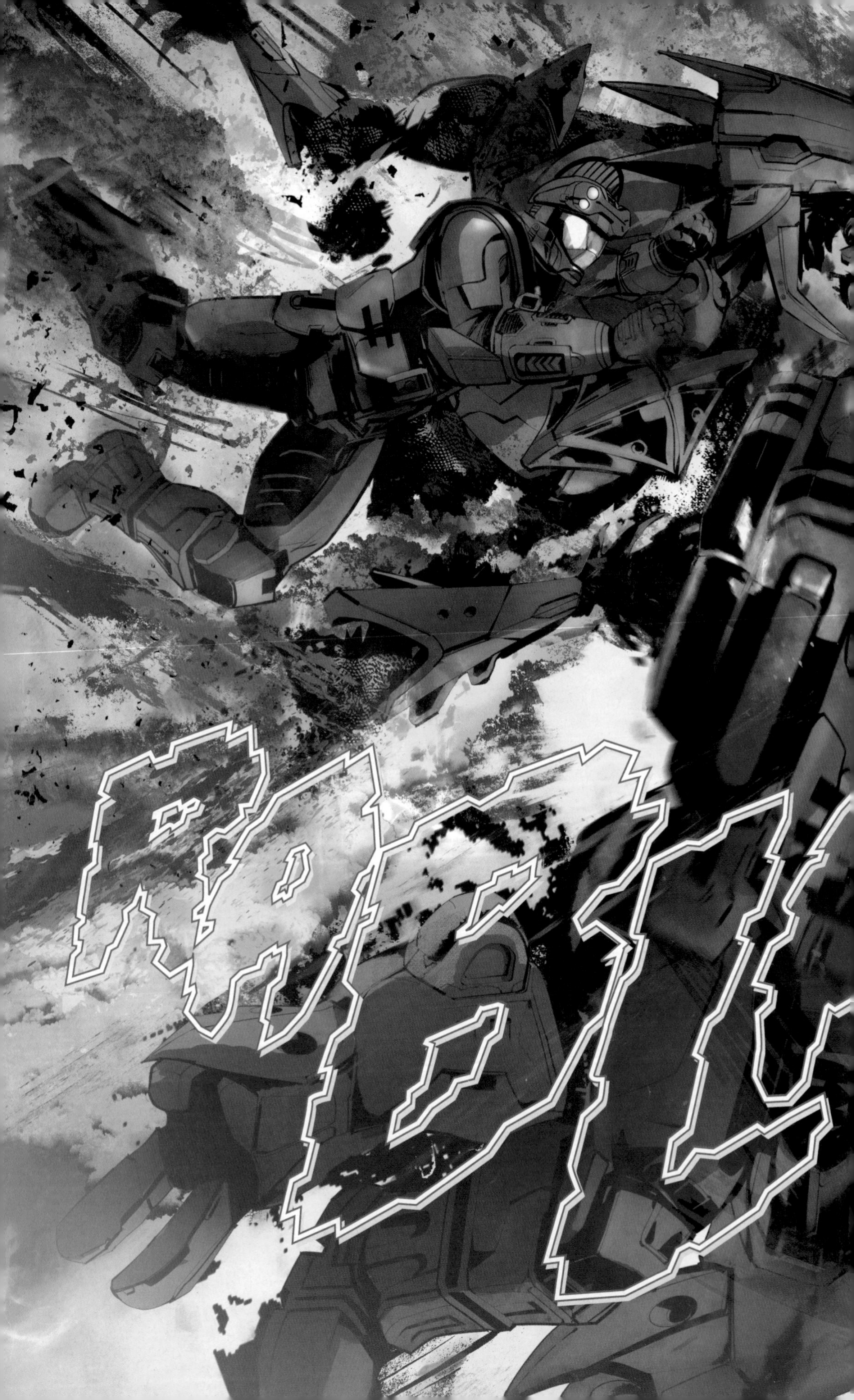

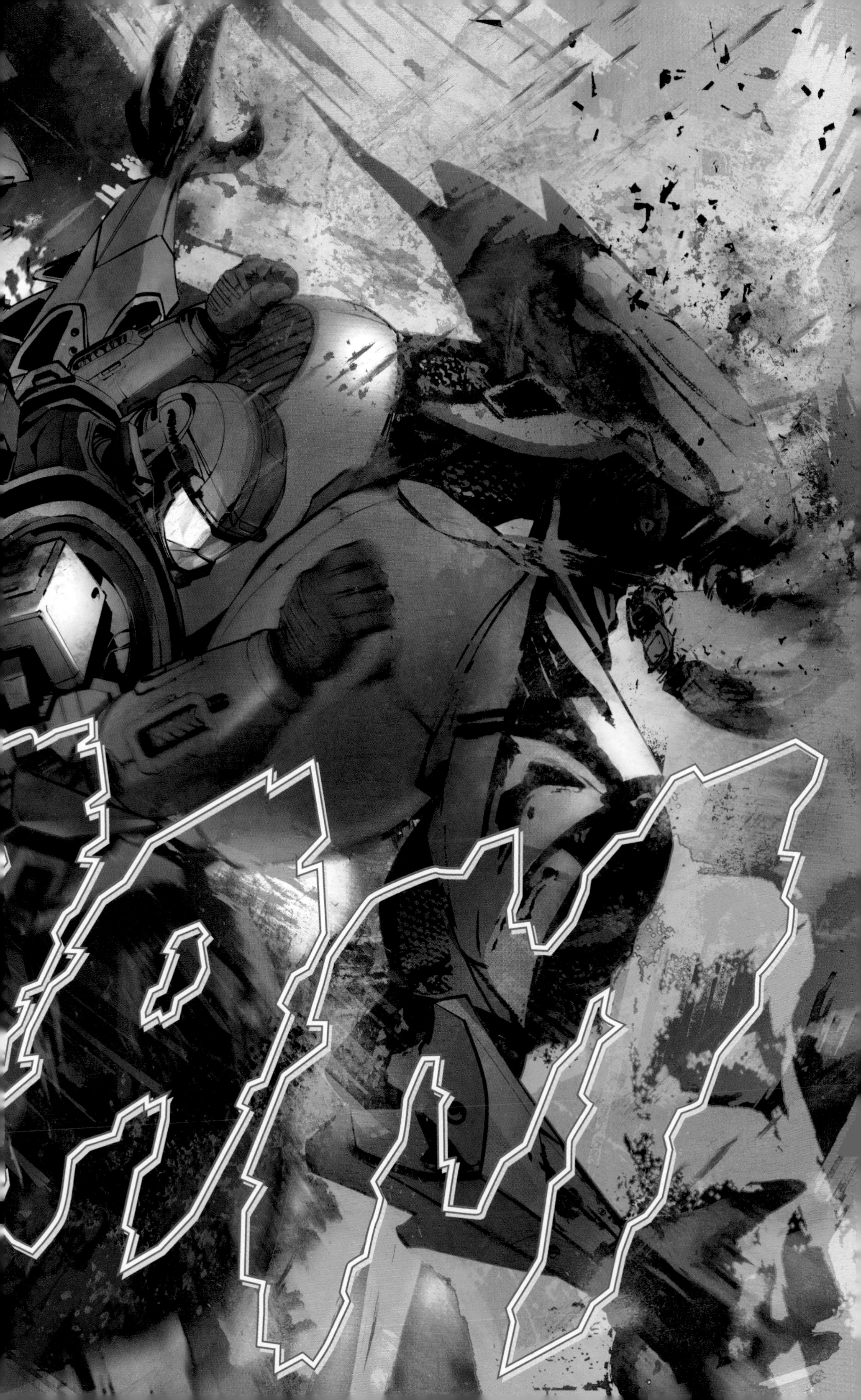

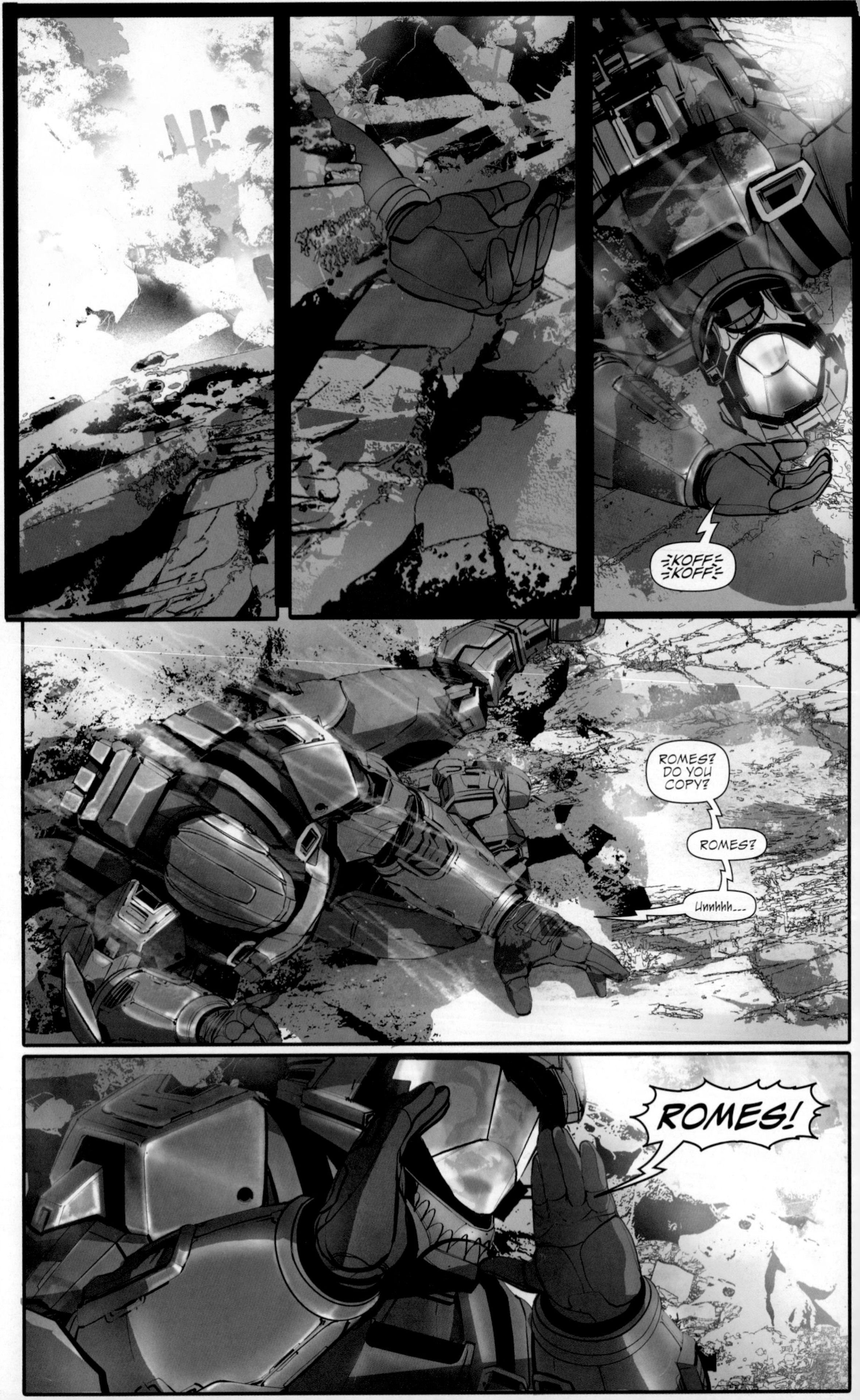
KOFF KOFF
ROMES? DO YOU COPY?
ROMES?
Unnhhh...
ROMES!

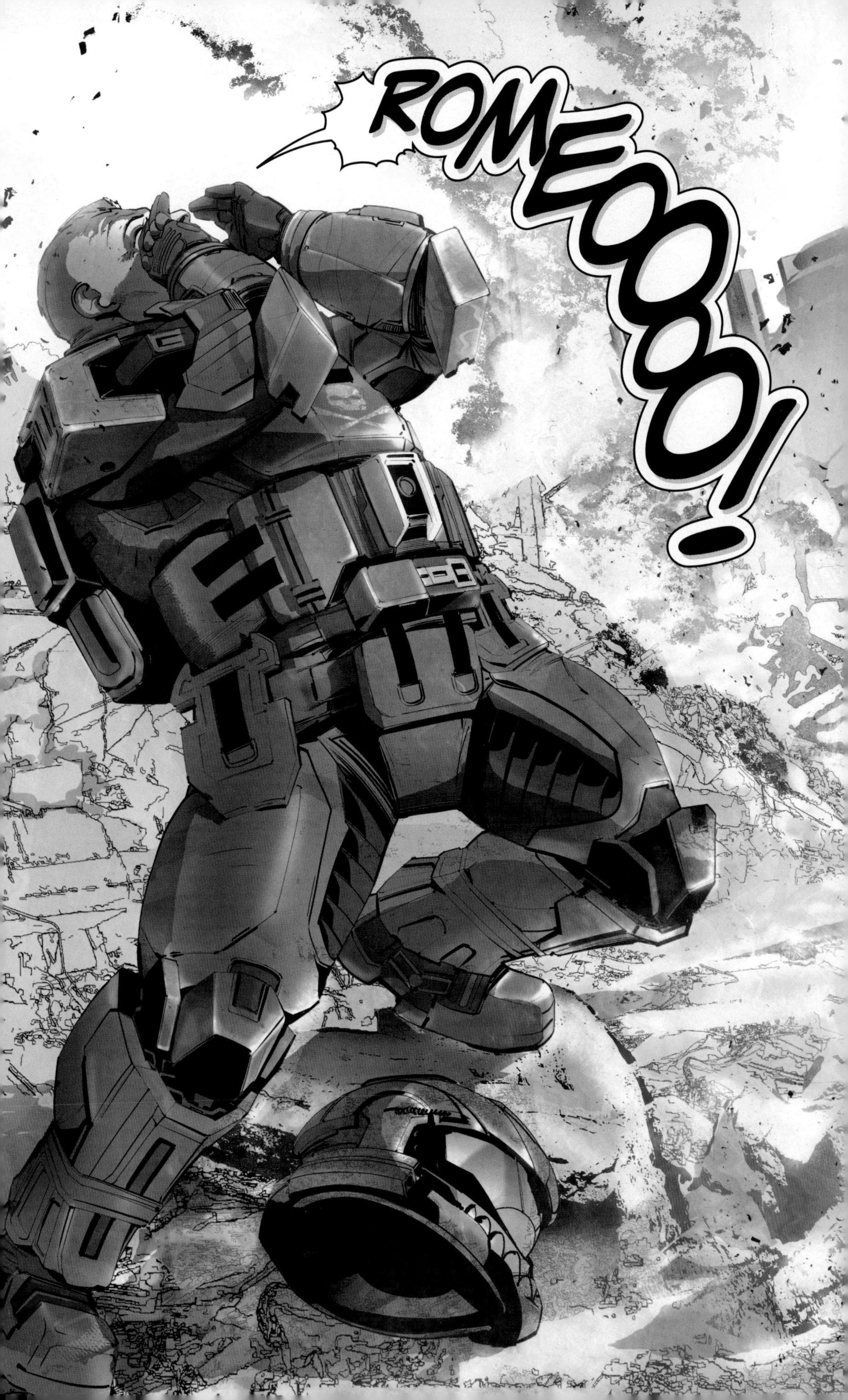
ROMEOOOO!

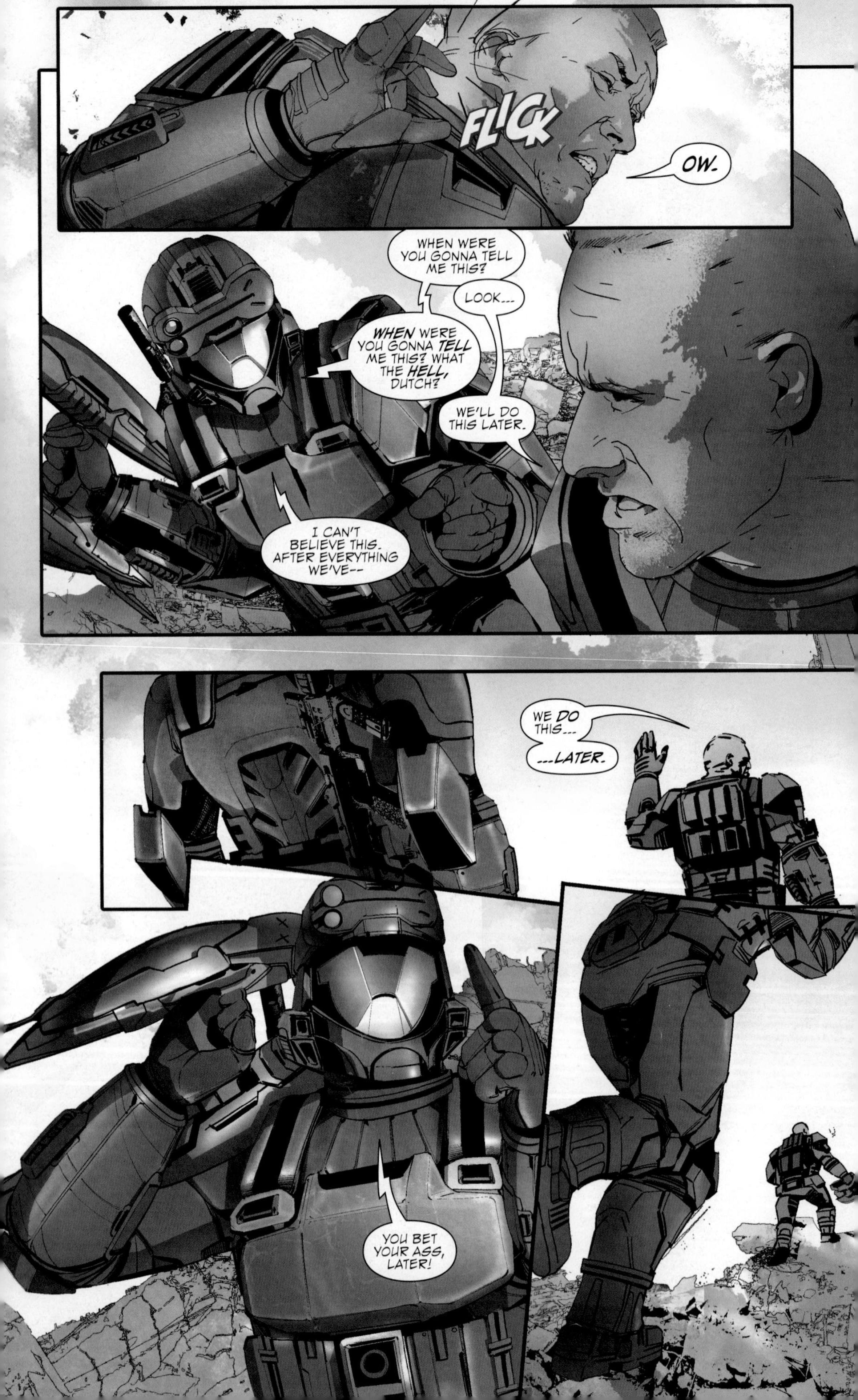

FLICK
OW.
WHEN WERE YOU GONNA TELL ME THIS?
LOOK...
WHEN WERE YOU GONNA TELL ME THIS? WHAT THE HELL, DUTCH?
WE'LL DO THIS LATER.
I CAN'T BELIEVE THIS. AFTER EVERYTHING WE'VE--
WE DO THIS...
...LATER.
YOU BET YOUR ASS, LATER!

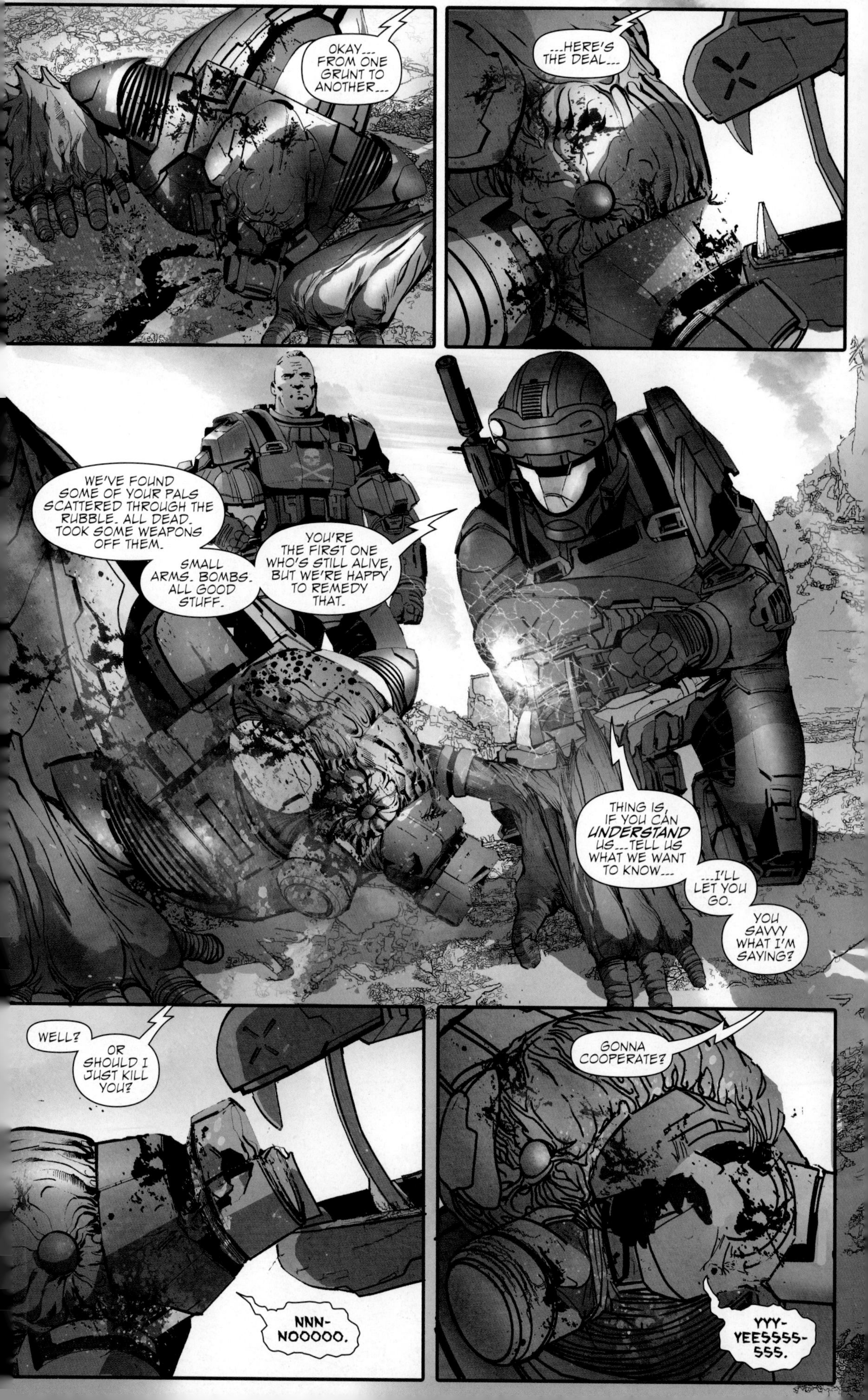
OKAY... FROM ONE GRUNT TO ANOTHER...
...HERE'S THE DEAL...
WE'VE FOUND SOME OF YOUR PALS SCATTERED THROUGH THE RUBBLE. ALL DEAD. TOOK SOME WEAPONS OFF THEM.
SMALL ARMS. BOMBS. ALL GOOD STUFF.
YOU'RE THE FIRST ONE WHO'S STILL ALIVE, BUT WE'RE HAPPY TO REMEDY THAT.
THING IS, IF YOU CAN UNDERSTAND US...TELL US WHAT WE WANT TO KNOW...
...I'LL LET YOU GO.
YOU SAVVY WHAT I'M SAYING?
WELL?
OR SHOULD I JUST KILL YOU?
NNN-NOOOOO.
GONNA COOPERATE?
YYY-YEESSSSS-SSS.

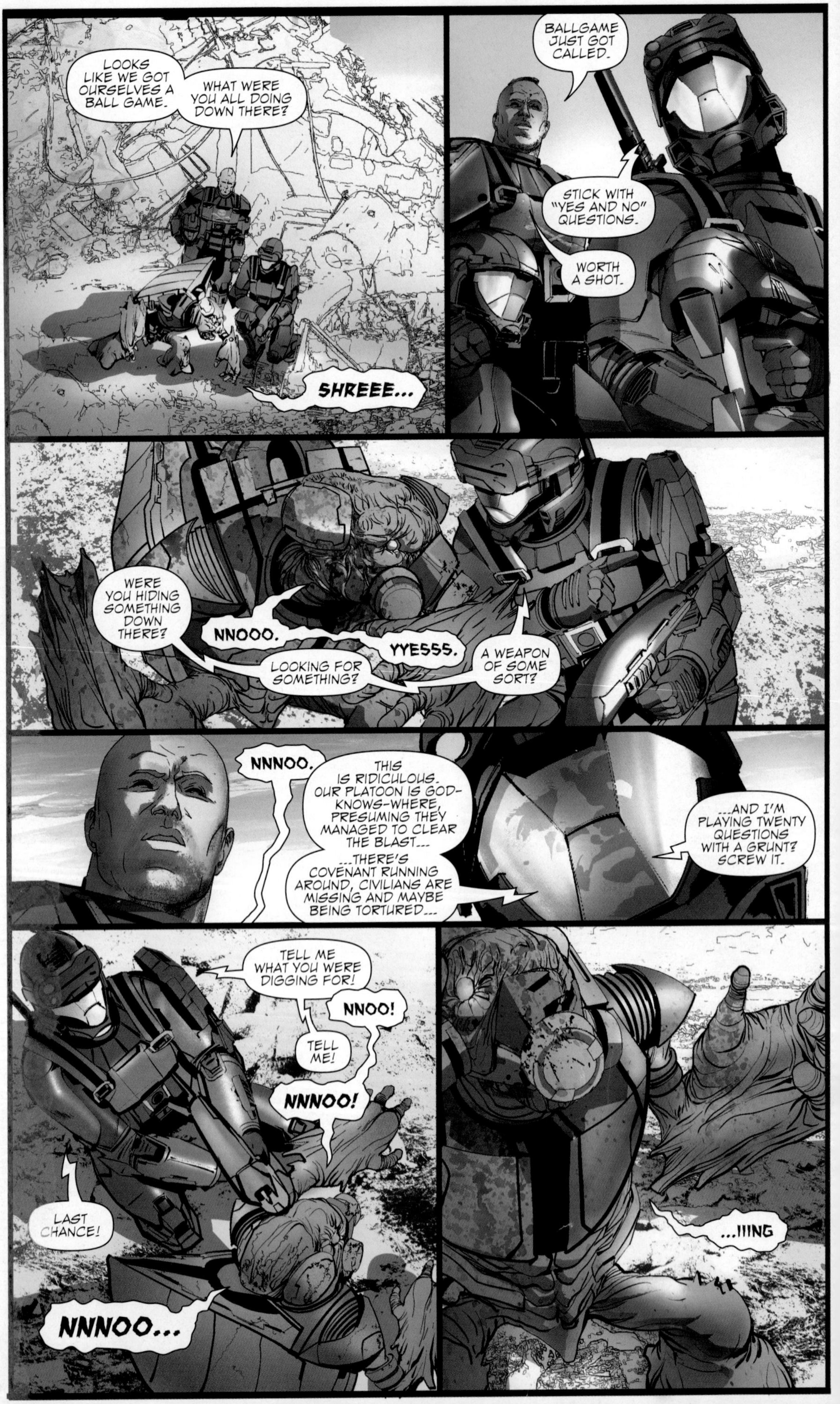
LOOKS LIKE WE GOT OURSELVES A BALL GAME.
WHAT WERE YOU ALL DOING DOWN THERE?
SHREEE...
BALLGAME JUST GOT CALLED.
STICK WITH "YES AND NO" QUESTIONS.
WORTH A SHOT.
WERE YOU HIDING SOMETHING DOWN THERE?
NNOOO.
LOOKING FOR SOMETHING?
YYESSS.
A WEAPON OF SOME SORT?
NNNOO.
THIS IS RIDICULOUS. OUR PLATOON IS GOD-KNOWS-WHERE, PRESUMING THEY MANAGED TO CLEAR THE BLAST...
...THERE'S COVENANT RUNNING AROUND, CIVILIANS ARE MISSING AND MAYBE BEING TORTURED...
...AND I'M PLAYING TWENTY QUESTIONS WITH A GRUNT? SCREW IT.
TELL ME WHAT YOU WERE DIGGING FOR!
NNOO!
TELL ME!
NNNOO!
LAST CHANCE!
NNNOO...
...IIING

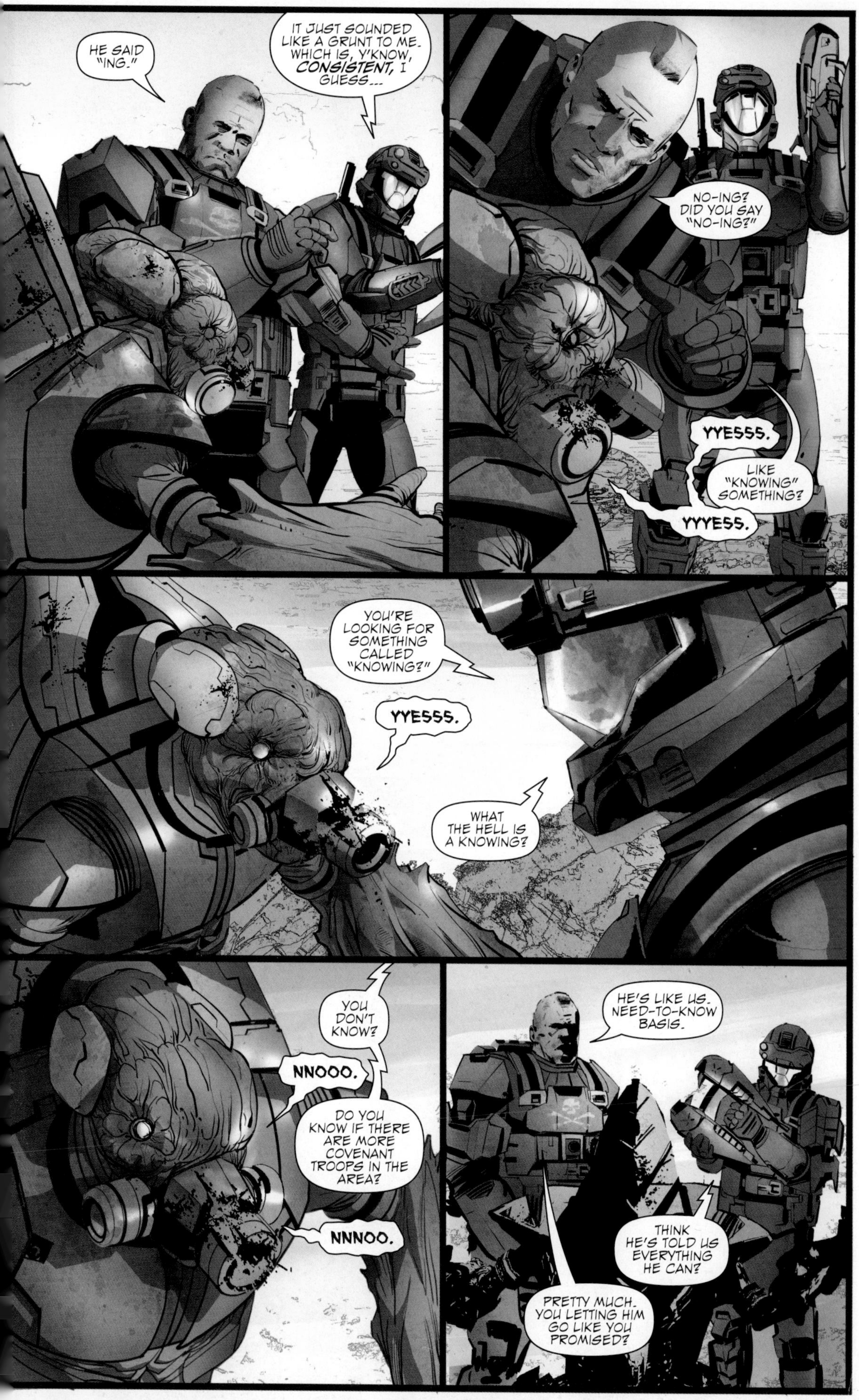
HE SAID "ING."
IT JUST SOUNDED LIKE A GRUNT TO ME. WHICH IS, Y'KNOW, CONSISTENT, I GUESS...
NO-ING? DID YOU SAY "NO-ING?"
YYESSS.
LIKE "KNOWING" SOMETHING?
YYYESS.
YOU'RE LOOKING FOR SOMETHING CALLED "KNOWING?"
YYESSS.
WHAT THE HELL IS A KNOWING?
YOU DON'T KNOW?
NNOOO.
DO YOU KNOW IF THERE ARE MORE COVENANT TROOPS IN THE AREA?
NNNOO.
HE'S LIKE US. NEED-TO-KNOW BASIS.
THINK HE'S TOLD US EVERYTHING HE CAN?
PRETTY MUCH. YOU LETTING HIM GO LIKE YOU PROMISED?

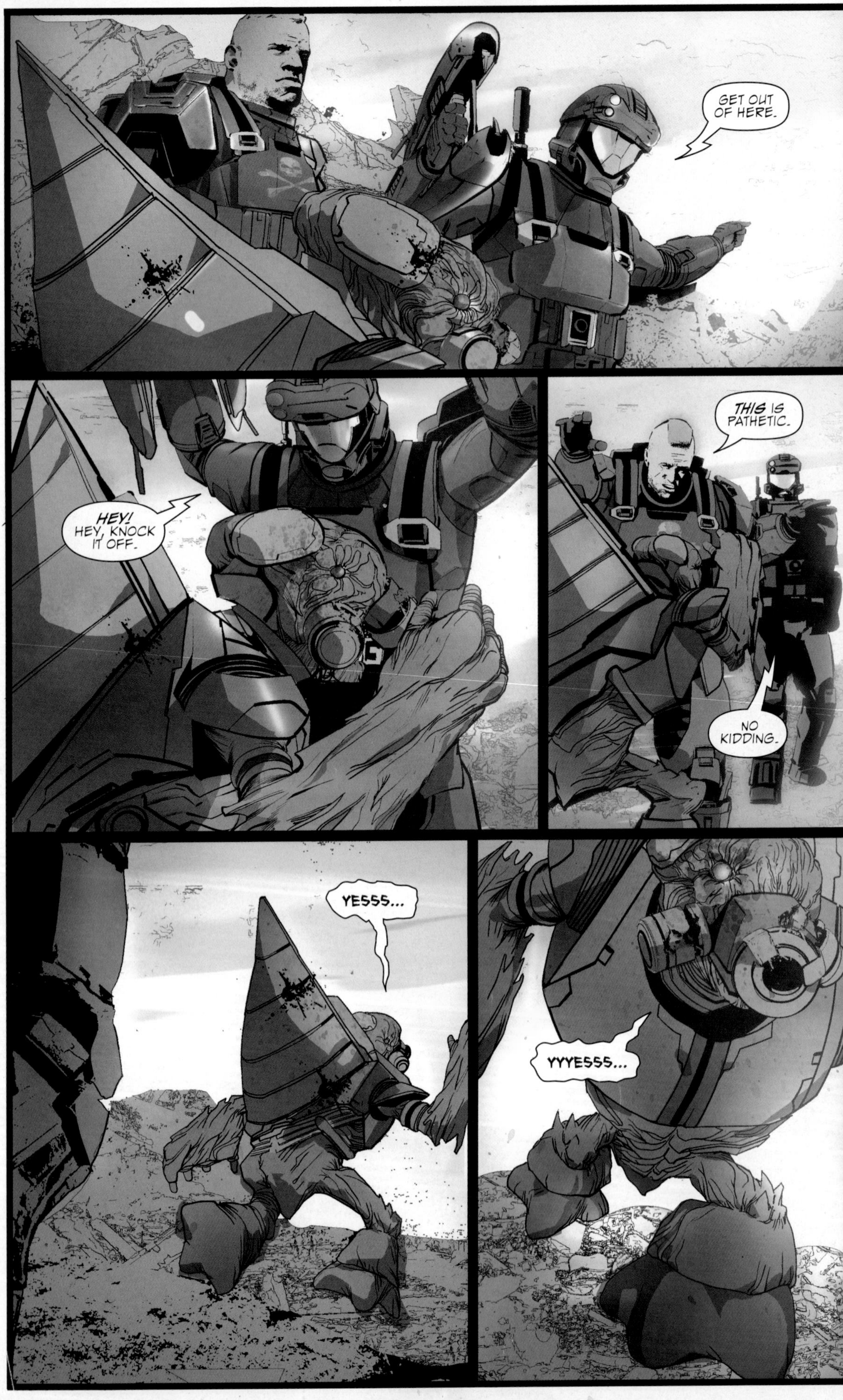
GET OUT OF HERE.
HEY! HEY, KNOCK IT OFF.
THIS IS PATHETIC.
NO KIDDING.
YESSS...
YYYESSS...

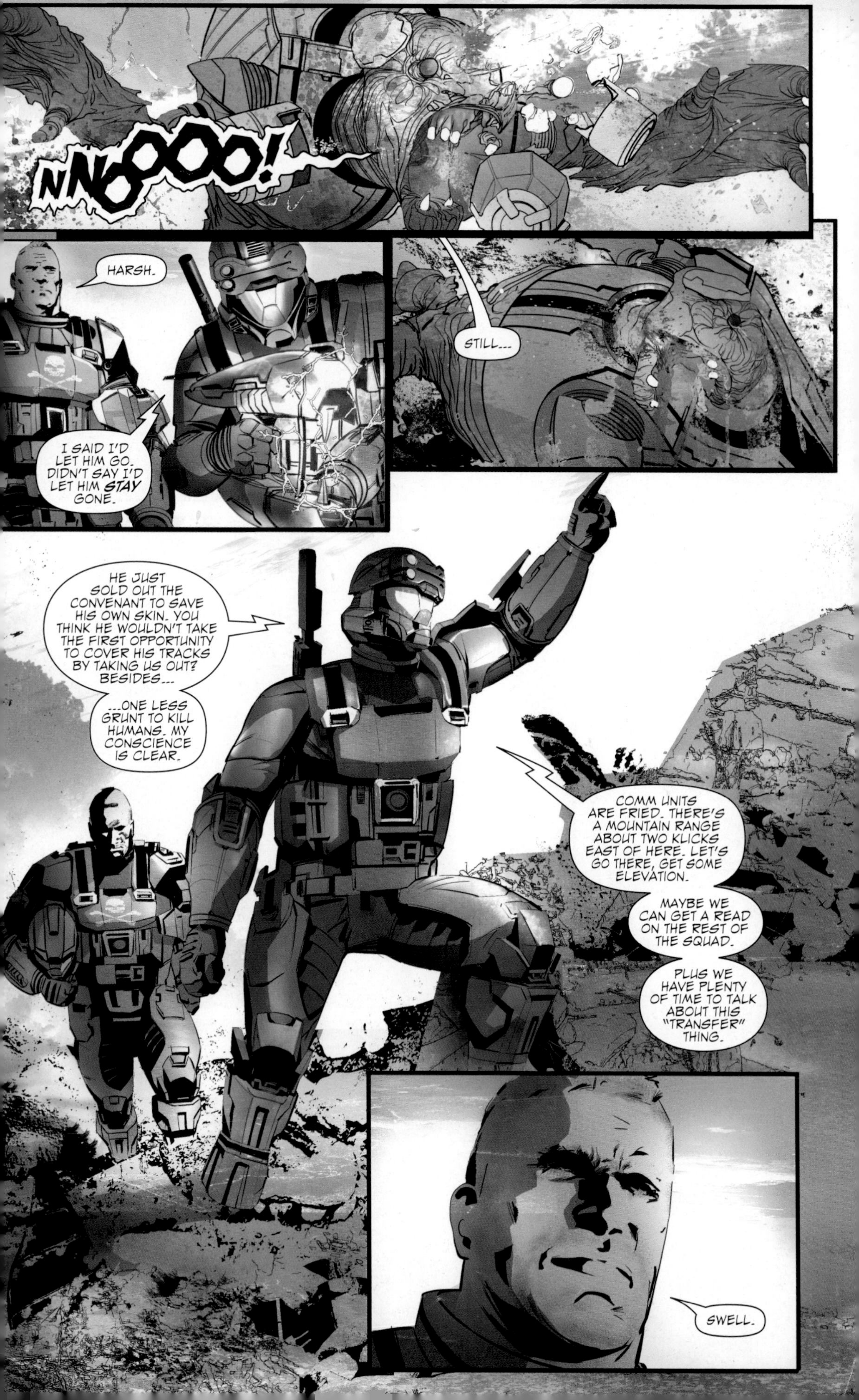
NNOOOO!
HARSH.
I SAID I'D LET HIM GO. DIDN'T SAY I'D LET HIM STAY GONE.
STILL...
HE JUST SOLD OUT THE CONVENANT TO SAVE HIS OWN SKIN. YOU THINK HE WOULDN'T TAKE THE FIRST OPPORTUNITY TO COVER HIS TRACKS BY TAKING US OUT? BESIDES...
...ONE LESS GRUNT TO KILL HUMANS. MY CONSCIENCE IS CLEAR.
COMM UNITS ARE FRIED. THERE'S A MOUNTAIN RANGE ABOUT TWO KLICKS EAST OF HERE. LET'S GO THERE, GET SOME ELEVATION.
MAYBE WE CAN GET A READ ON THE REST OF THE SQUAD.
PLUS WE HAVE PLENTY OF TIME TO TALK ABOUT THIS "TRANSFER" THING.
SWELL.

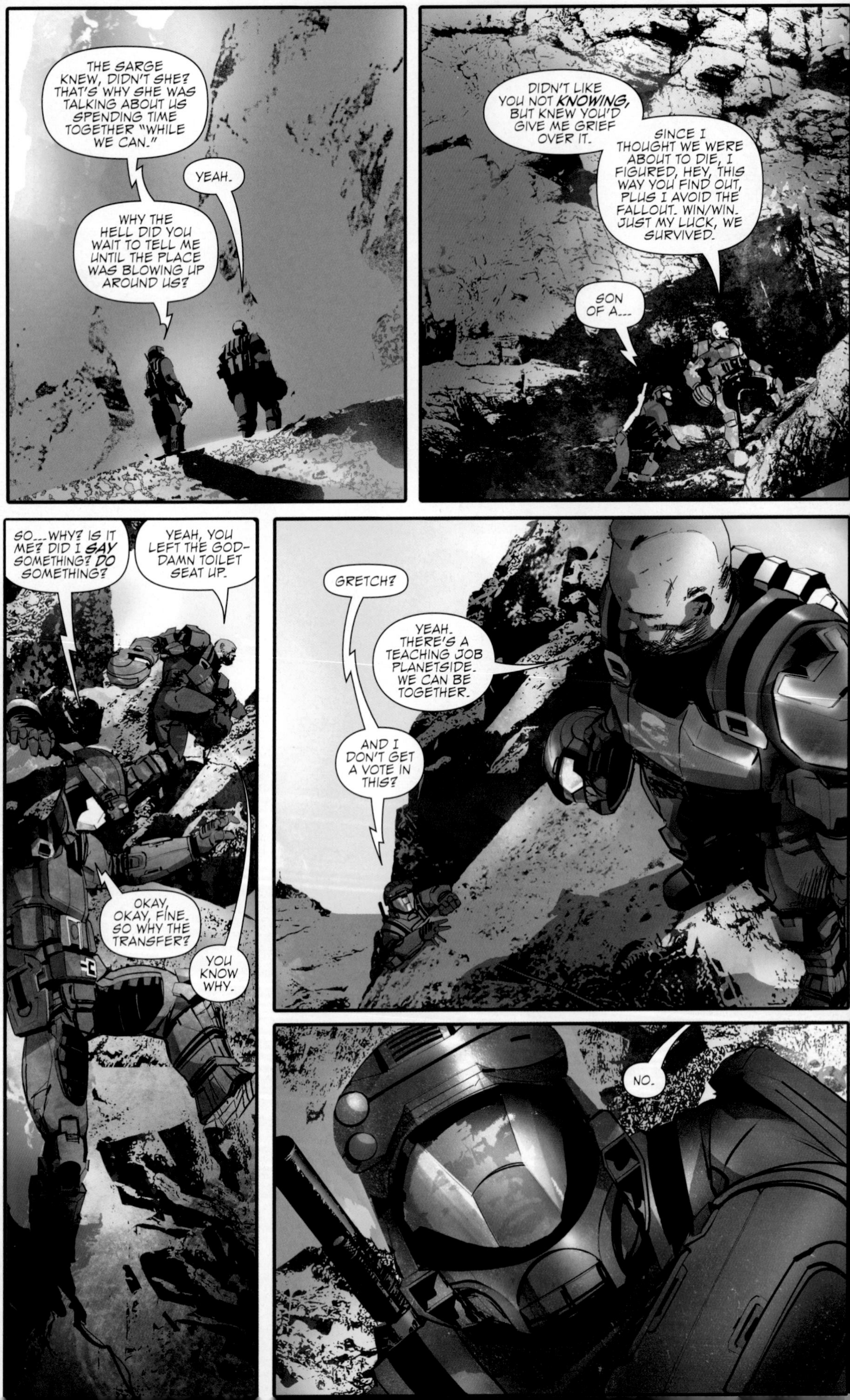
THE SARGE KNEW, DIDN'T SHE? THAT'S WHY SHE WAS TALKING ABOUT US SPENDING TIME TOGETHER "WHILE WE CAN."
YEAH.
WHY THE HELL DID YOU WAIT TO TELL ME UNTIL THE PLACE WAS BLOWING UP AROUND US?
DIDN'T LIKE YOU NOT KNOWING, BUT KNEW YOU'D GIVE ME GRIEF OVER IT.
SINCE I THOUGHT WE WERE ABOUT TO DIE, I FIGURED, HEY, THIS WAY YOU FIND OUT, PLUS I AVOID THE FALLOUT. WIN/WIN. JUST MY LUCK, WE SURVIVED.
SON OF A...
SO...WHY? IS IT ME? DID I SAY SOMETHING? DO SOMETHING?
YEAH, YOU LEFT THE GOD-DAMN TOILET SEAT UP.
OKAY, OKAY, FINE. SO WHY THE TRANSFER?
YOU KNOW WHY.
GRETCH?
YEAH. THERE'S A TEACHING JOB PLANETSIDE. WE CAN BE TOGETHER.
AND I DON'T GET A VOTE IN THIS?
NO.

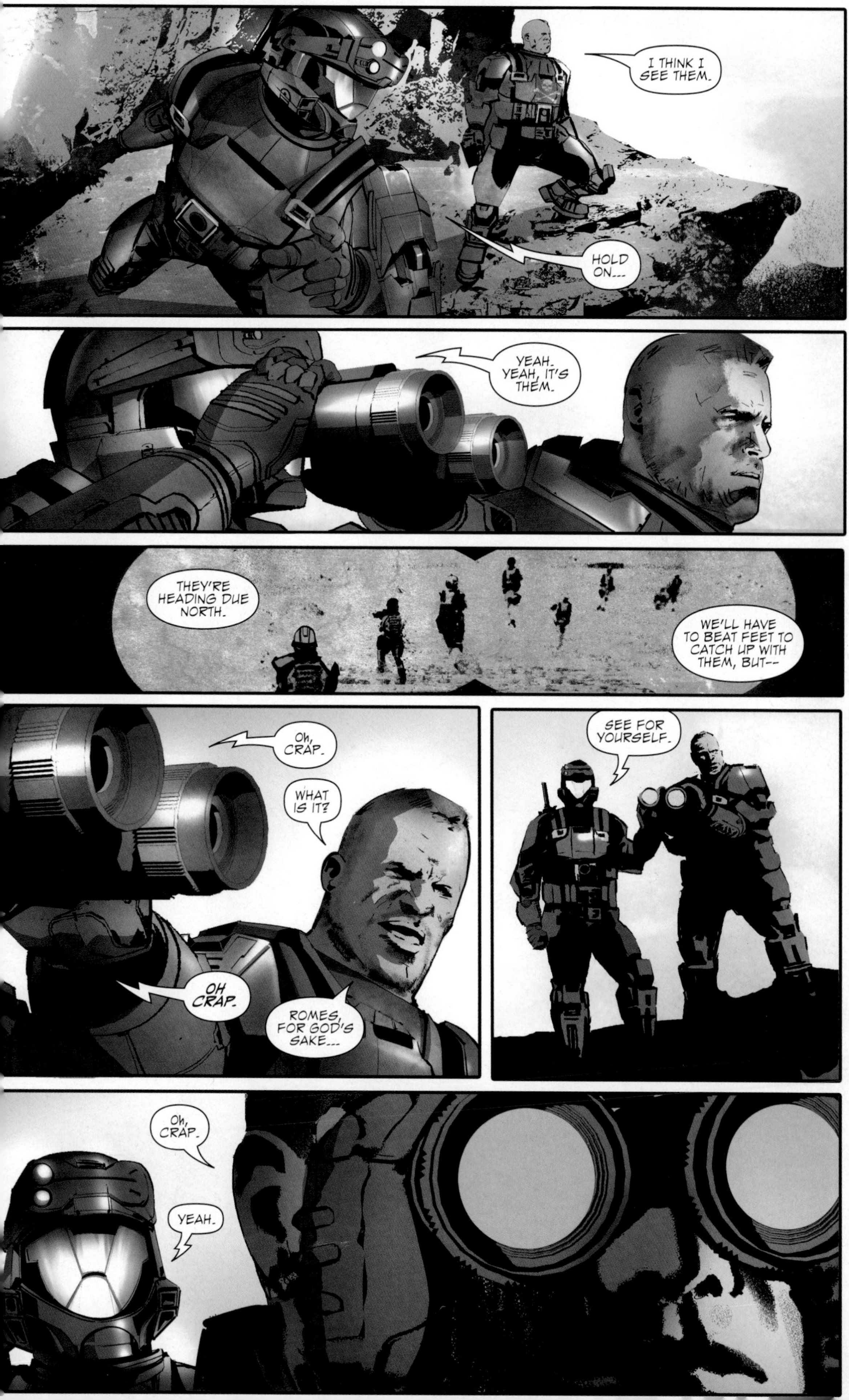
I THINK I SEE THEM.
HOLD ON...
YEAH. YEAH, IT'S THEM.
THEY'RE HEADING DUE NORTH.
WE'LL HAVE TO BEAT FEET TO CATCH UP WITH THEM, BUT--
Oh, CRAP.
WHAT IS IT?
OH CRAP.
ROMES, FOR GOD'S SAKE...
SEE FOR YOURSELF.
Oh, CRAP.
YEAH.

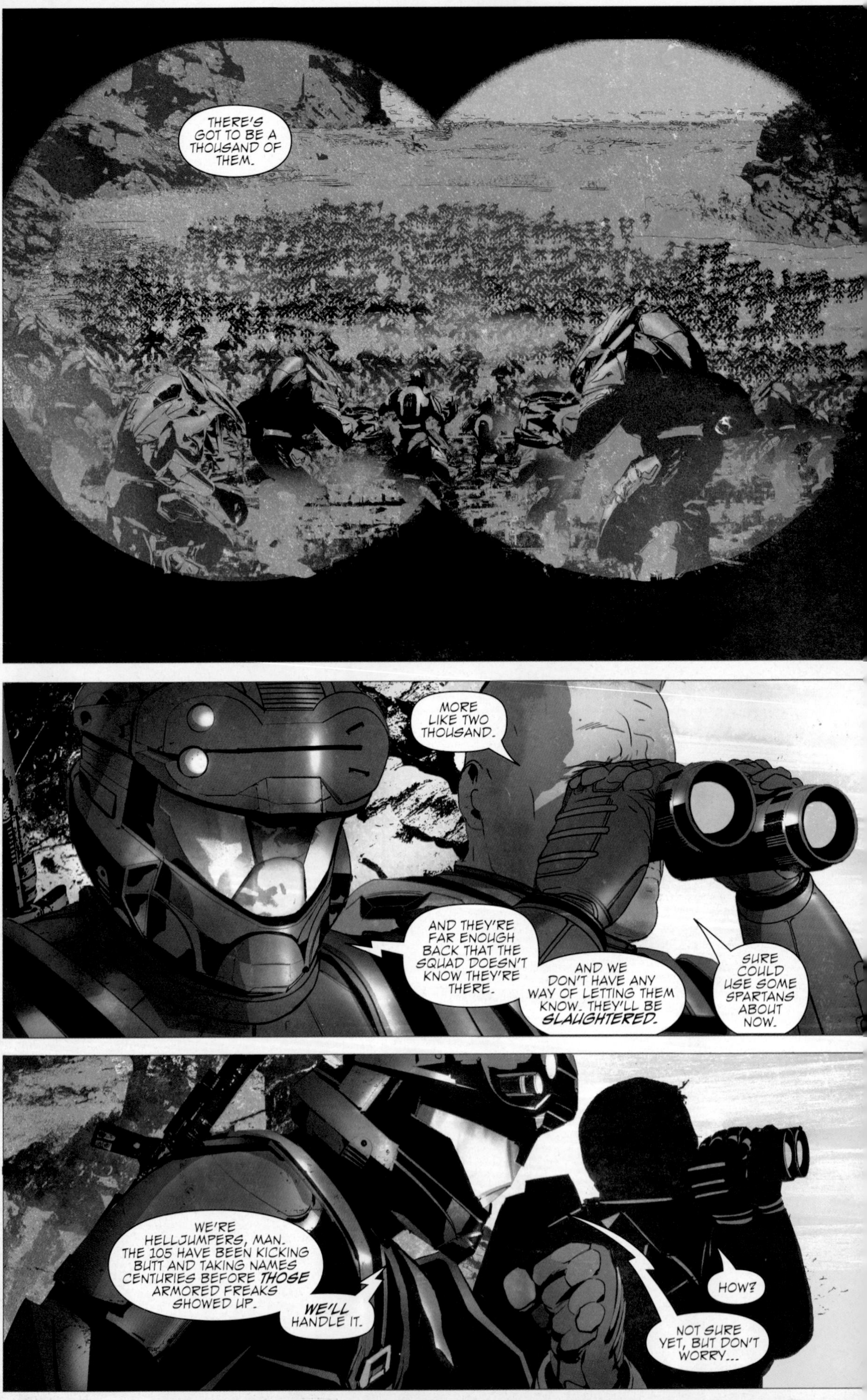
THERE'S GOT TO BE A THOUSAND OF THEM.
MORE LIKE TWO THOUSAND.
AND THEY'RE FAR ENOUGH BACK THAT THE SQUAD DOESN'T KNOW THEY'RE THERE.
AND WE DON'T HAVE ANY WAY OF LETTING THEM KNOW. THEY'LL BE SLAUGHTERED.
SURE COULD USE SOME SPARTANS ABOUT NOW.
WE'RE HELLJUMPERS, MAN. THE 105 HAVE BEEN KICKING BUTT AND TAKING NAMES CENTURIES BEFORE THOSE ARMORED FREAKS SHOWED UP.
WE'LL HANDLE IT.
HOW?
NOT SURE YET, BUT DON'T WORRY...

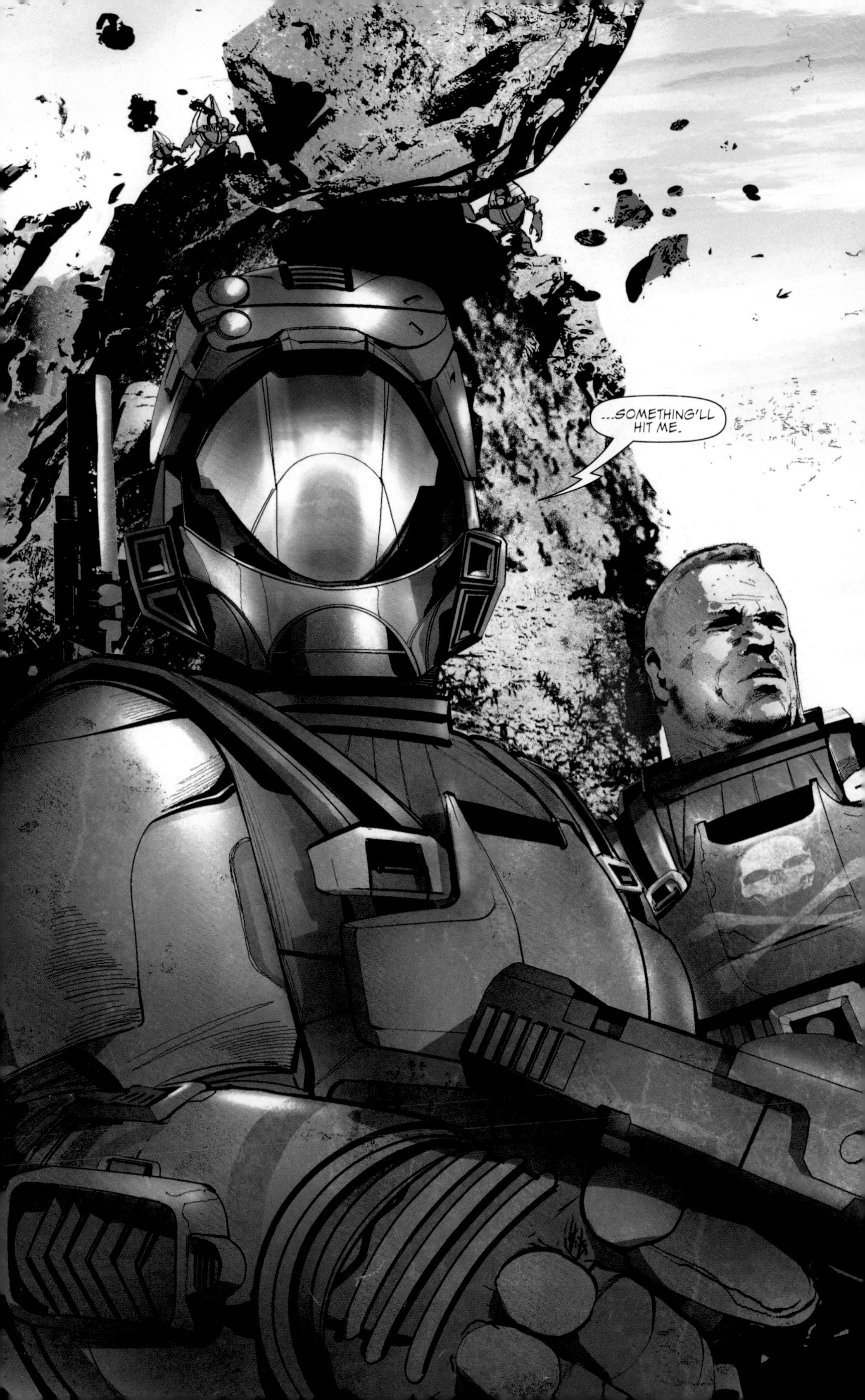
...SOMETHING'LL HIT ME.

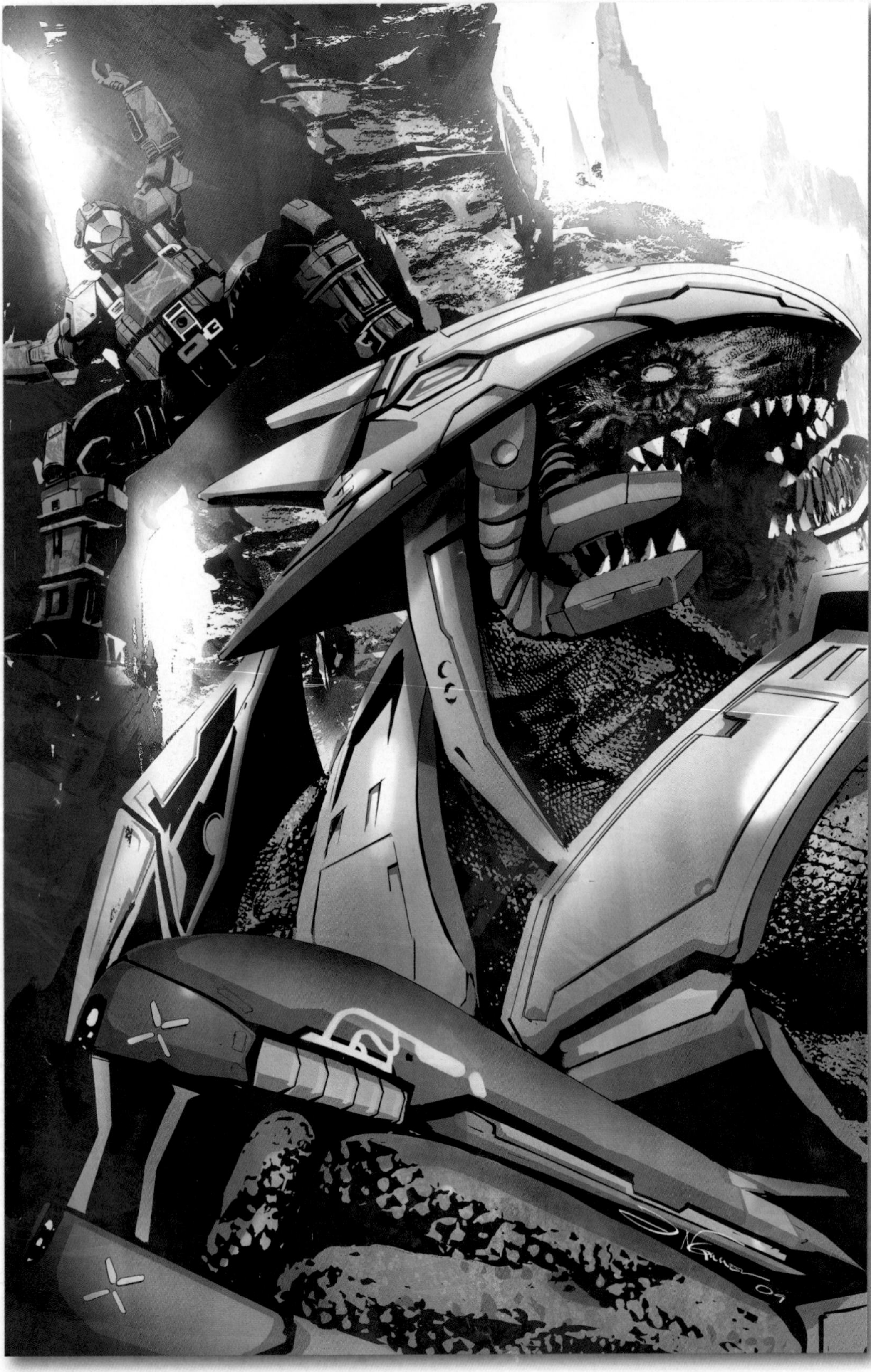

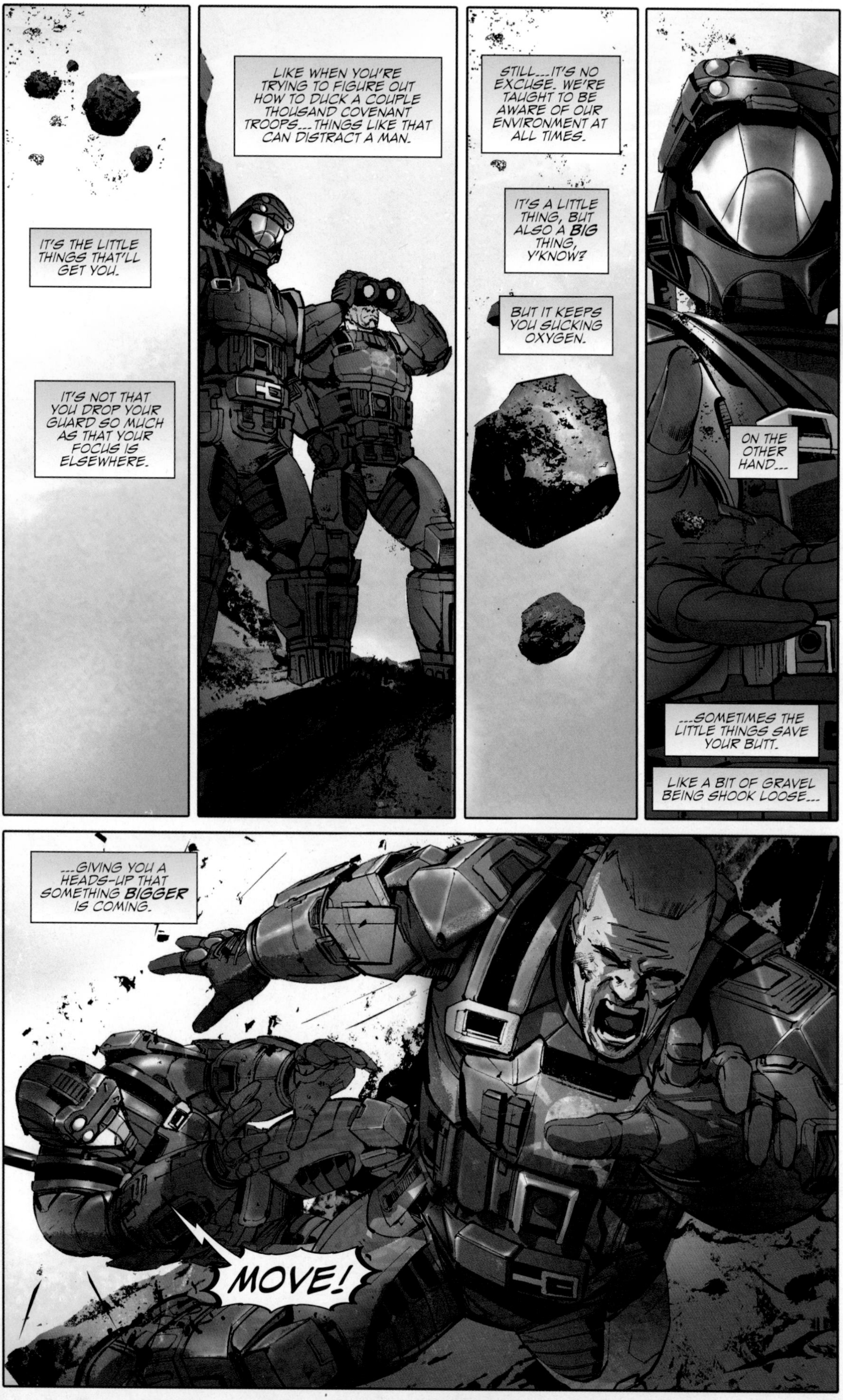
IT'S THE LITTLE THINGS THAT'LL GET YOU.
IT'S NOT THAT YOU DROP YOUR GUARD SO MUCH AS THAT YOUR FOCUS IS ELSEWHERE.
LIKE WHEN YOU'RE TRYING TO FIGURE OUT HOW TO DUCK A COUPLE THOUSAND COVENANT TROOPS... THINGS LIKE THAT CAN DISTRACT A MAN.
STILL... IT'S NO EXCUSE. WE'RE TAUGHT TO BE AWARE OF OUR ENVIRONMENT AT ALL TIMES.
IT'S A LITTLE THING, BUT ALSO A BIG THING, Y'KNOW?
BUT IT KEEPS YOU SUCKING OXYGEN.
ON THE OTHER HAND...
...SOMETIMES THE LITTLE THINGS SAVE YOUR BUTT.
LIKE A BIT OF GRAVEL BEING SHOOK LOOSE...
...GIVING YOU A HEADS-UP THAT SOMETHING BIGGER IS COMING.
MOVE!

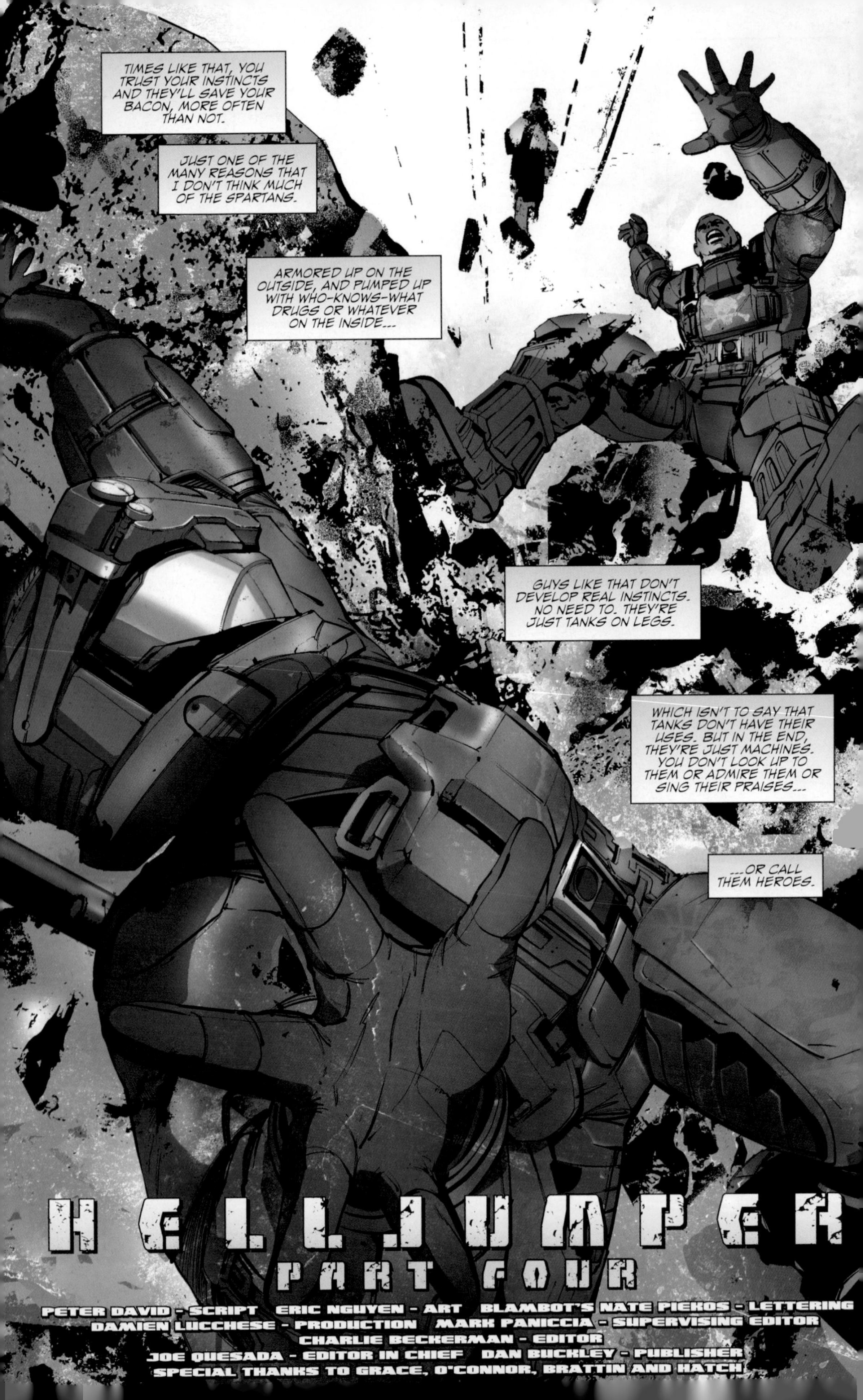
TIMES LIKE THAT, YOU TRUST YOUR INSTINCTS AND THEY'LL SAVE YOUR BACON, MORE OFTEN THAN NOT.
JUST ONE OF THE MANY REASONS THAT I DON'T THINK MUCH OF THE SPARTANS.
ARMORED UP ON THE OUTSIDE, AND PUMPED UP WITH WHO-KNOWS-WHAT DRUGS OR WHATEVER ON THE INSIDE...
GUYS LIKE THAT DON'T DEVELOP REAL INSTINCTS. NO NEED TO. THEY'RE JUST TANKS ON LEGS.
WHICH ISN'T TO SAY THAT TANKS DON'T HAVE THEIR USES. BUT IN THE END, THEY'RE JUST MACHINES. YOU DON'T LOOK UP TO THEM OR ADMIRE THEM OR SING THEIR PRAISES...
...OR CALL THEM HEROES.
HELLJUMPER
PART FOUR
PETER DAVID - SCRIPT ERIC NGUYEN - ART BLAMBOT'S NATE PIEKOS - LETTERING
DAMIEN LUCCHESE - PRODUCTION MARK PANICCIA - SUPERVISING EDITOR
CHARLIE BECKERMAN - EDITOR
JOE QUESADA - EDITOR IN CHIEF DAN BUCKLEY - PUBLISHER
SPECIAL THANKS TO GRACE, O'CONNOR, BRATTIN AND HATCH

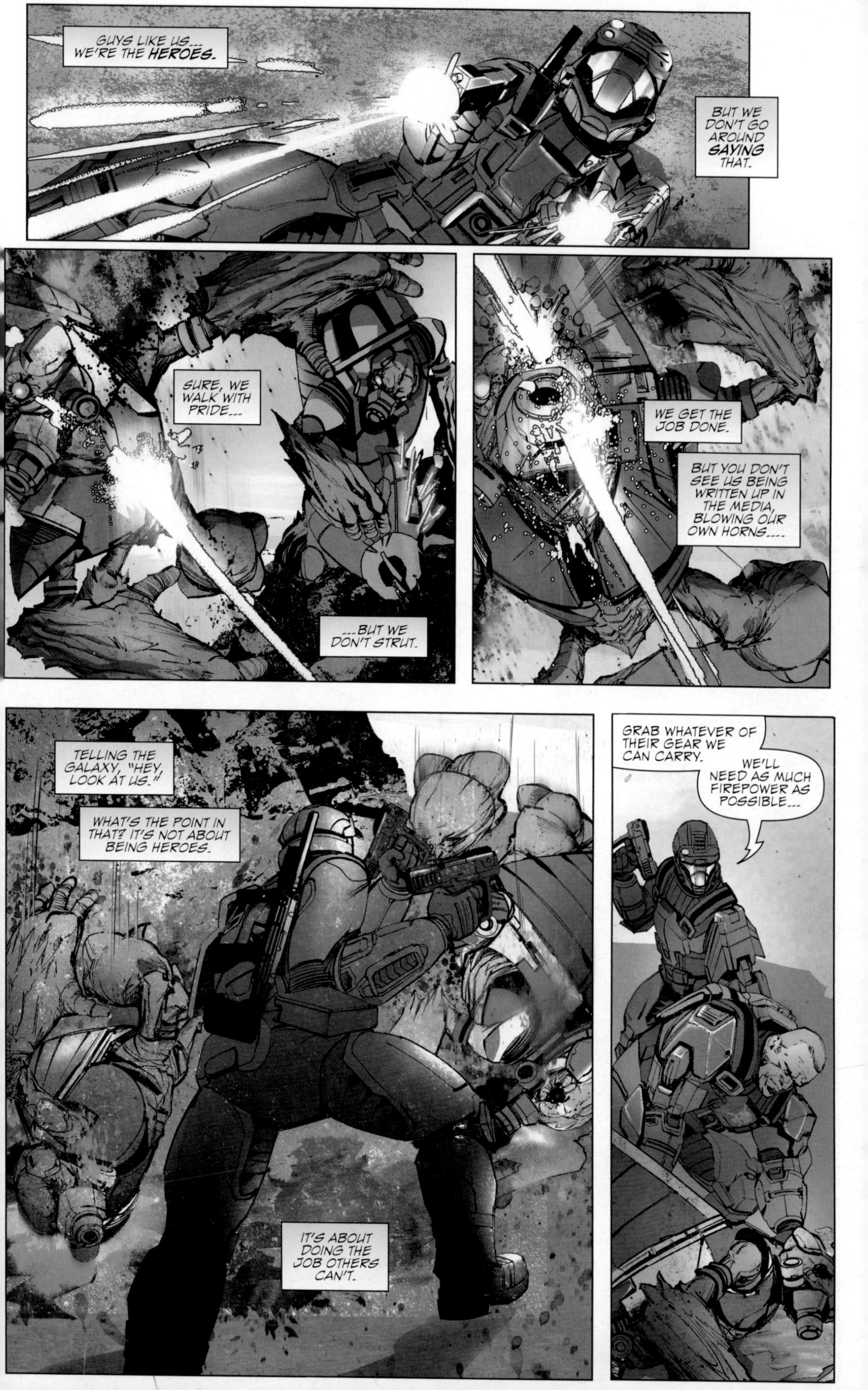
GUYS LIKE US...
WE'RE THE HEROES.
BUT WE DON'T GO AROUND SAYING THAT.
SURE, WE WALK WITH PRIDE...
...BUT WE DON'T STRUT.
WE GET THE JOB DONE.
BUT YOU DON'T SEE US BEING WRITTEN UP IN THE MEDIA, BLOWING OUR OWN HORNS....
TELLING THE GALAXY, "HEY, LOOK AT US."
WHAT'S THE POINT IN THAT? IT'S NOT ABOUT BEING HEROES.
IT'S ABOUT DOING THE JOB OTHERS CAN'T.
GRAB WHATEVER OF THEIR GEAR WE CAN CARRY.
WE'LL NEED AS MUCH FIREPOWER AS POSSIBLE...

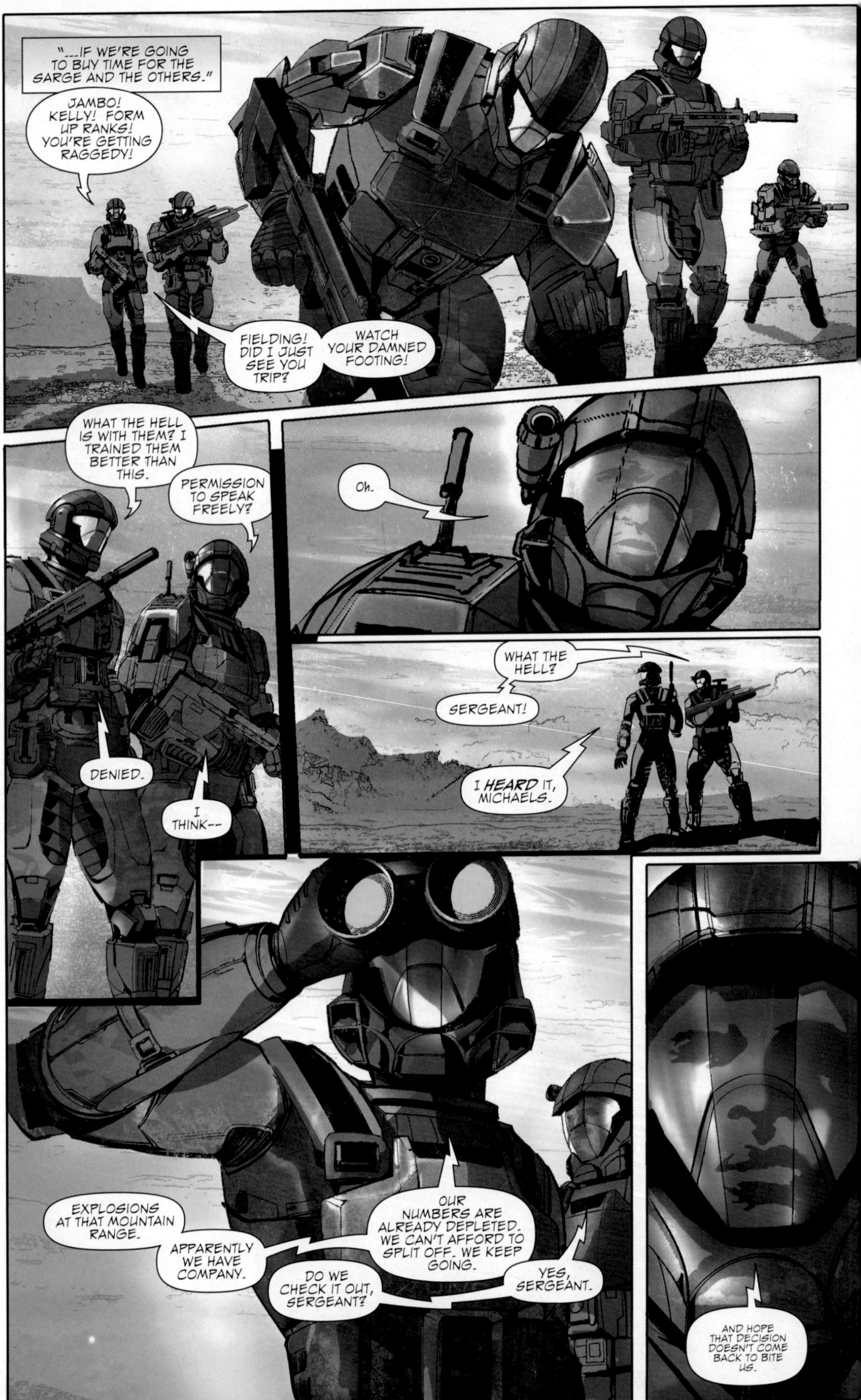
"...IF WE'RE GOING TO BUY TIME FOR THE SARGE AND THE OTHERS."
JAMBO! KELLY! FORM UP RANKS! YOU'RE GETTING RAGGEDY!
FIELDING! DID I JUST SEE YOU TRIP?
WATCH YOUR DAMNED FOOTING!
WHAT THE HELL IS WITH THEM? I TRAINED THEM BETTER THAN THIS.
PERMISSION TO SPEAK FREELY?
DENIED.
I THINK--
Oh.
WHAT THE HELL?
SERGEANT!
I HEARD IT, MICHAELS.
EXPLOSIONS AT THAT MOUNTAIN RANGE.
APPARENTLY WE HAVE COMPANY.
DO WE CHECK IT OUT, SERGEANT?
OUR NUMBERS ARE ALREADY DEPLETED. WE CAN'T AFFORD TO SPLIT OFF. WE KEEP GOING.
YES, SERGEANT.
AND HOPE THAT DECISION DOESN'T COME BACK TO BITE US.

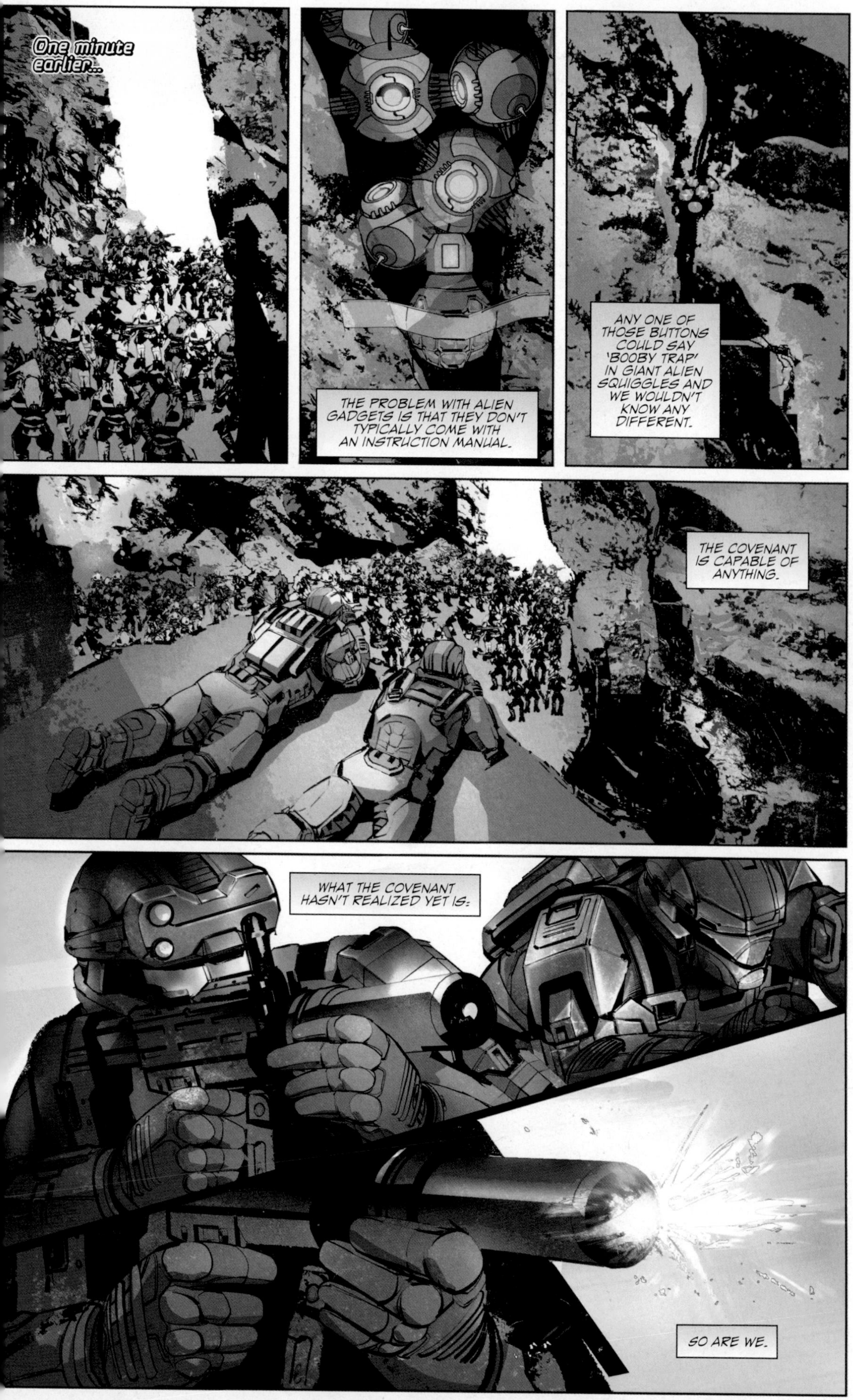
One minute earlier...
THE PROBLEM WITH ALIEN GADGETS IS THAT THEY DON'T TYPICALLY COME WITH AN INSTRUCTION MANUAL.
ANY ONE OF THOSE BUTTONS COULD SAY 'BOOBY TRAP' IN GIANT ALIEN SQUIGGLES AND WE WOULDN'T KNOW ANY DIFFERENT.
THE COVENANT IS CAPABLE OF ANYTHING.
WHAT THE COVENANT HASN'T REALIZED YET IS:
SO ARE WE.

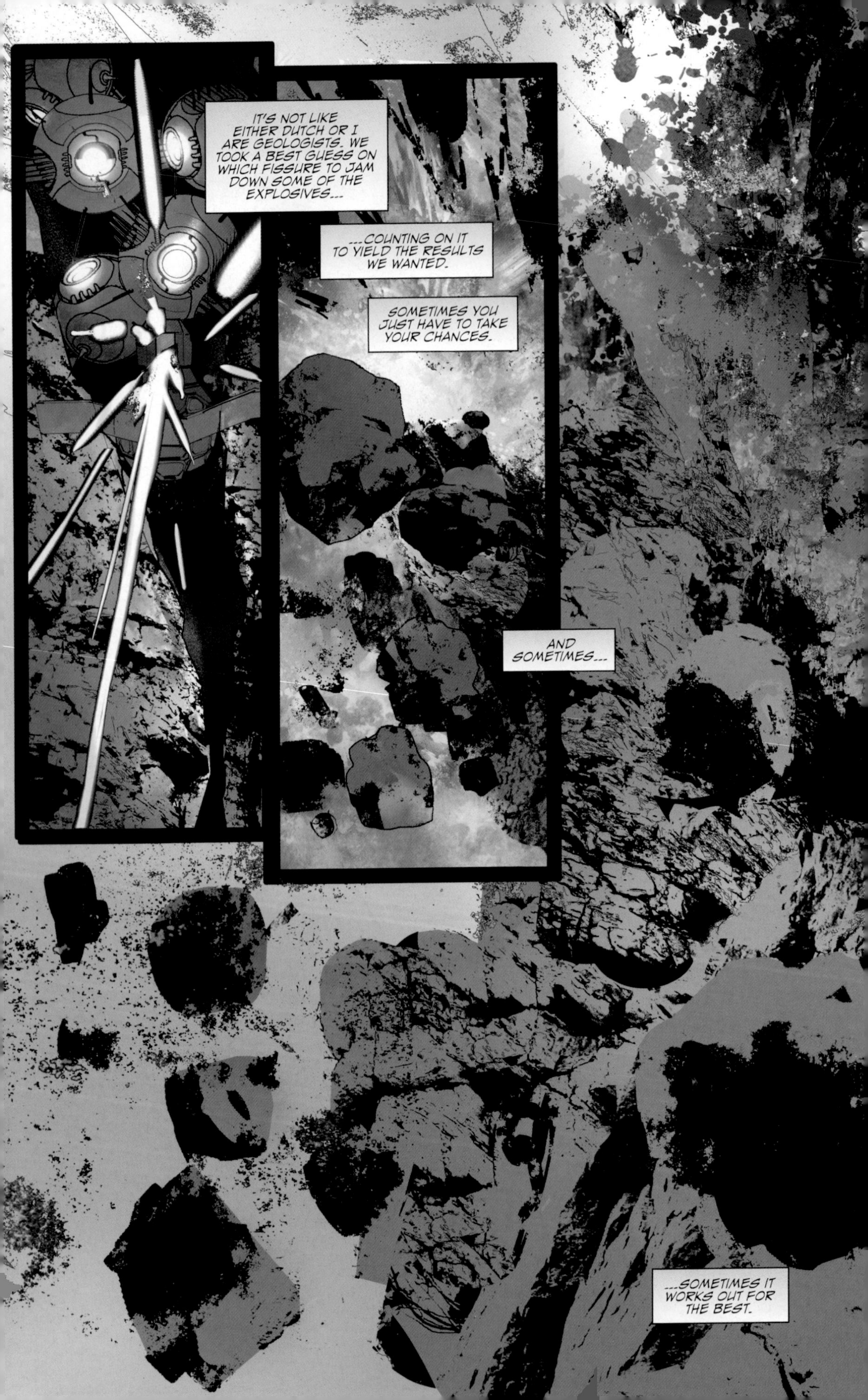
IT'S NOT LIKE EITHER DUTCH OR I ARE GEOLOGISTS. WE TOOK A BEST GUESS ON WHICH FISSURE TO JAM DOWN SOME OF THE EXPLOSIVES...
...COUNTING ON IT TO YIELD THE RESULTS WE WANTED.
SOMETIMES YOU JUST HAVE TO TAKE YOUR CHANCES.
AND SOMETIMES...
...SOMETIMES IT WORKS OUT FOR THE BEST.

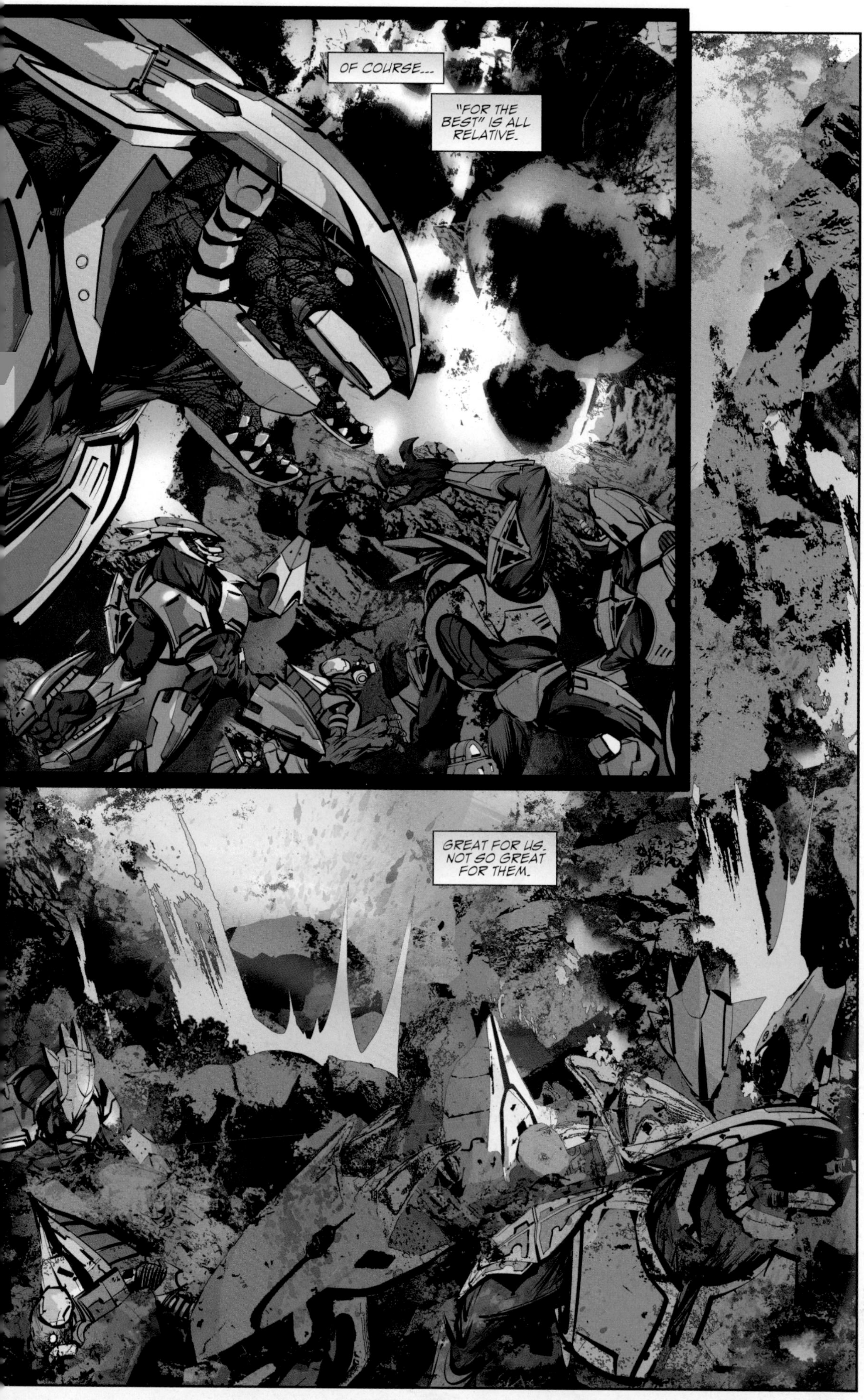
OF COURSE...
"FOR THE BEST" IS ALL RELATIVE.
GREAT FOR US. NOT SO GREAT FOR THEM.

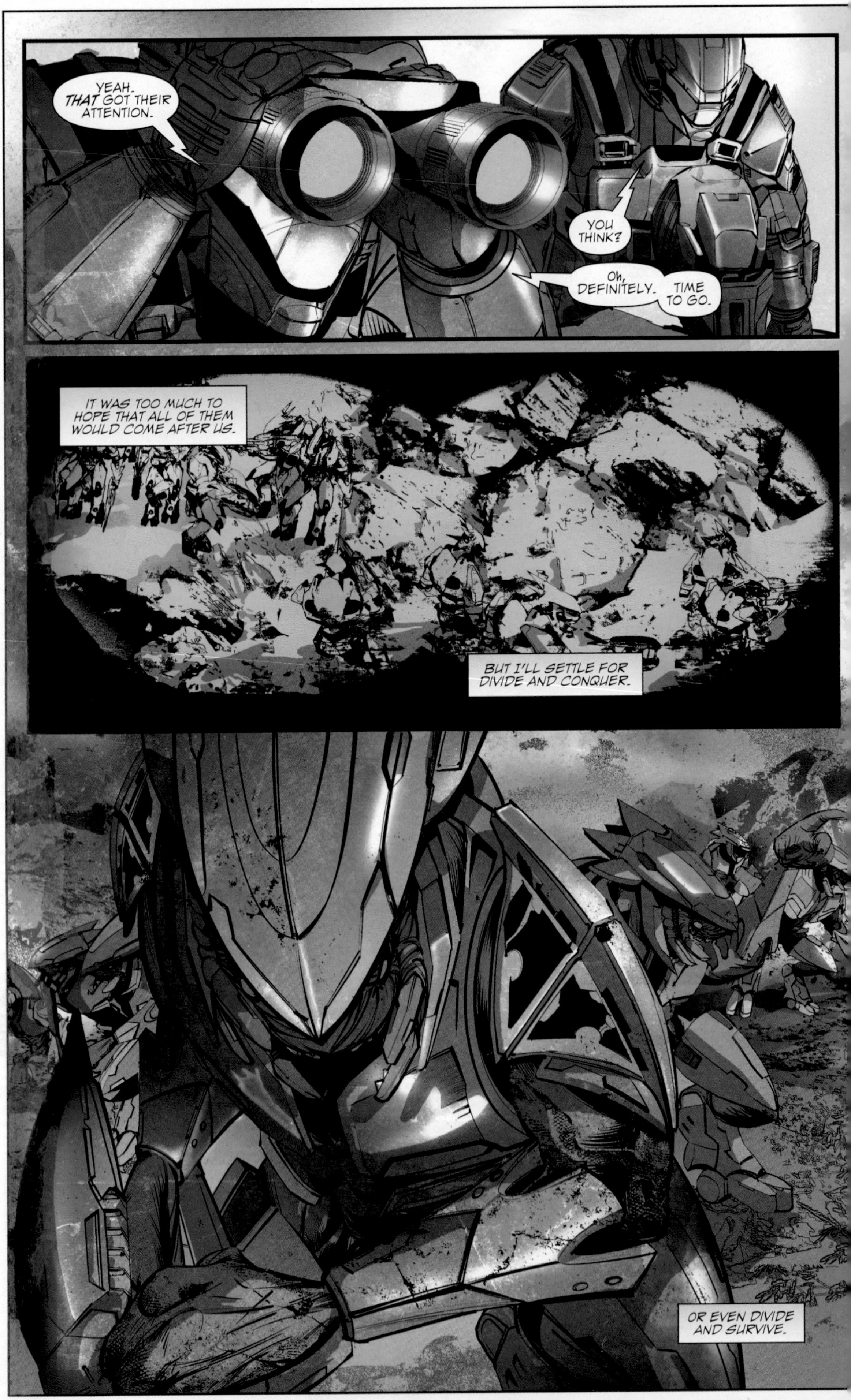
YEAH. THAT GOT THEIR ATTENTION.
YOU THINK?
Oh, DEFINITELY.
TIME TO GO.
IT WAS TOO MUCH TO HOPE THAT ALL OF THEM WOULD COME AFTER US.
BUT I'LL SETTLE FOR DIVIDE AND CONQUER.
OR EVEN DIVIDE AND SURVIVE.

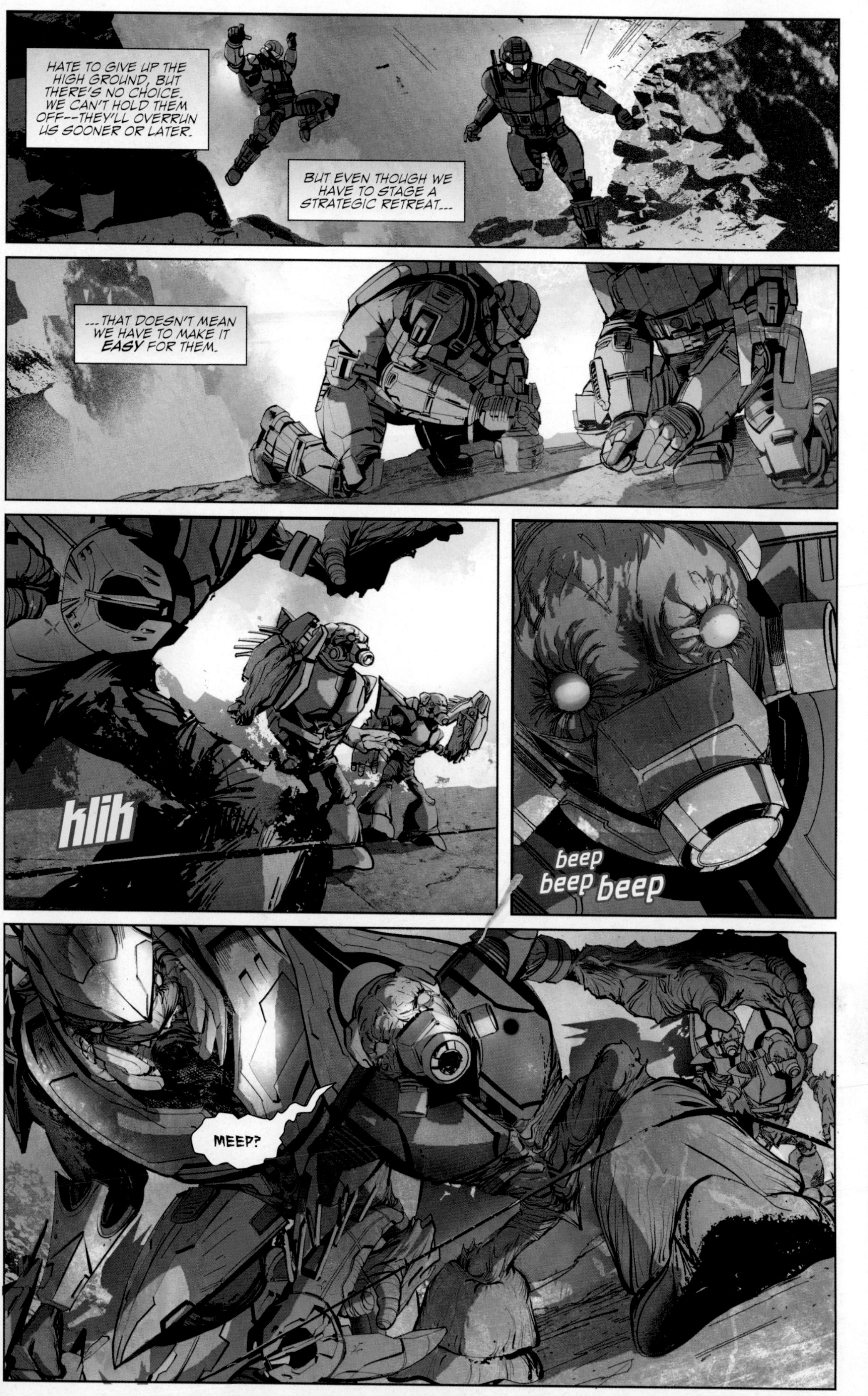
HATE TO GIVE UP THE HIGH GROUND, BUT THERE'S NO CHOICE. WE CAN'T HOLD THEM OFF--THEY'LL OVERRUN US SOONER OR LATER.
BUT EVEN THOUGH WE HAVE TO STAGE A STRATEGIC RETREAT...
...THAT DOESN'T MEAN WE HAVE TO MAKE IT EASY FOR THEM.
klik
beep beep beep
MEEP?

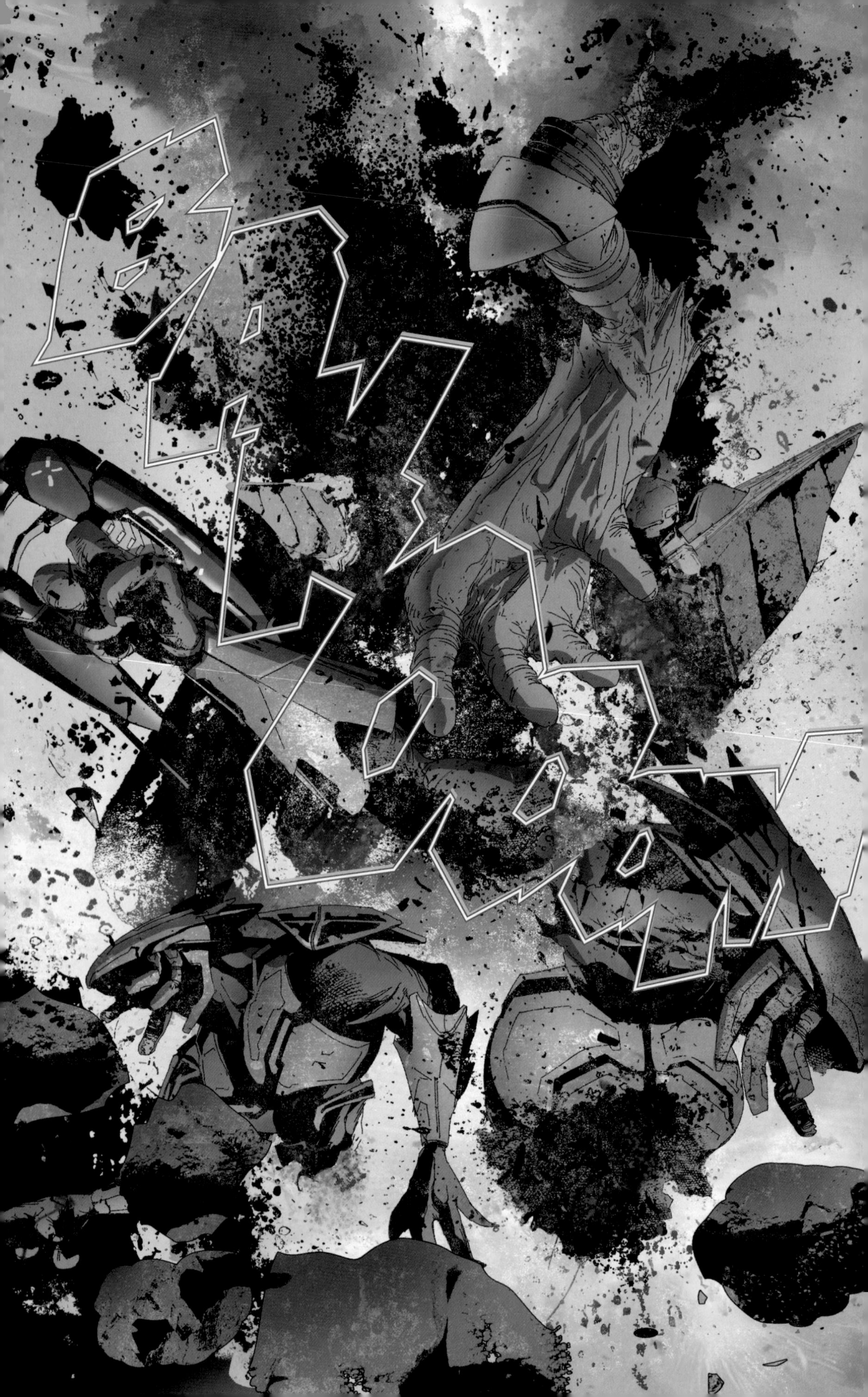

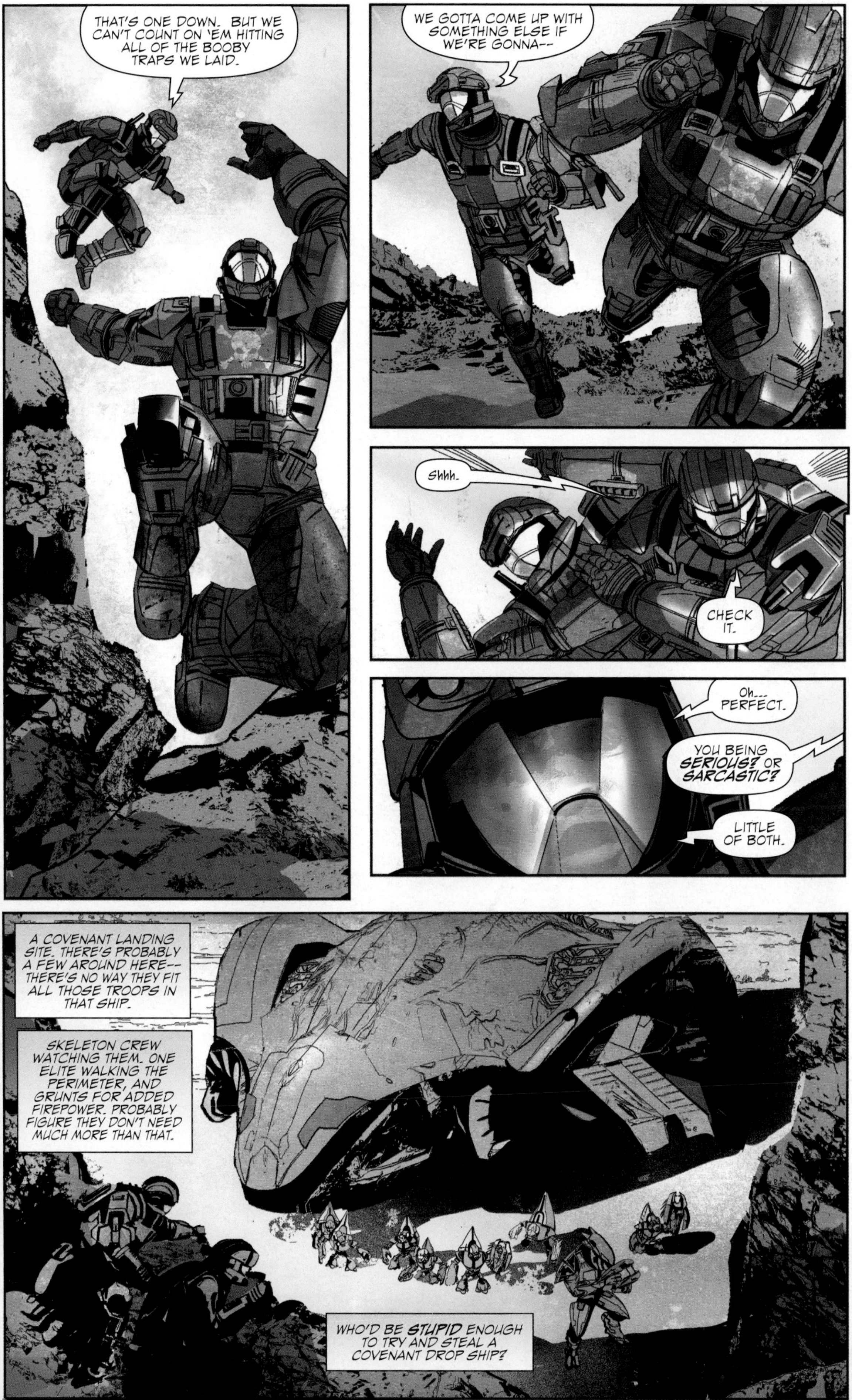
THAT'S ONE DOWN. BUT WE CAN'T COUNT ON 'EM HITTING ALL OF THE BOOBY TRAPS WE LAID.
WE GOTTA COME UP WITH SOMETHING ELSE IF WE'RE GONNA--
Shhh.
CHECK IT.
Oh... PERFECT.
YOU BEING SERIOUS? OR SARCASTIC?
LITTLE OF BOTH.
A COVENANT LANDING SITE. THERE'S PROBABLY A FEW AROUND HERE-- THERE'S NO WAY THEY FIT ALL THOSE TROOPS IN THAT SHIP.
SKELETON CREW WATCHING THEM. ONE ELITE WALKING THE PERIMETER, AND GRUNTS FOR ADDED FIREPOWER. PROBABLY FIGURE THEY DON'T NEED MUCH MORE THAN THAT.
WHO'D BE STUPID ENOUGH TO TRY AND STEAL A COVENANT DROP SHIP?

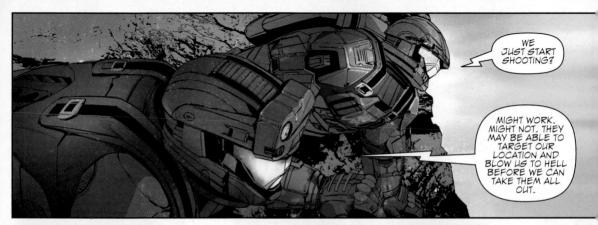

WE JUST START SHOOTING?

MIGHT WORK. MIGHT NOT. THEY MAY BE ABLE TO TARGET OUR LOCATION AND BLOW US TO HELL BEFORE WE CAN TAKE THEM ALL OUT.

I THINK THERE'S ANOTHER WAY, IF WE CAN REPOSITION OURSELVES.

"THE ELITE KEEPS WALKING THE EXACT SAME COURSE.

"THE WAY THE ROCKS ARE POSITIONED, THERE'S A POINT WHERE HE'S BRIEFLY OUT OF SIGHT OF THE GRUNTS.

"THAT'S WHEN WE MAKE OUR MOVE.

"PROBLEM IS, A SHOT WOULD ALERT THE GRUNTS.

"THAT, DUTCH, IS WHERE YOU COME IN."

WGHHH?!

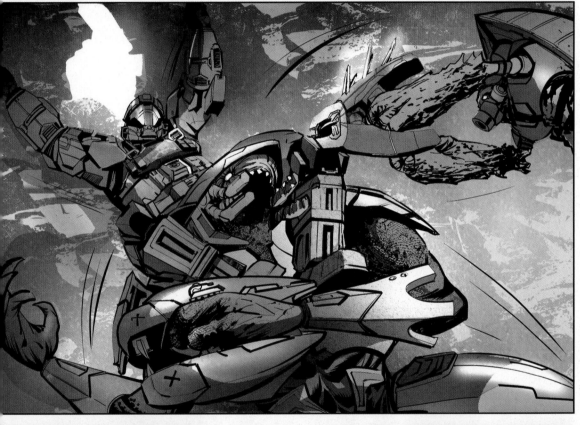

DIE, YOU BASTARD.

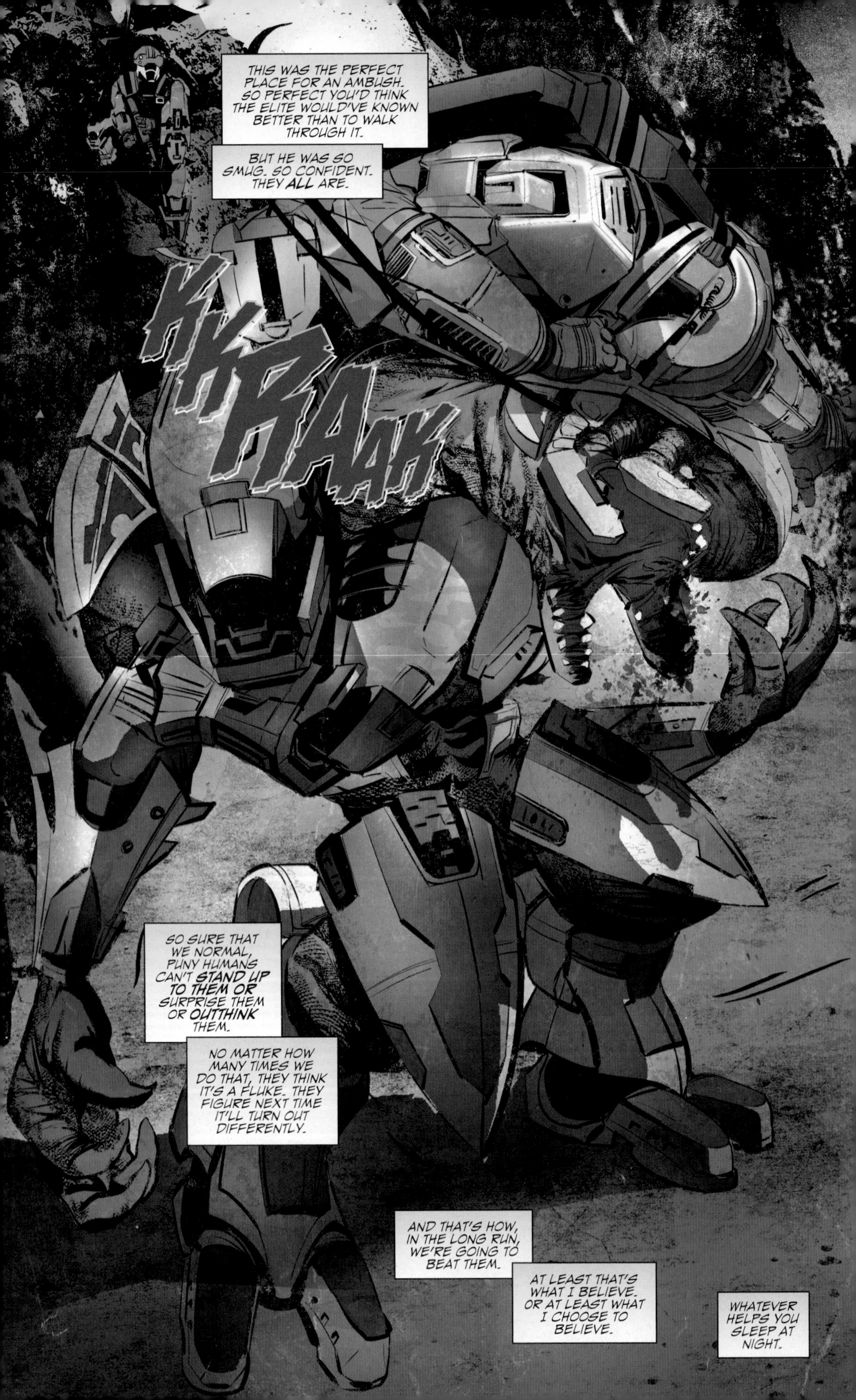
THIS WAS THE PERFECT PLACE FOR AN AMBUSH. SO PERFECT YOU'D THINK THE ELITE WOULD'VE KNOWN BETTER THAN TO WALK THROUGH IT.
BUT HE WAS SO SMUG. SO CONFIDENT. THEY ALL ARE.
KKRAAK
SO SURE THAT WE NORMAL, PUNY HUMANS CAN'T STAND UP TO THEM OR SURPRISE THEM OR OUTTHINK THEM.
NO MATTER HOW MANY TIMES WE DO THAT, THEY THINK IT'S A FLUKE. THEY FIGURE NEXT TIME IT'LL TURN OUT DIFFERENTLY.
AND THAT'S HOW, IN THE LONG RUN, WE'RE GOING TO BEAT THEM.
AT LEAST THAT'S WHAT I BELIEVE. OR AT LEAST WHAT I CHOOSE TO BELIEVE.
WHATEVER HELPS YOU SLEEP AT NIGHT.

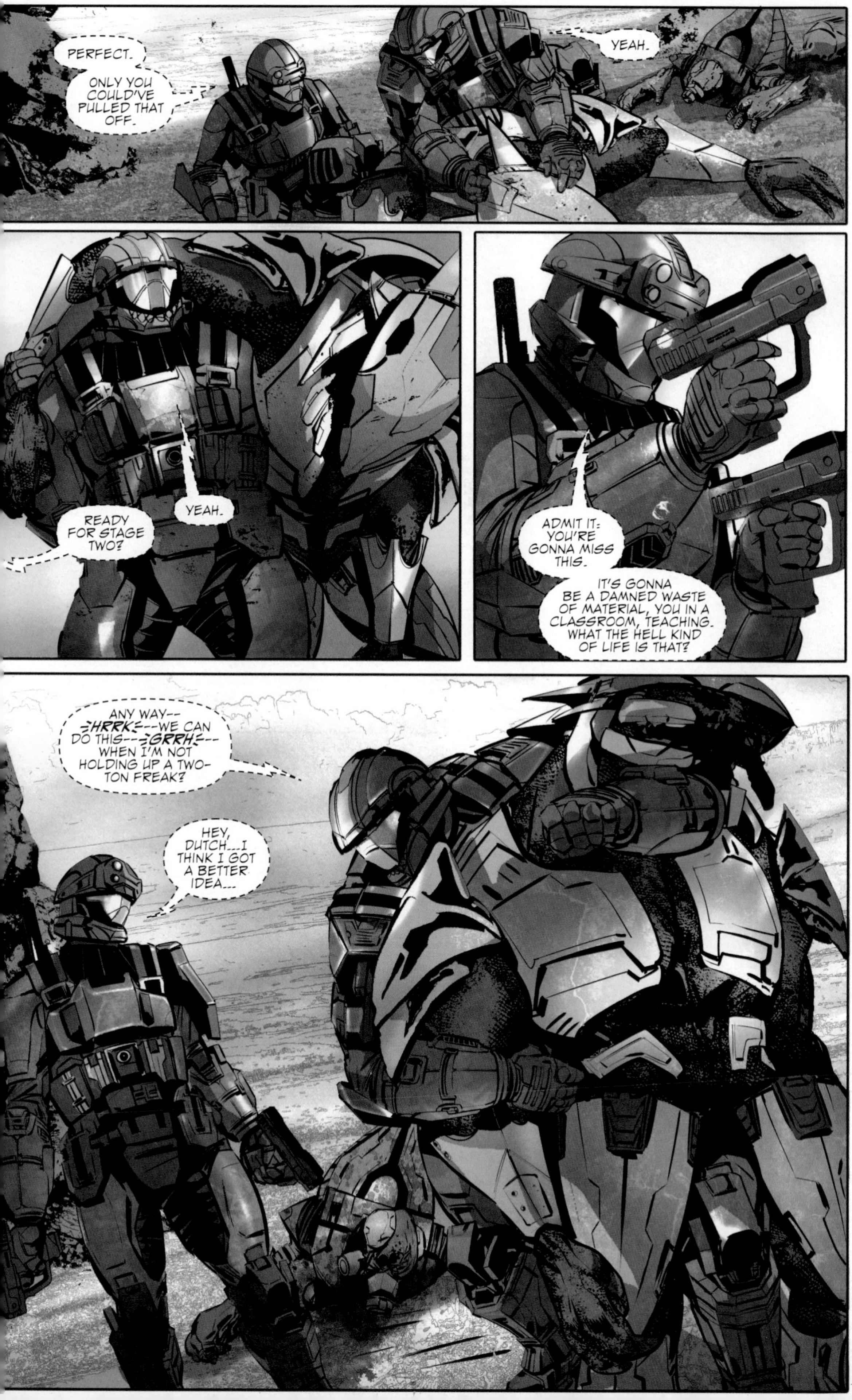
PERFECT.
ONLY YOU COULD'VE PULLED THAT OFF.
YEAH.
READY FOR STAGE TWO?
YEAH.
ADMIT IT: YOU'RE GONNA MISS THIS.
IT'S GONNA BE A DAMNED WASTE OF MATERIAL, YOU IN A CLASSROOM, TEACHING. WHAT THE HELL KIND OF LIFE IS THAT?
ANY WAY-- HRRK--WE CAN DO THIS--GRRH--WHEN I'M NOT HOLDING UP A TWO-TON FREAK?
HEY, DUTCH...I THINK I GOT A BETTER IDEA...

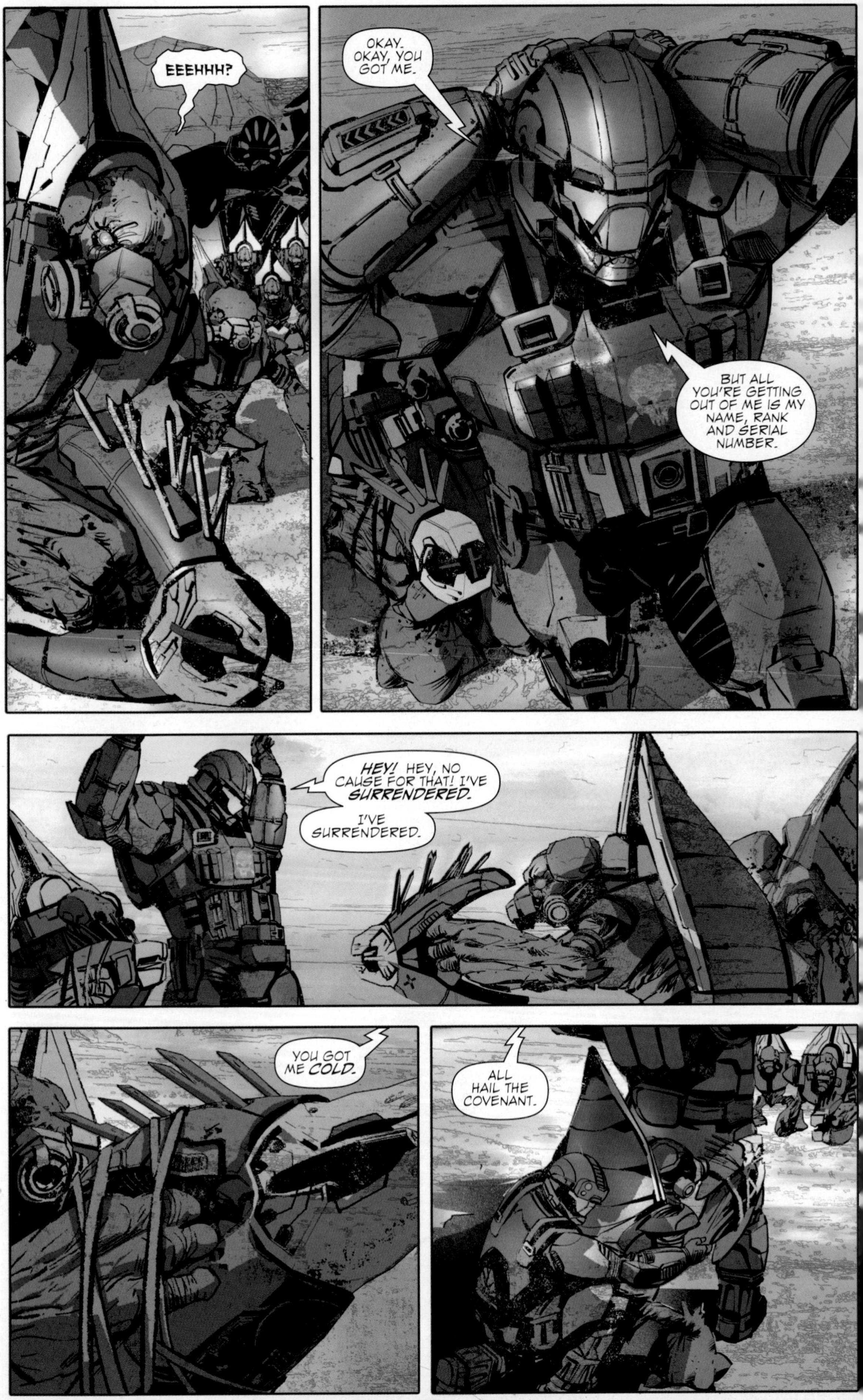
EEEHHH?
OKAY. OKAY, YOU GOT ME.
BUT ALL YOU'RE GETTING OUT OF ME IS MY NAME, RANK AND SERIAL NUMBER.
HEY! HEY, NO CAUSE FOR THAT! I'VE SURRENDERED.
I'VE SURRENDERED.
YOU GOT ME COLD.
ALL HAIL THE COVENANT.

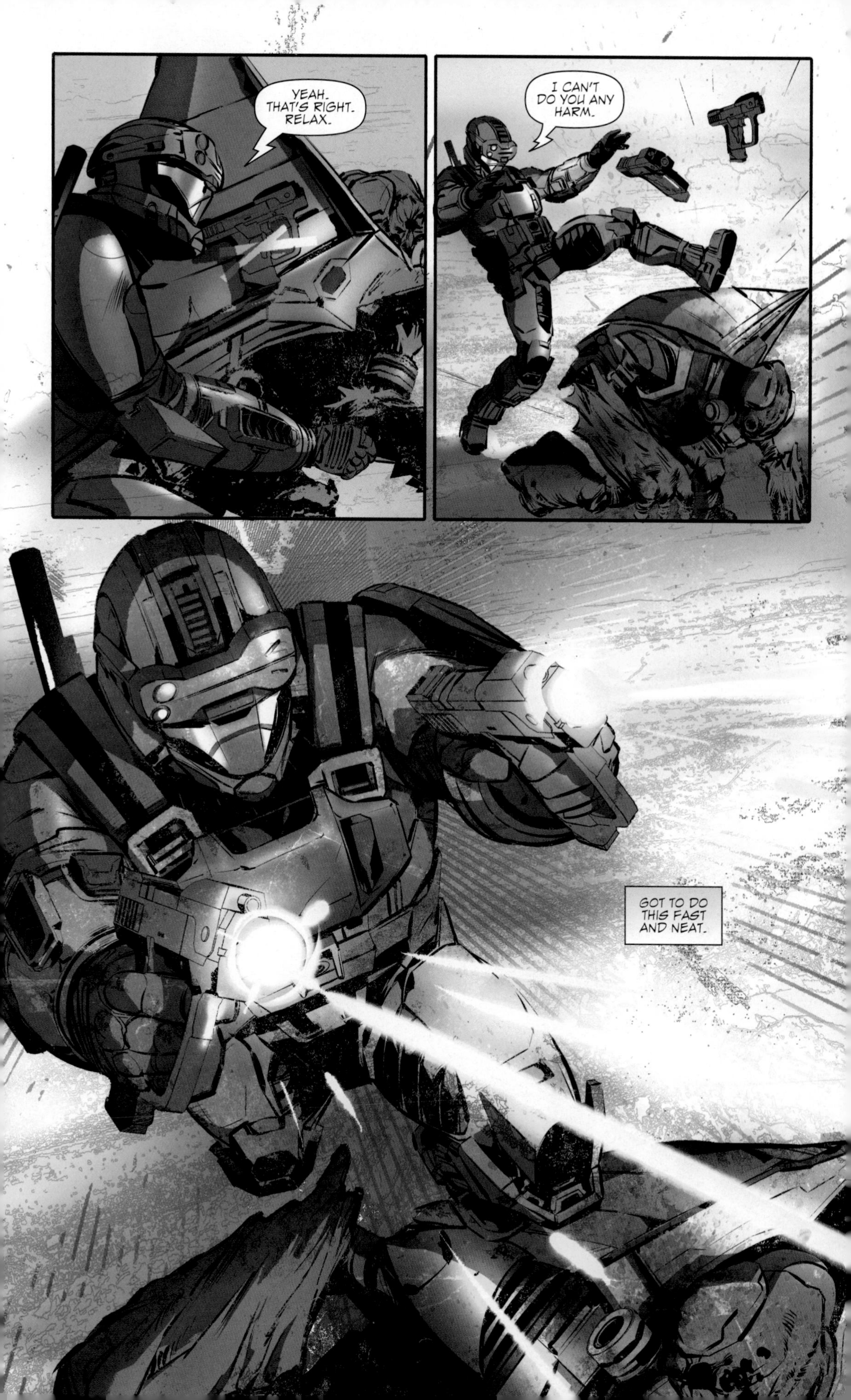
YEAH. THAT'S RIGHT. RELAX.
I CAN'T DO YOU ANY HARM.
GOT TO DO THIS FAST AND NEAT.

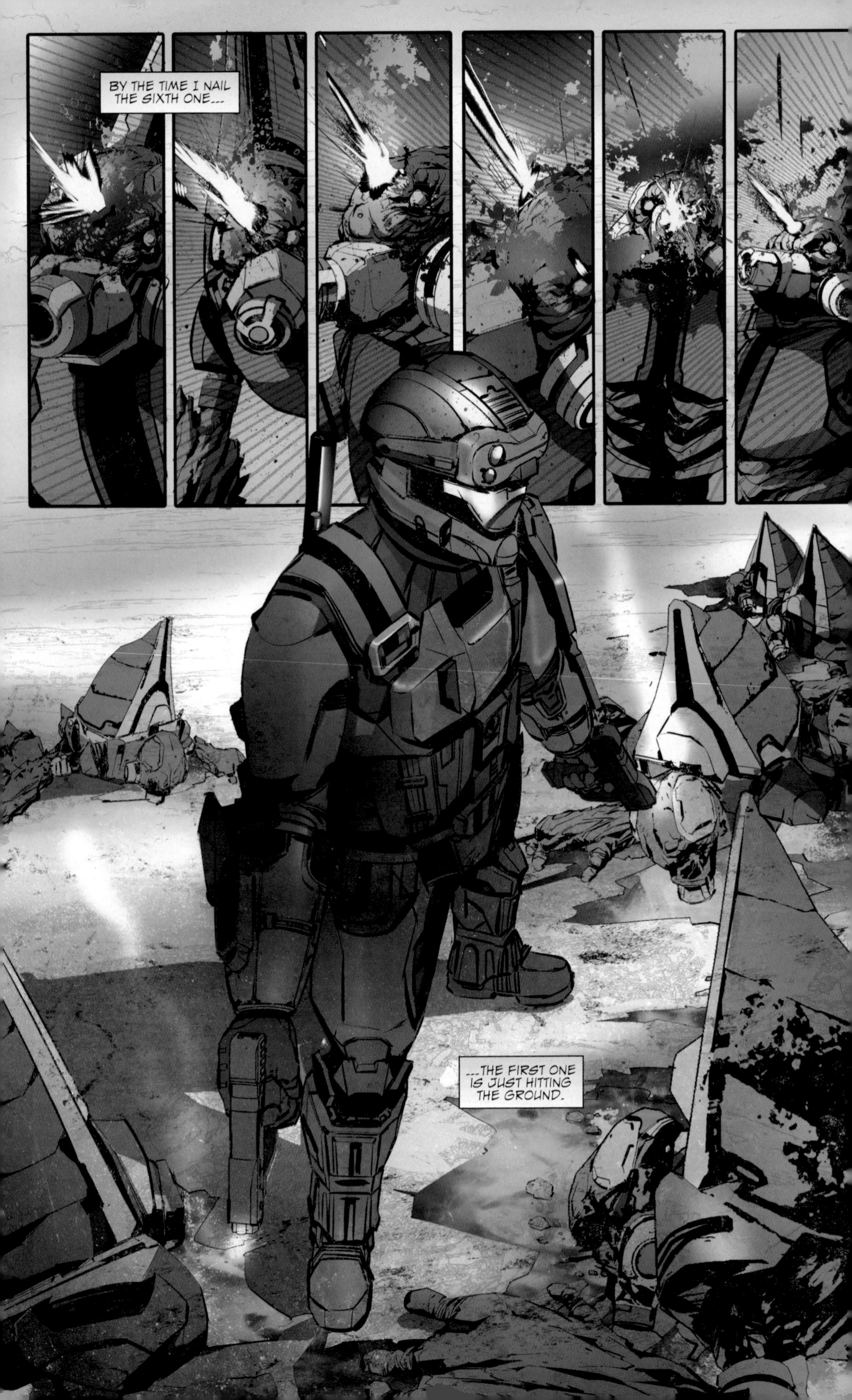
BY THE TIME I NAIL THE SIXTH ONE...
...THE FIRST ONE IS JUST HITTING THE GROUND.

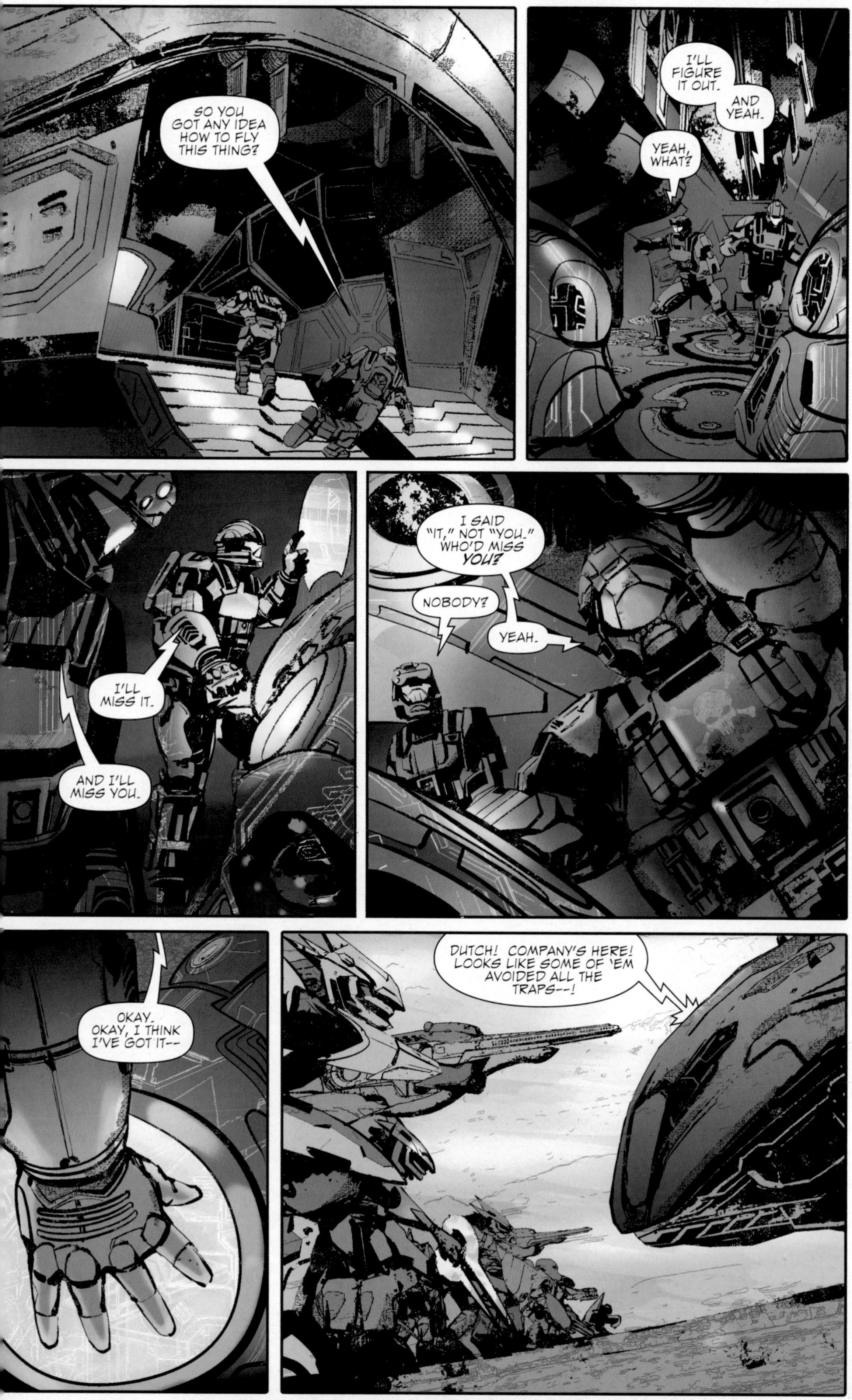
SO YOU GOT ANY IDEA HOW TO FLY THIS THING?
I'LL FIGURE IT OUT.
AND YEAH.
YEAH, WHAT?
I'LL MISS IT.
AND I'LL MISS YOU.
I SAID "IT," NOT "YOU." WHO'D MISS YOU?
NOBODY?
YEAH.
OKAY. OKAY, I THINK I'VE GOT IT--
DUTCH! COMPANY'S HERE! LOOKS LIKE SOME OF 'EM AVOIDED ALL THE TRAPS--!

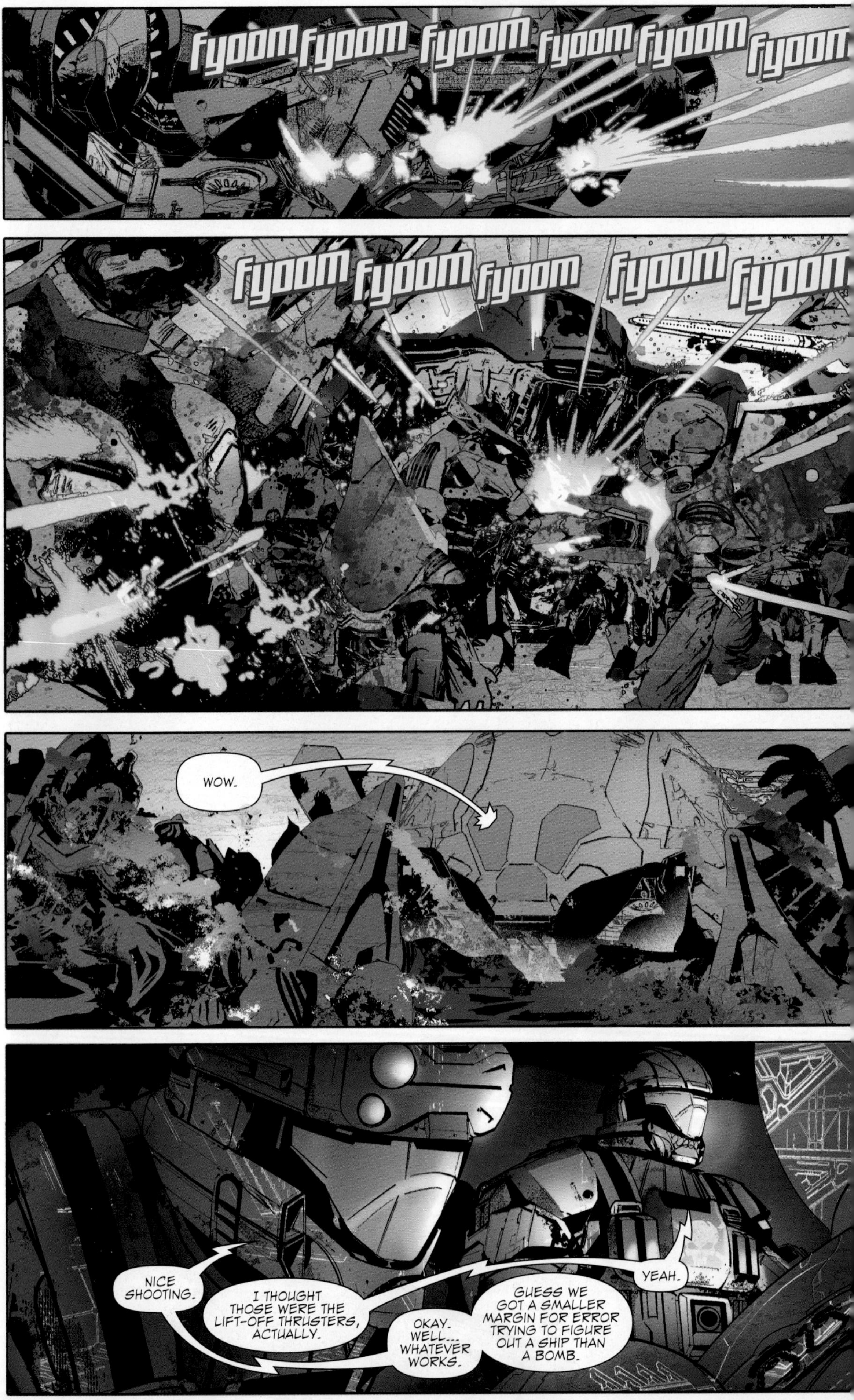
fyoom fyoom fyoom fyoom fyoom fyoom
fyoom fyoom fyoom fyoom fyoom
WOW.
NICE SHOOTING.
I THOUGHT THOSE WERE THE LIFT-OFF THRUSTERS, ACTUALLY.
OKAY. WELL... WHATEVER WORKS.
GUESS WE GOT A SMALLER MARGIN FOR ERROR TRYING TO FIGURE OUT A SHIP THAN A BOMB.
YEAH.

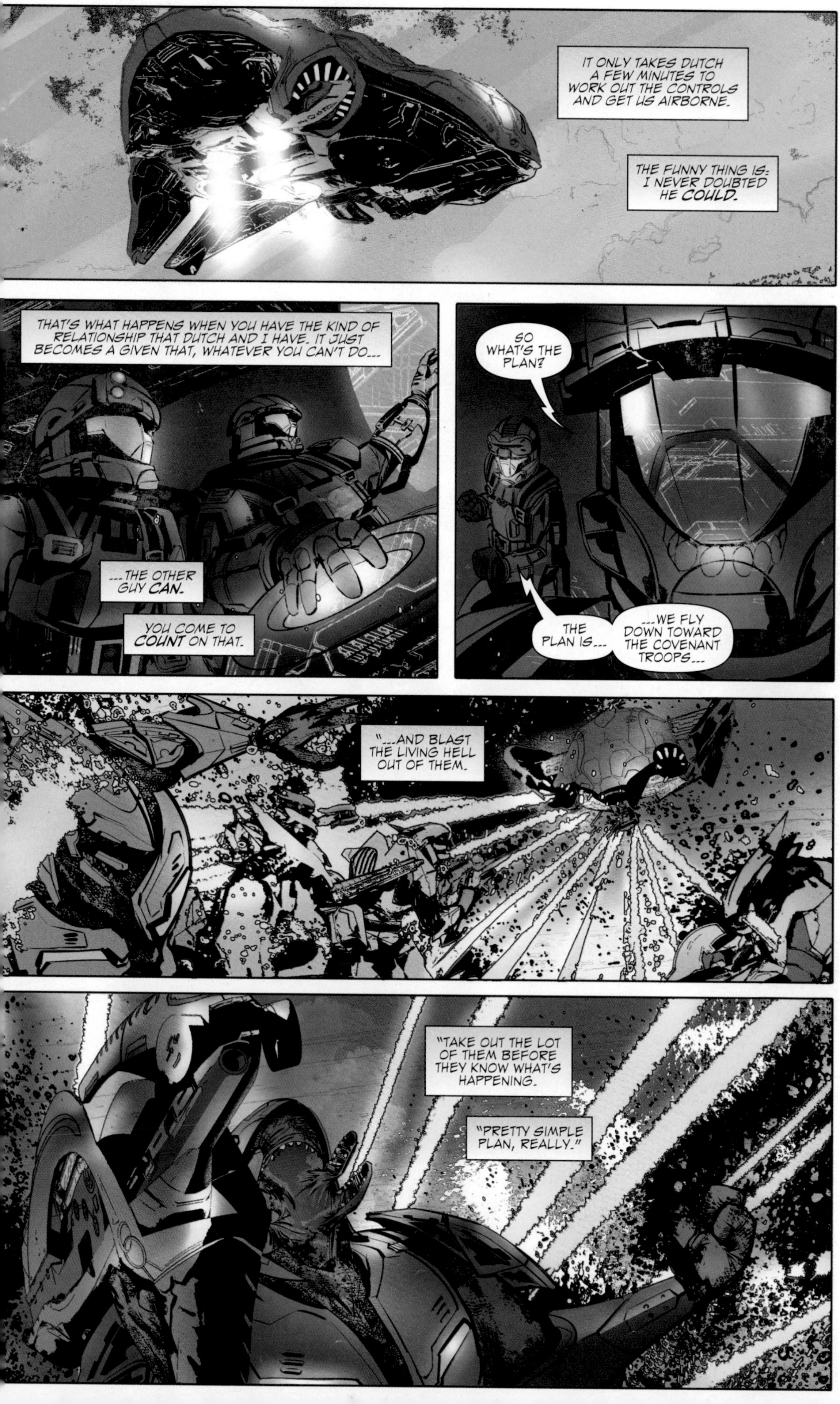
IT ONLY TAKES DUTCH A FEW MINUTES TO WORK OUT THE CONTROLS AND GET US AIRBORNE.
THE FUNNY THING IS: I NEVER DOUBTED HE COULD.
THAT'S WHAT HAPPENS WHEN YOU HAVE THE KIND OF RELATIONSHIP THAT DUTCH AND I HAVE. IT JUST BECOMES A GIVEN THAT, WHATEVER YOU CAN'T DO...
...THE OTHER GUY CAN.
YOU COME TO COUNT ON THAT.
SO WHAT'S THE PLAN?
THE PLAN IS...
...WE FLY DOWN TOWARD THE COVENANT TROOPS...
"...AND BLAST THE LIVING HELL OUT OF THEM.
"TAKE OUT THE LOT OF THEM BEFORE THEY KNOW WHAT'S HAPPENING.
"PRETTY SIMPLE PLAN, REALLY."

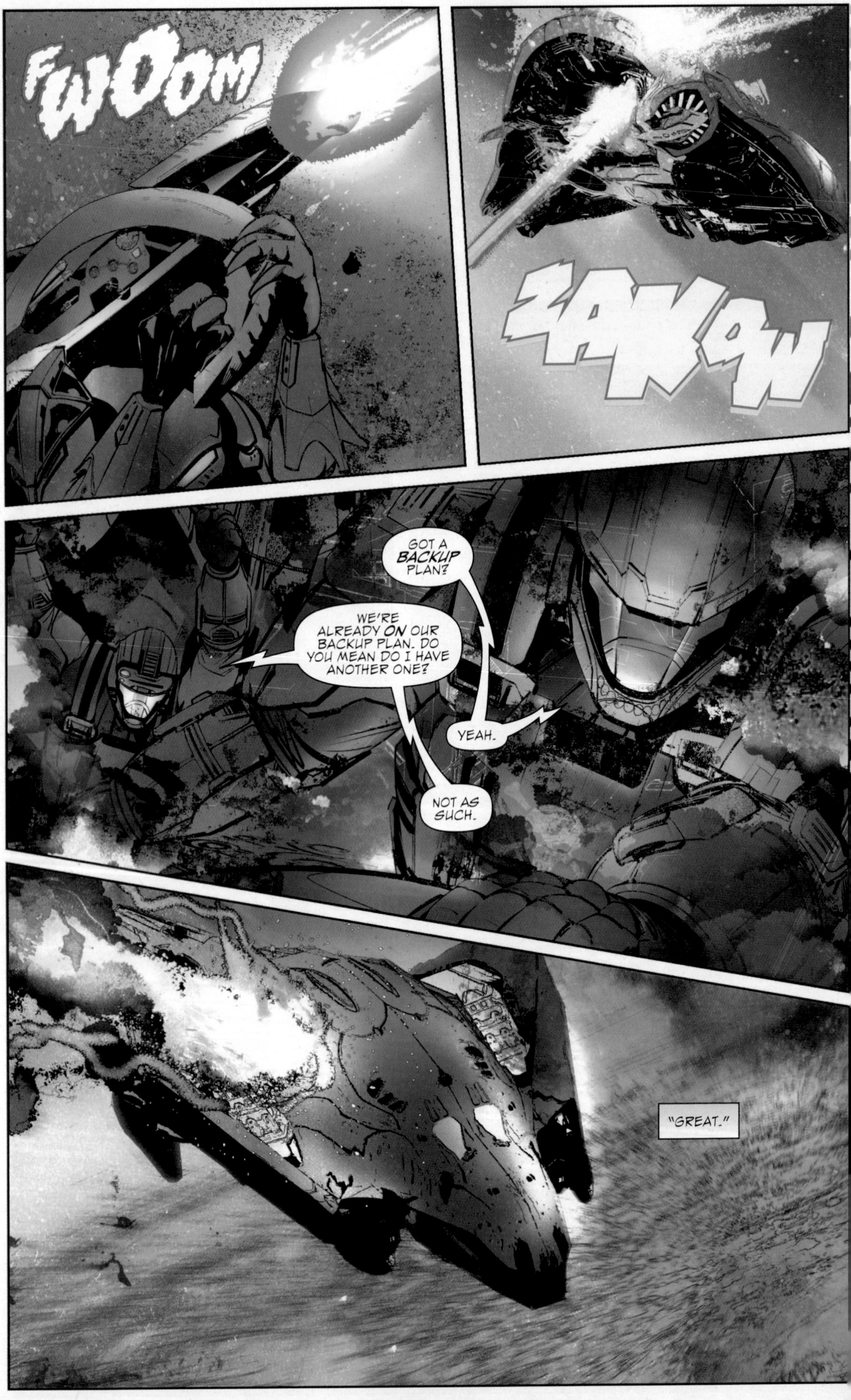
FWOOM
ZAKOW
GOT A BACKUP PLAN?
WE'RE ALREADY ON OUR BACKUP PLAN. DO YOU MEAN DO I HAVE ANOTHER ONE?
YEAH.
NOT AS SUCH.
"GREAT."

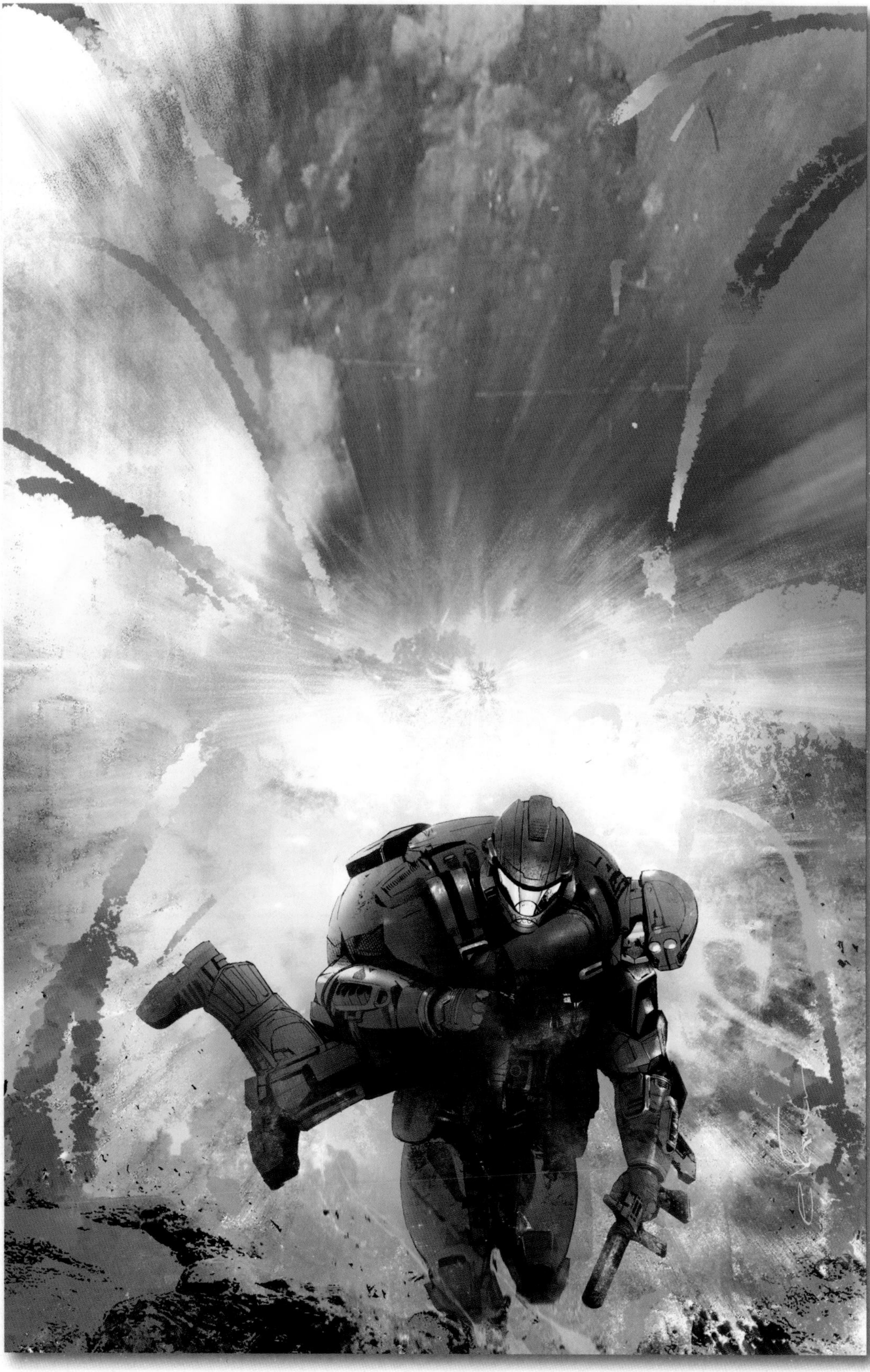

SERGEANT!

IF THAT'S WHERE IT'S BOUND, IT MEANS WE CAN EXPECT COVENANT TROOPS TO BE THERE WHEN WE ARRIVE.

INFORM THE REST OF THE SQUAD. THE STAKES HAVE JUST GONE UP.

IT'S A COVENANT DROP SHIP, HEADING TOWARD THE SECOND DIG SITE.

AND IT'S IN SERIOUS DISTRESS.

WHAT ABOUT THE DROP SHIP?

I SEE IT, MICHAELS.

WHAT *ABOUT* IT?

WITH ANY LUCK, IT CRASHES...

"...AND ALL HANDS ABOARD ARE KILLED.

"IT'S A COVENANT SHIP WITH COVENANT TROOPS.

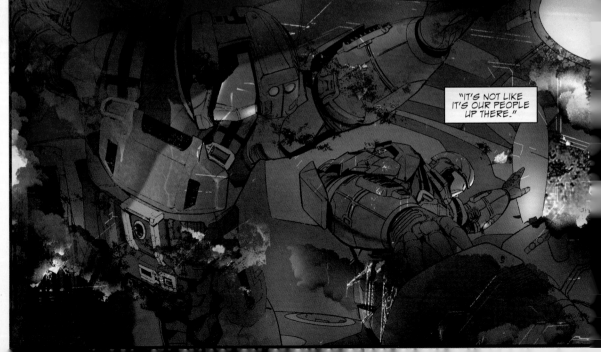

"IT'S NOT LIKE IT'S OUR PEOPLE UP THERE."

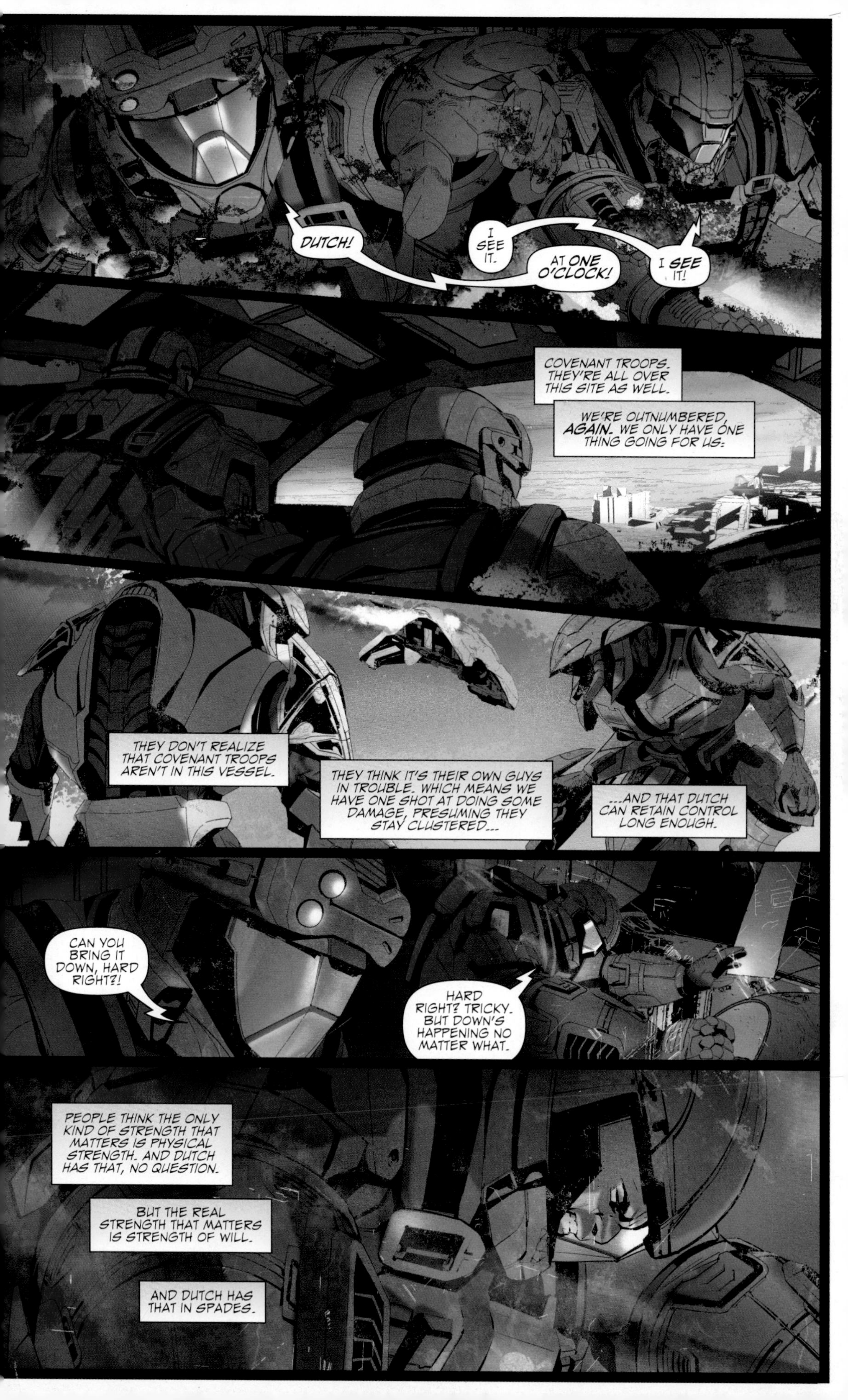
DUTCH!
I SEE IT.
AT ONE O'CLOCK!
I SEE IT!
COVENANT TROOPS. THEY'RE ALL OVER THIS SITE AS WELL.
WE'RE OUTNUMBERED, AGAIN. WE ONLY HAVE ONE THING GOING FOR US:
THEY DON'T REALIZE THAT COVENANT TROOPS AREN'T IN THIS VESSEL.
THEY THINK IT'S THEIR OWN GUYS IN TROUBLE. WHICH MEANS WE HAVE ONE SHOT AT DOING SOME DAMAGE, PRESUMING THEY STAY CLUSTERED...
...AND THAT DUTCH CAN RETAIN CONTROL LONG ENOUGH.
CAN YOU BRING IT DOWN, HARD RIGHT?!
HARD RIGHT? TRICKY. BUT DOWN'S HAPPENING NO MATTER WHAT.
PEOPLE THINK THE ONLY KIND OF STRENGTH THAT MATTERS IS PHYSICAL STRENGTH. AND DUTCH HAS THAT, NO QUESTION.
BUT THE REAL STRENGTH THAT MATTERS IS STRENGTH OF WILL.
AND DUTCH HAS THAT IN SPADES.

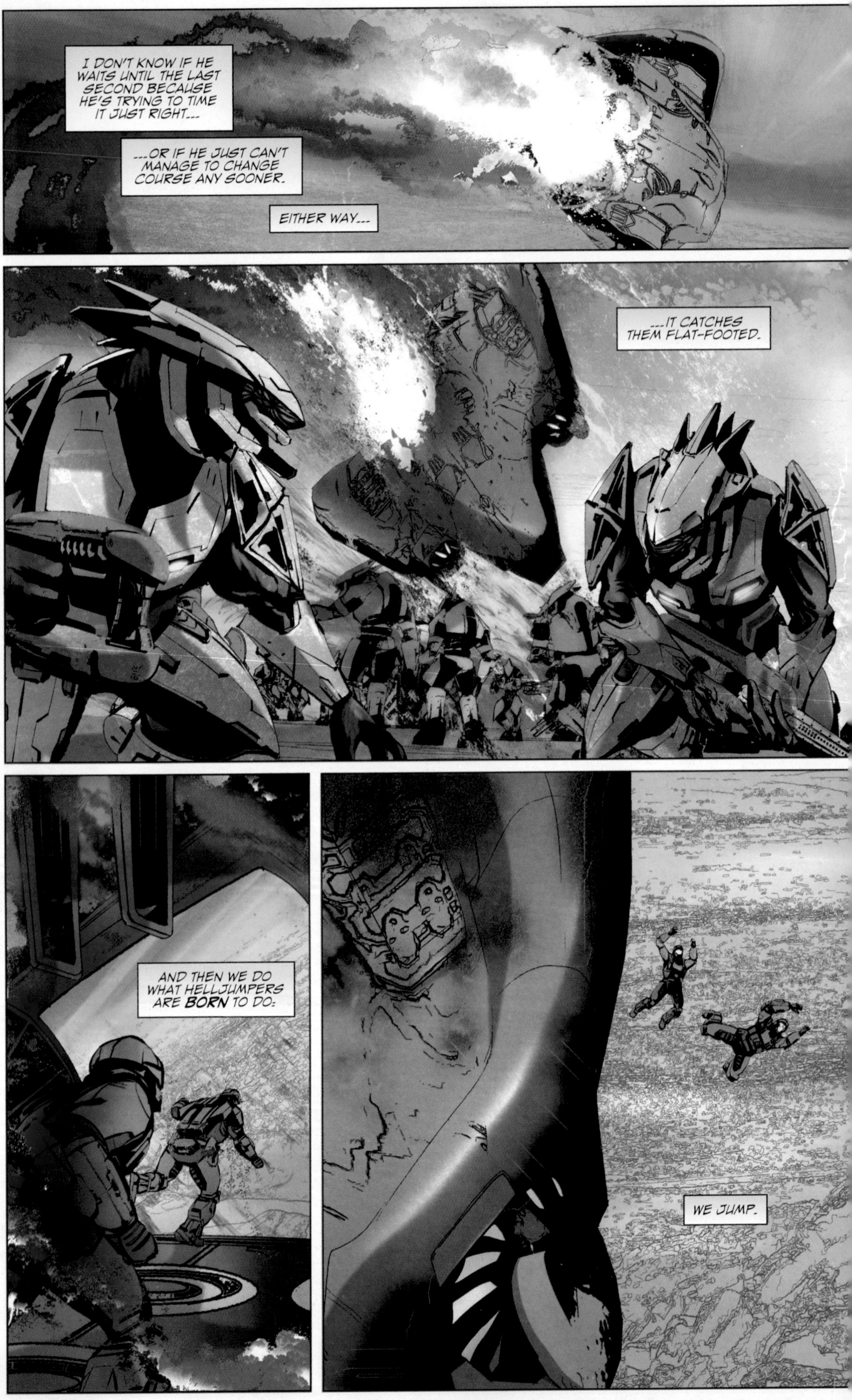
I DON'T KNOW IF HE WAITS UNTIL THE LAST SECOND BECAUSE HE'S TRYING TO TIME IT JUST RIGHT...
...OR IF HE JUST CAN'T MANAGE TO CHANGE COURSE ANY SOONER.
EITHER WAY...
...IT CATCHES THEM FLAT-FOOTED.
AND THEN WE DO WHAT HELLJUMPERS ARE **BORN** TO DO:
WE JUMP.

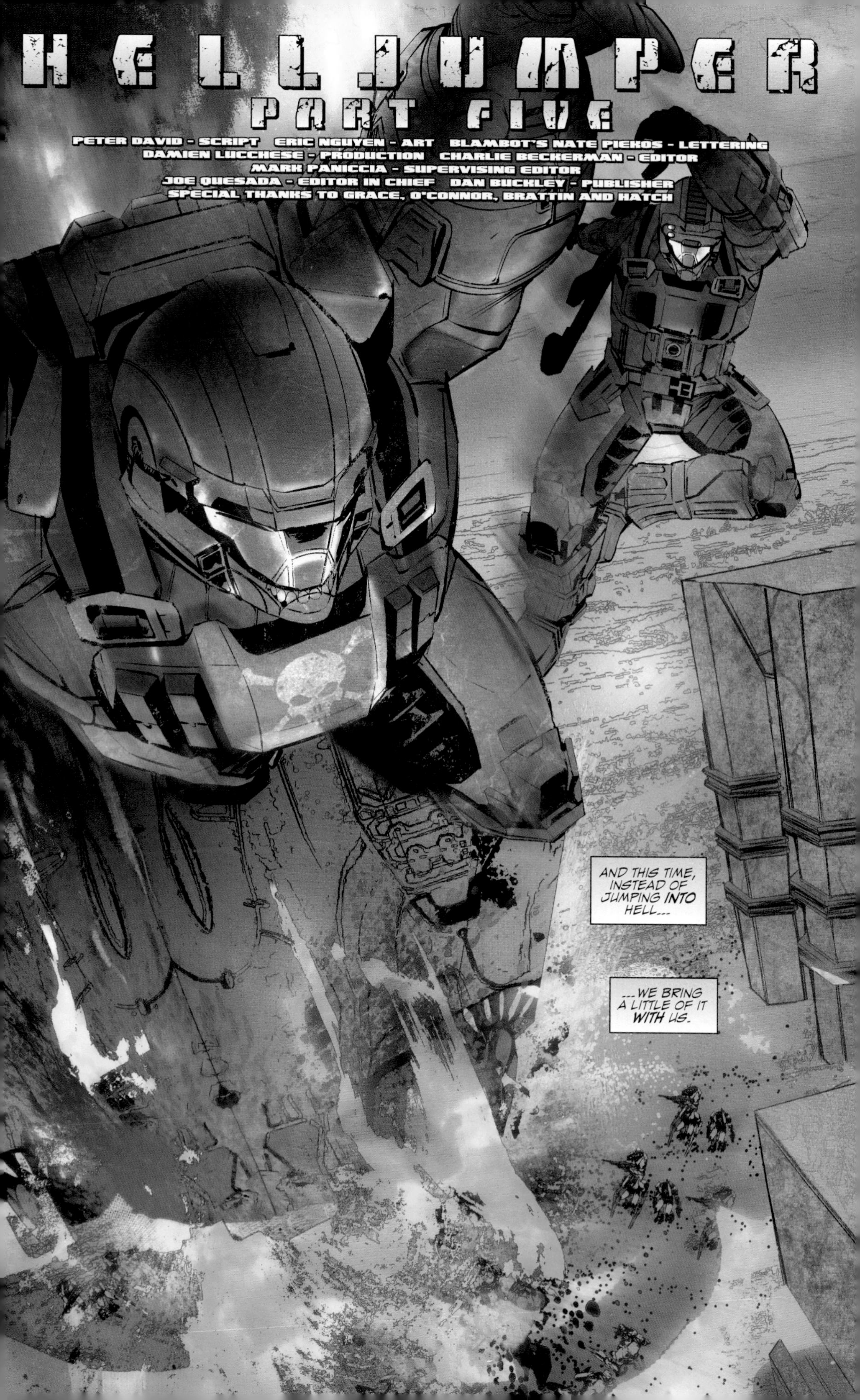
HELLJUMPER
PART FIVE
PETER DAVID - SCRIPT ERIC NGUYEN - ART BLAMBOT'S NATE PIEKOS - LETTERING
DAMIEN LUCCHESE - PRODUCTION CHARLIE BECKERMAN - EDITOR
MARK PANICCIA - SUPERVISING EDITOR
JOE QUESADA - EDITOR IN CHIEF DAN BUCKLEY - PUBLISHER
SPECIAL THANKS TO GRACE, O'CONNOR, BRATTIN AND HATCH
AND THIS TIME, INSTEAD OF JUMPING INTO HELL...
...WE BRING A LITTLE OF IT WITH US.

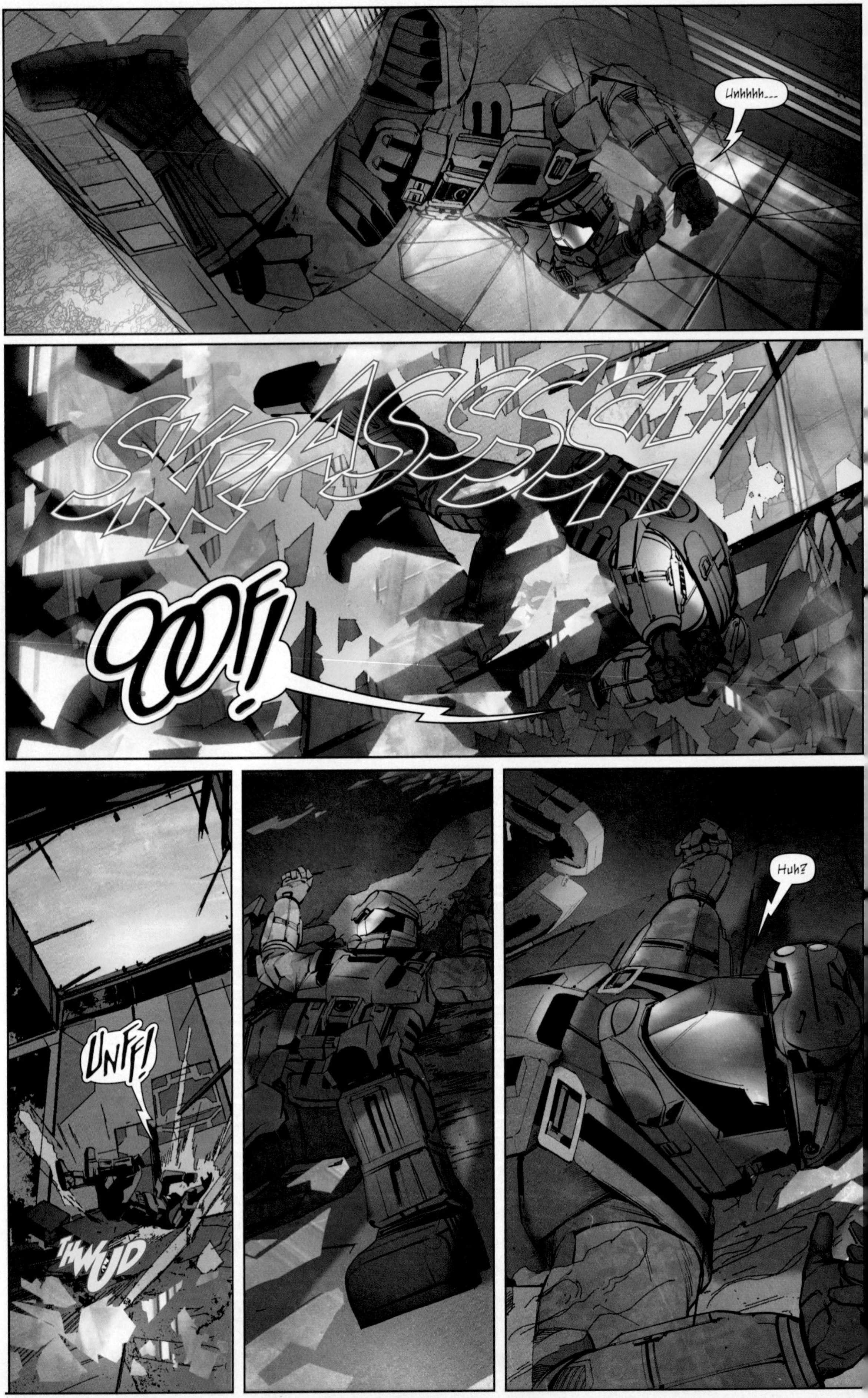
Unhhhh...
SMASSSSH
OOF!
UNFF!
THWUD
Huh?

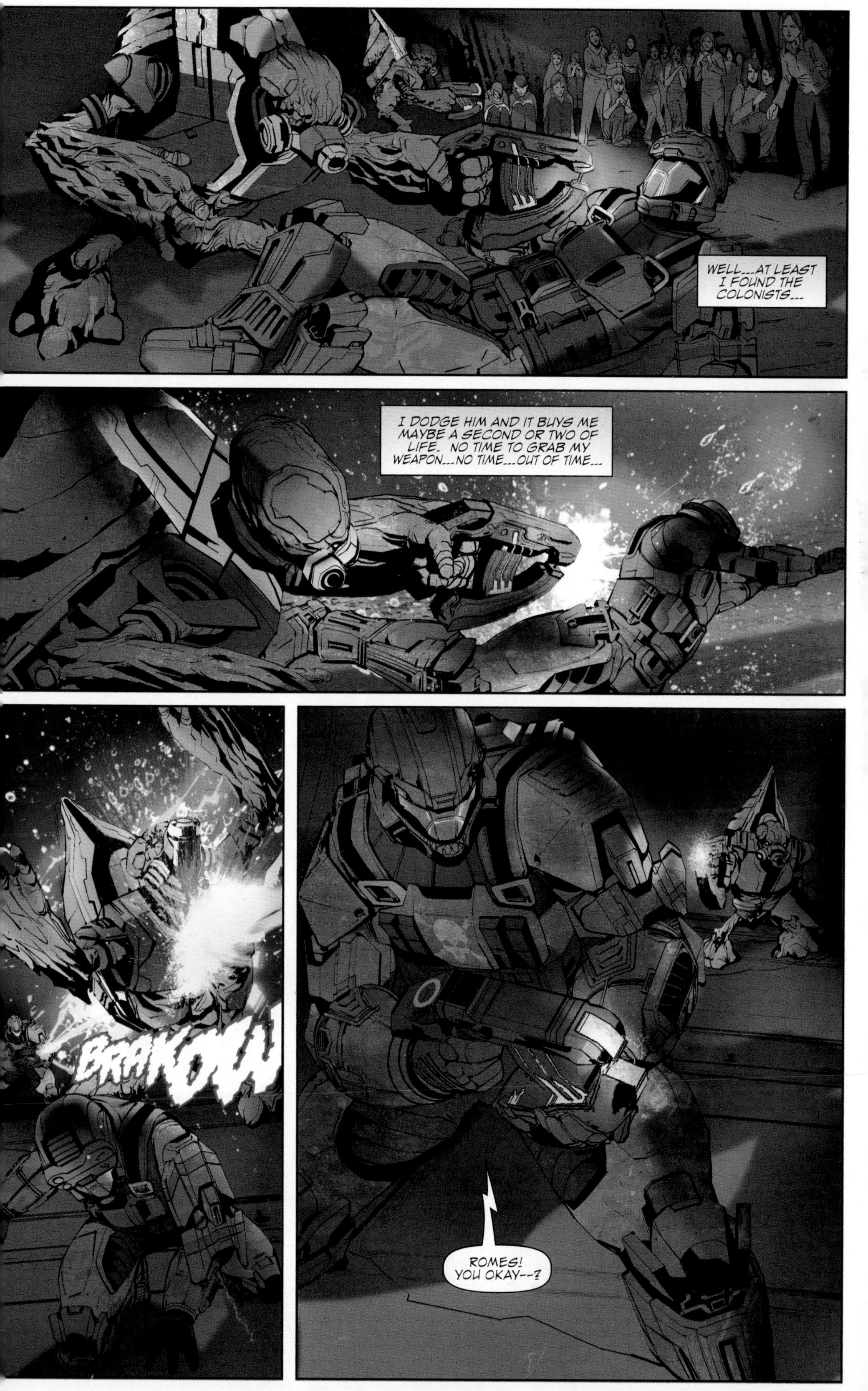
WELL...AT LEAST I FOUND THE COLONISTS...
I DODGE HIM AND IT BUYS ME MAYBE A SECOND OR TWO OF LIFE. NO TIME TO GRAB MY WEAPON...NO TIME...OUT OF TIME...
BRAKOW
ROMES! YOU OKAY--?

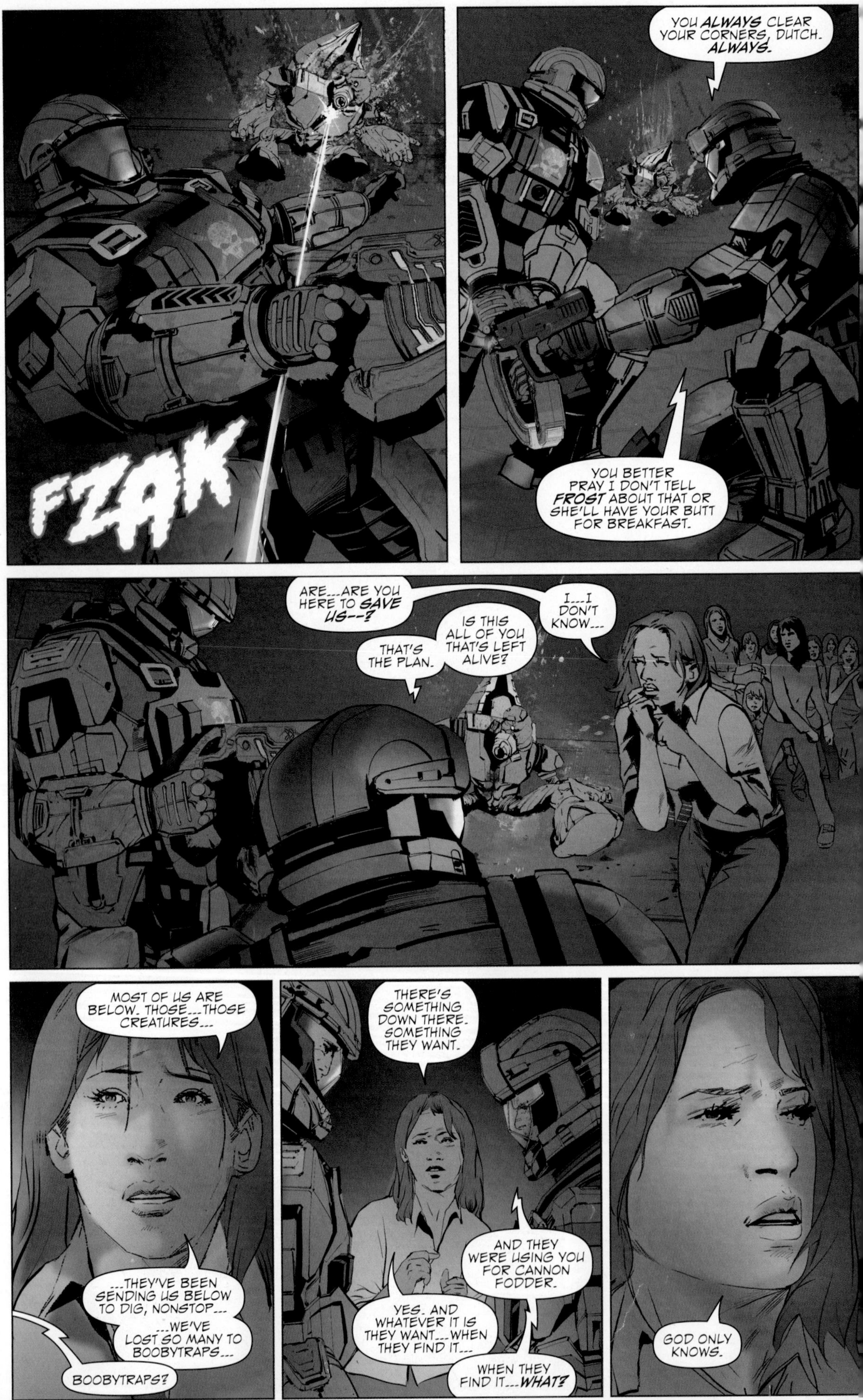
FZAK
YOU ALWAYS CLEAR YOUR CORNERS, DUTCH. ALWAYS.
YOU BETTER PRAY I DON'T TELL FROST ABOUT THAT OR SHE'LL HAVE YOUR BUTT FOR BREAKFAST.
ARE... ARE YOU HERE TO SAVE US--?
THAT'S THE PLAN.
IS THIS ALL OF YOU THAT'S LEFT ALIVE?
I... I DON'T KNOW...
MOST OF US ARE BELOW. THOSE... THOSE CREATURES...
...THEY'VE BEEN SENDING US BELOW TO DIG, NONSTOP...
...WE'VE LOST SO MANY TO BOOBYTRAPS...
BOOBYTRAPS?
THERE'S SOMETHING DOWN THERE. SOMETHING THEY WANT.
AND THEY WERE USING YOU FOR CANNON FODDER.
YES. AND WHATEVER IT IS THEY WANT... WHEN THEY FIND IT...
WHEN THEY FIND IT... WHAT?
GOD ONLY KNOWS.

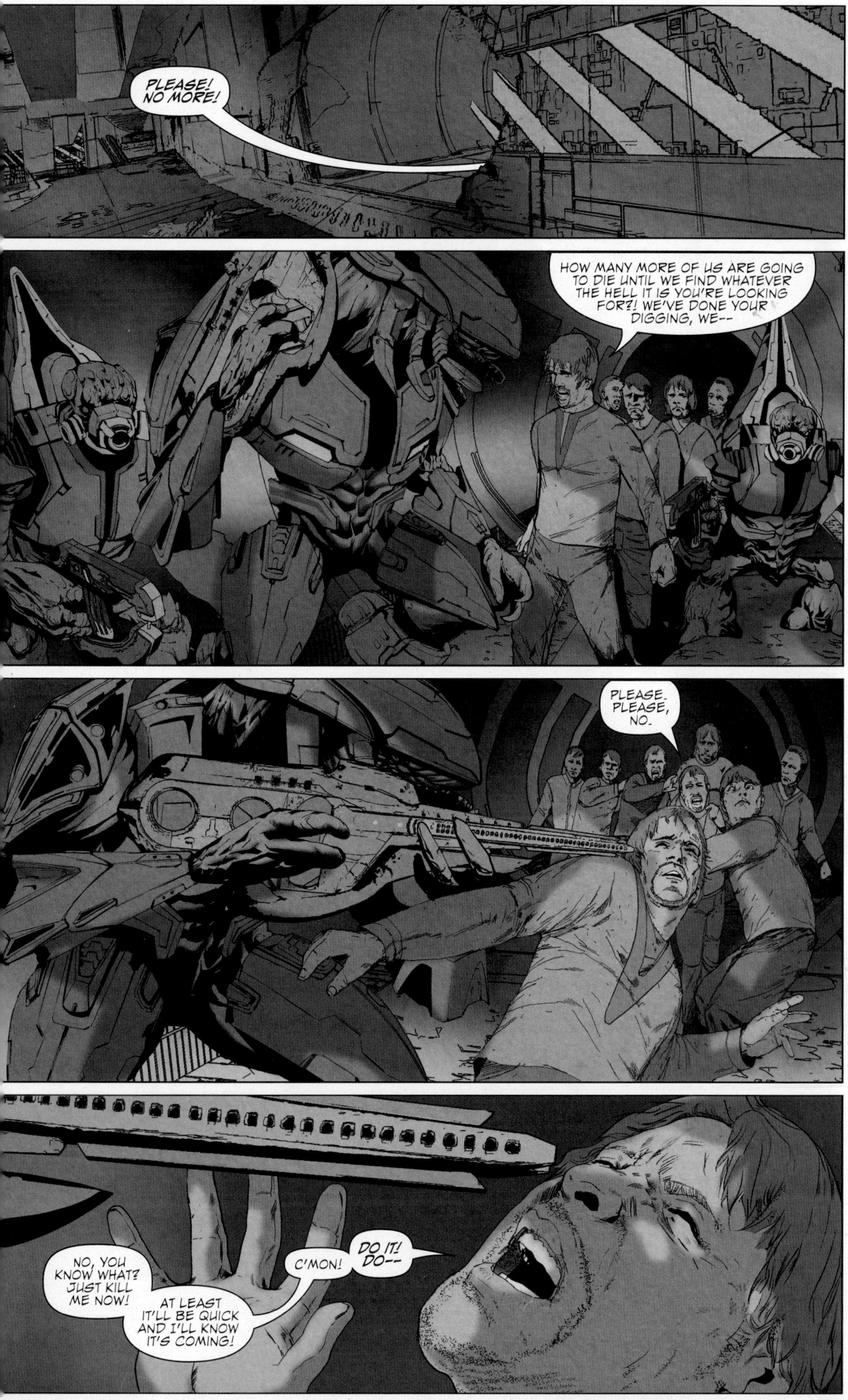
PLEASE! NO MORE!
HOW MANY MORE OF US ARE GOING TO DIE UNTIL WE FIND WHATEVER THE HELL IT IS YOU'RE LOOKING FOR?! WE'VE DONE YOUR DIGGING, WE--
PLEASE. PLEASE, NO.
NO, YOU KNOW WHAT? JUST KILL ME NOW!
AT LEAST IT'LL BE QUICK AND I'LL KNOW IT'S COMING!
C'MON!
DO IT! DO--

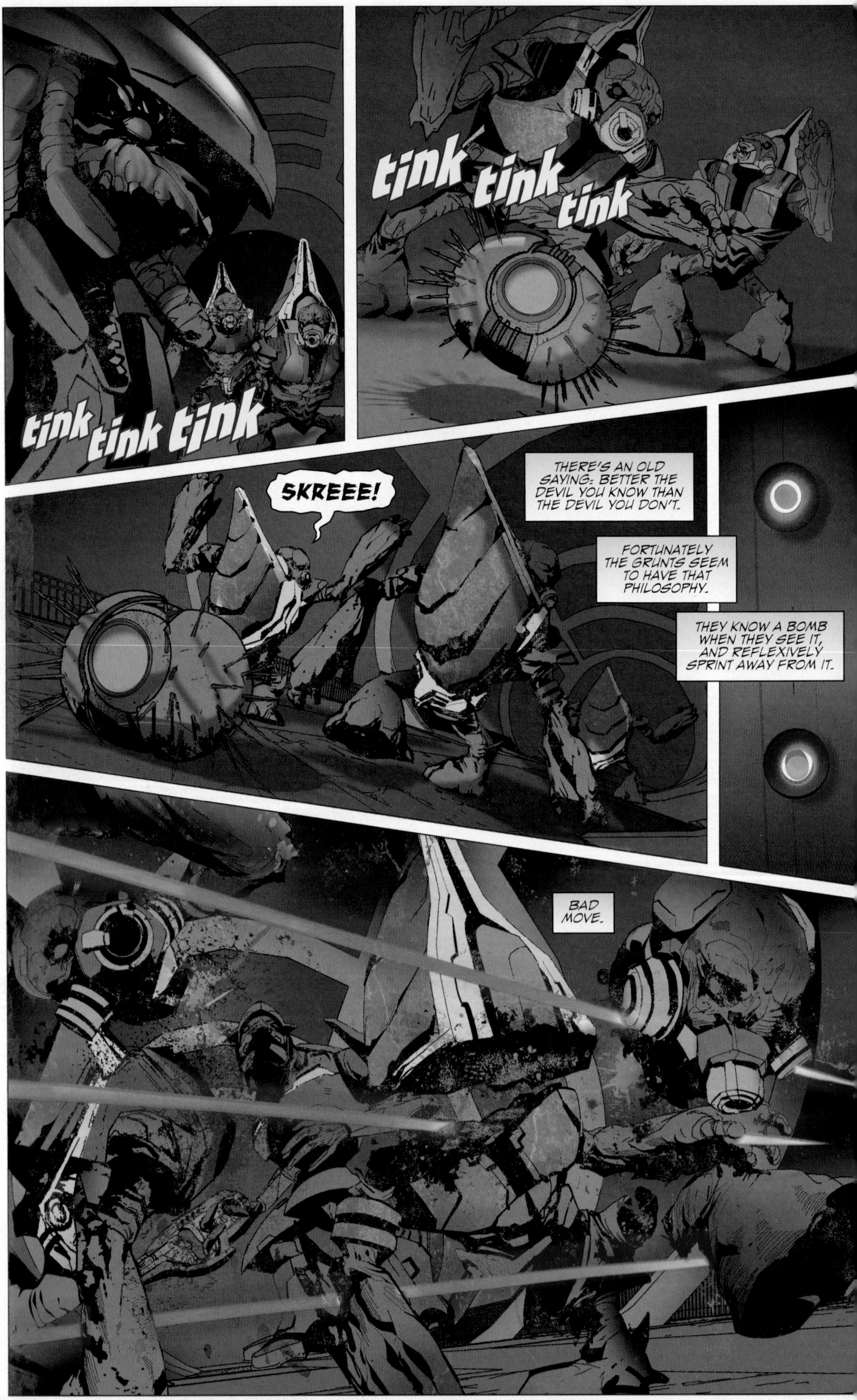
tink tink tink
tink tink tink
SKREEE!
THERE'S AN OLD SAYING: BETTER THE DEVIL YOU KNOW THAN THE DEVIL YOU DON'T.
FORTUNATELY THE GRUNTS SEEM TO HAVE THAT PHILOSOPHY.
THEY KNOW A BOMB WHEN THEY SEE IT, AND REFLEXIVELY SPRINT AWAY FROM IT.
BAD MOVE.

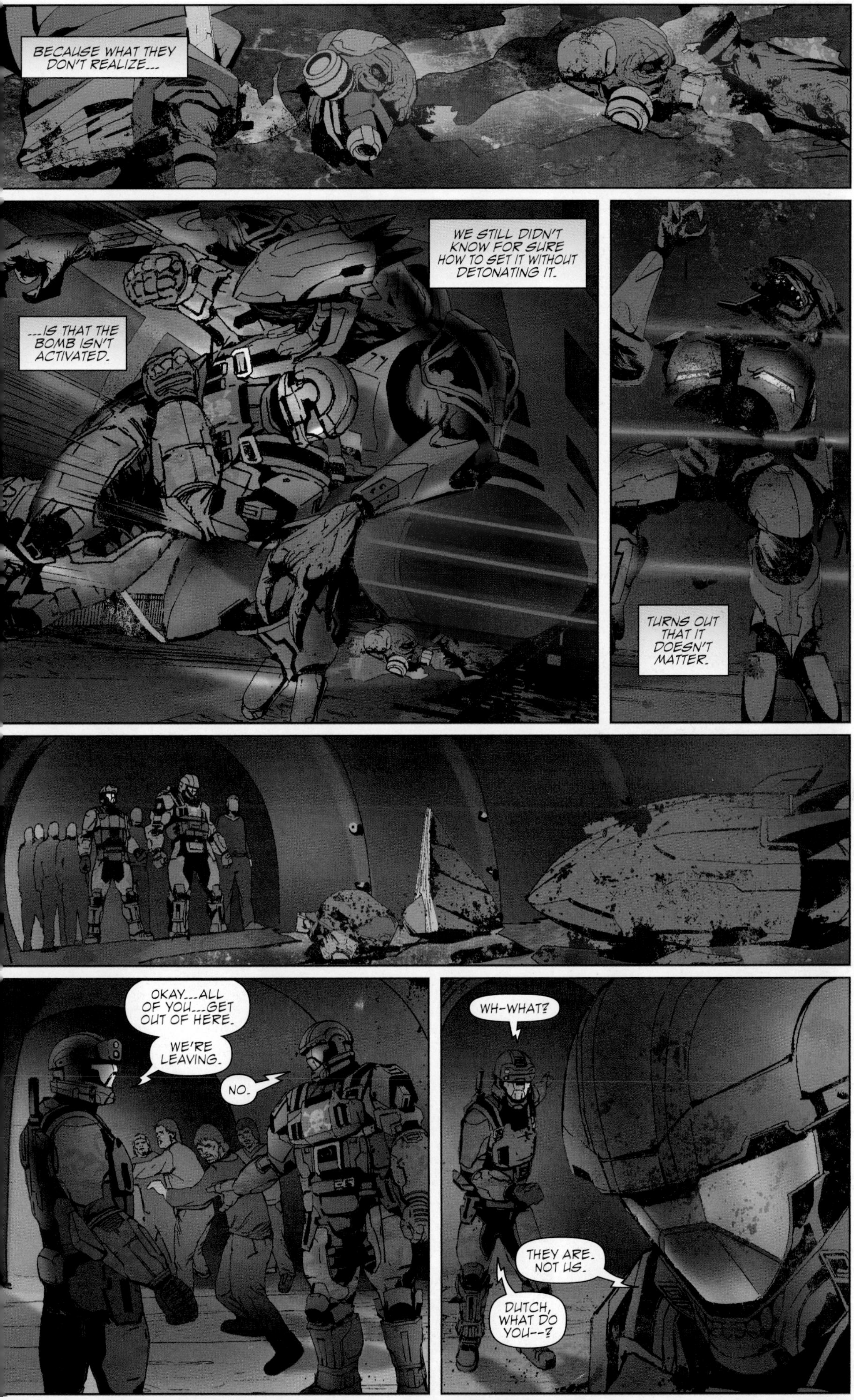

BECAUSE WHAT THEY DON'T REALIZE...
...IS THAT THE BOMB ISN'T ACTIVATED.
WE STILL DIDN'T KNOW FOR SURE HOW TO SET IT WITHOUT DETONATING IT.
TURNS OUT THAT IT DOESN'T MATTER.
OKAY...ALL OF YOU...GET OUT OF HERE.
WE'RE LEAVING.
NO.
WH-WHAT?
THEY ARE. NOT US.
DUTCH, WHAT DO YOU--?

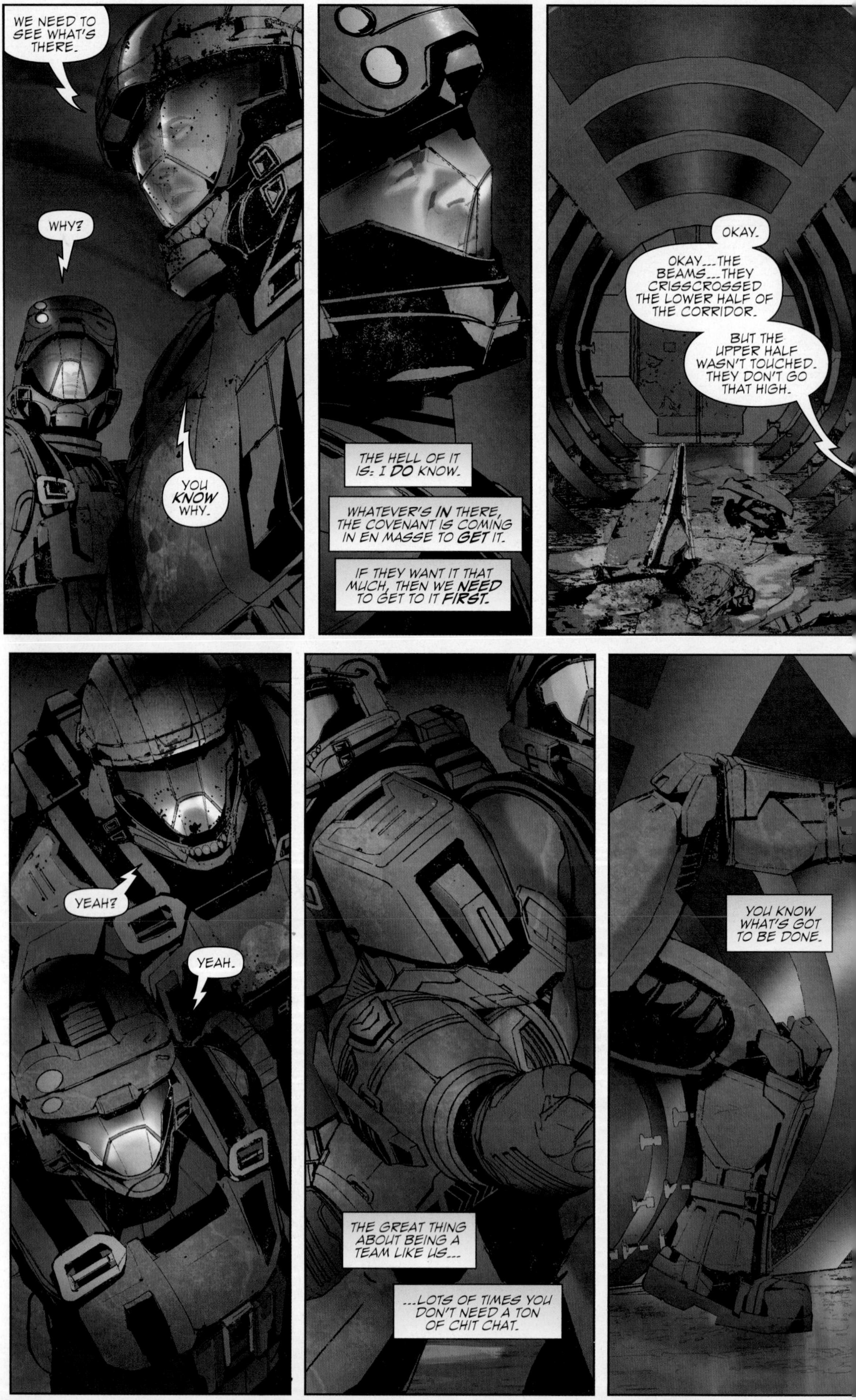
WE NEED TO SEE WHAT'S THERE.
WHY?
YOU KNOW WHY.
THE HELL OF IT IS: I DO KNOW.
WHATEVER'S IN THERE, THE COVENANT IS COMING IN EN MASSE TO GET IT.
IF THEY WANT IT THAT MUCH, THEN WE NEED TO GET TO IT FIRST.
OKAY.
OKAY... THE BEAMS... THEY CRISSCROSSED THE LOWER HALF OF THE CORRIDOR.
BUT THE UPPER HALF WASN'T TOUCHED. THEY DON'T GO THAT HIGH.
YEAH?
YEAH.
THE GREAT THING ABOUT BEING A TEAM LIKE US...
...LOTS OF TIMES YOU DON'T NEED A TON OF CHIT CHAT.
YOU KNOW WHAT'S GOT TO BE DONE.

AND YOU DO IT.

HOLD STEADY.

TAKE YOUR TIME. NO PRESSURE.

FWZZK

OKAY! ONE-- TWO--

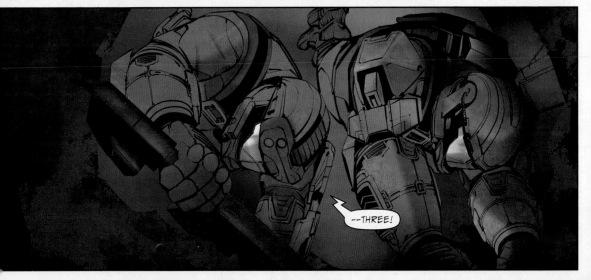

--THREE!

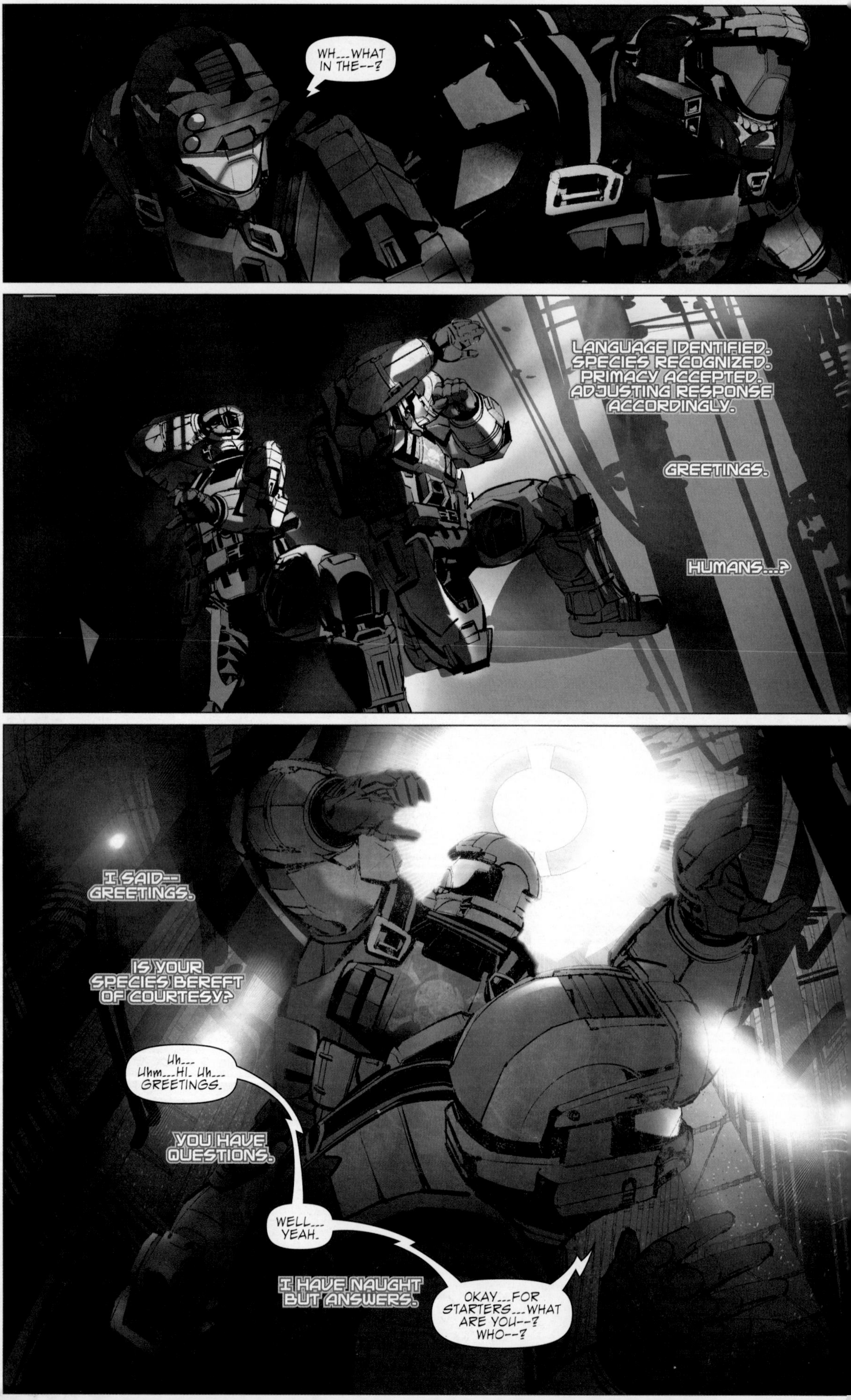
WH...WHAT IN THE--?
LANGUAGE IDENTIFIED. SPECIES RECOGNIZED. PRIMACY ACCEPTED. ADJUSTING RESPONSE ACCORDINGLY.
GREETINGS.
HUMANS...?
I SAID-- GREETINGS.
IS YOUR SPECIES BEREFT OF COURTESY?
Uh... Uhm...HI. Uh... GREETINGS.
YOU HAVE QUESTIONS.
WELL... YEAH.
I HAVE NAUGHT BUT ANSWERS.
OKAY...FOR STARTERS...WHAT ARE YOU--? WHO--?

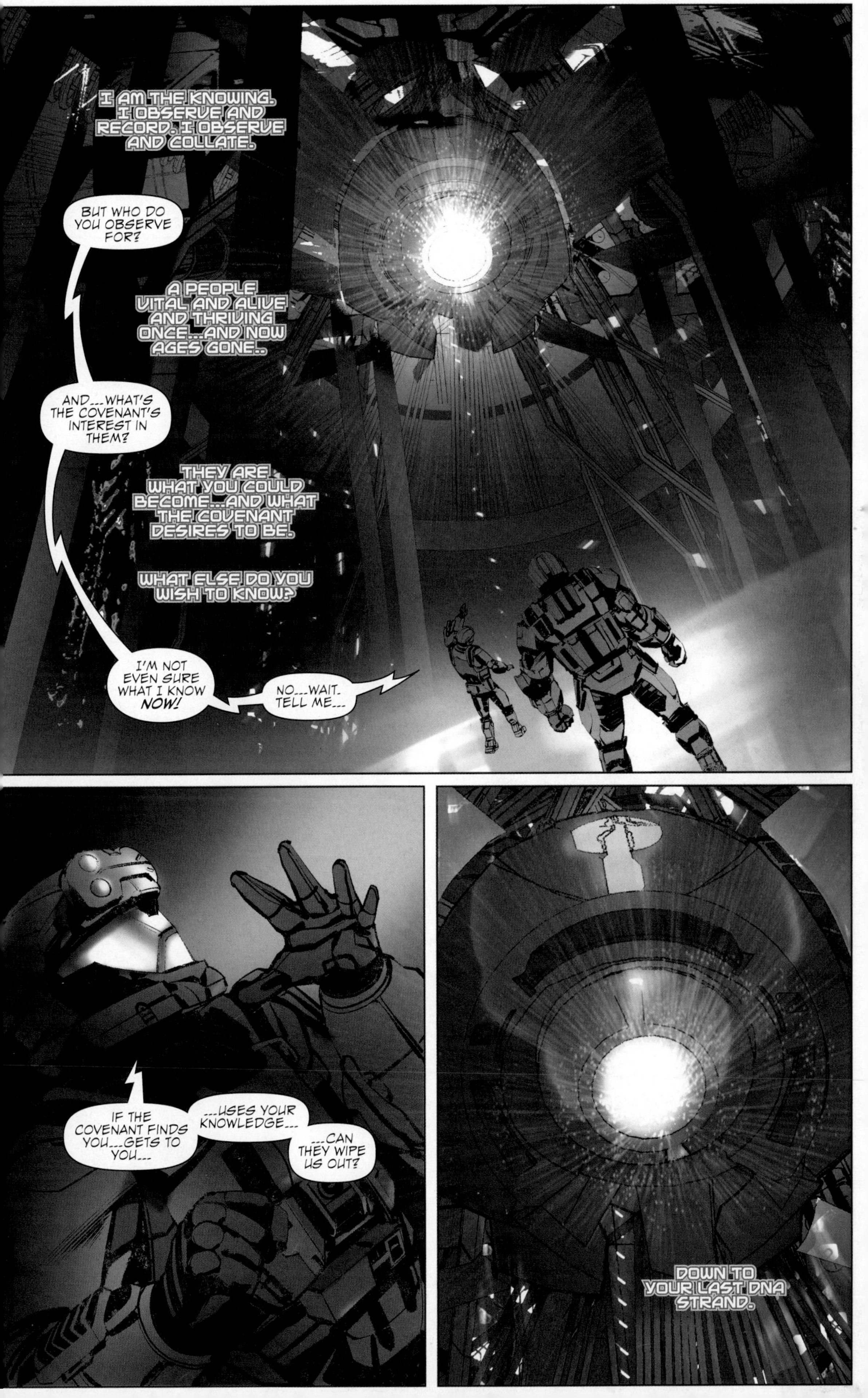
I AM THE KNOWING. I OBSERVE AND RECORD. I OBSERVE AND COLLATE.
BUT WHO DO YOU OBSERVE FOR?
A PEOPLE VITAL AND ALIVE AND THRIVING ONCE...AND NOW AGES GONE..
AND...WHAT'S THE COVENANT'S INTEREST IN THEM?
THEY ARE WHAT YOU COULD BECOME...AND WHAT THE COVENANT DESIRES TO BE.
WHAT ELSE DO YOU WISH TO KNOW?
I'M NOT EVEN SURE WHAT I KNOW *NOW!*
NO...WAIT. TELL ME...
IF THE COVENANT FINDS YOU...GETS TO YOU...
...USES YOUR KNOWLEDGE...
...CAN THEY WIPE US OUT?
DOWN TO YOUR LAST DNA STRAND.

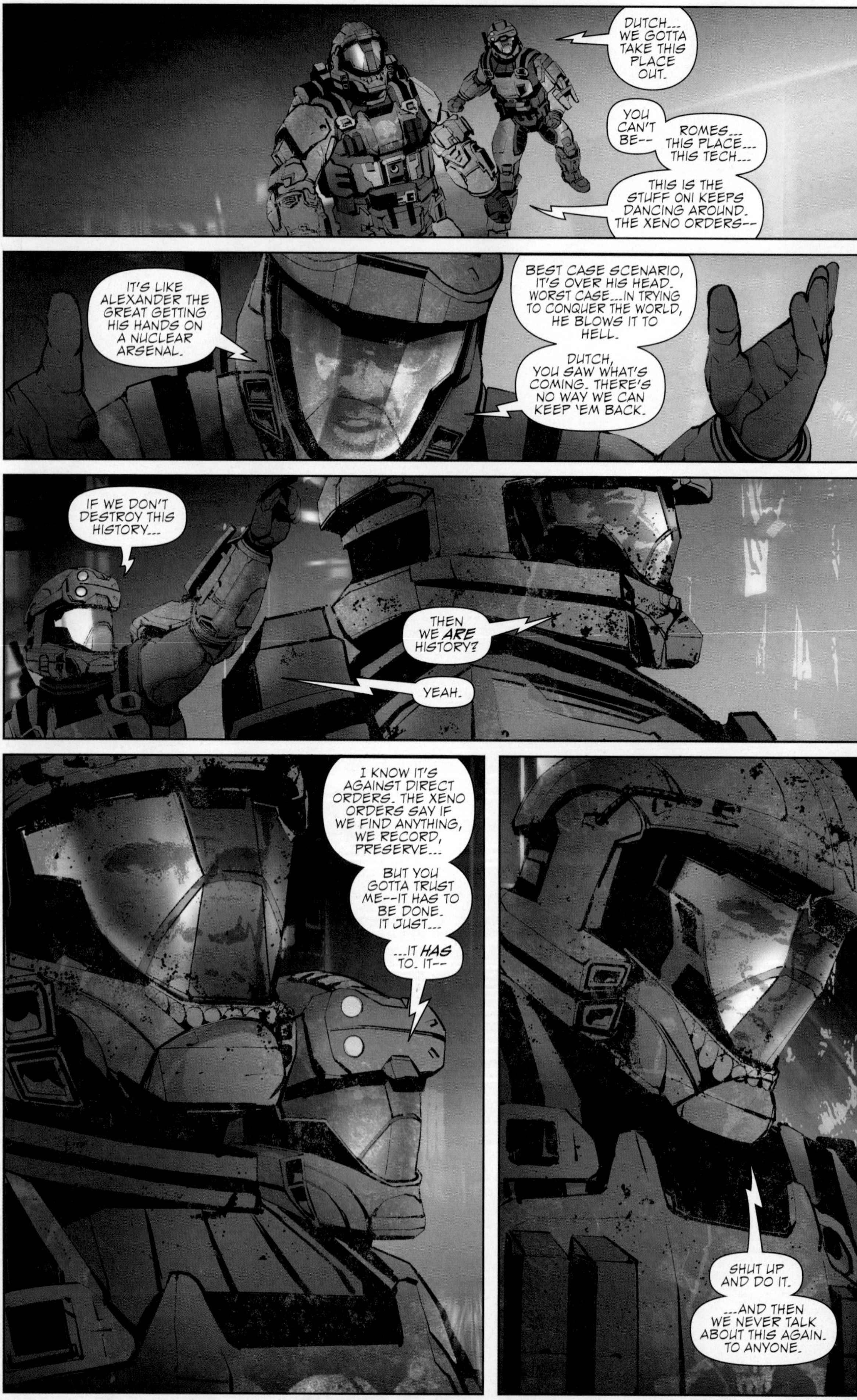
DUTCH... WE GOTTA TAKE THIS PLACE OUT.
YOU CAN'T BE--
ROMES... THIS PLACE... THIS TECH...
THIS IS THE STUFF ONI KEEPS DANCING AROUND. THE XENO ORDERS--
IT'S LIKE ALEXANDER THE GREAT GETTING HIS HANDS ON A NUCLEAR ARSENAL.
BEST CASE SCENARIO, IT'S OVER HIS HEAD. WORST CASE...IN TRYING TO CONQUER THE WORLD, HE BLOWS IT TO HELL.
DUTCH, YOU SAW WHAT'S COMING. THERE'S NO WAY WE CAN KEEP 'EM BACK.
IF WE DON'T DESTROY THIS HISTORY...
THEN WE ***ARE*** HISTORY?
YEAH.
I KNOW IT'S AGAINST DIRECT ORDERS. THE XENO ORDERS SAY IF WE FIND ANYTHING, WE RECORD, PRESERVE...
BUT YOU GOTTA TRUST ME--IT HAS TO BE DONE. IT JUST...
...IT ***HAS*** TO. IT--
SHUT UP AND DO IT.
...AND THEN WE NEVER TALK ABOUT THIS AGAIN. TO ANYONE.

KNOWING! I HAVE TWO LAST QUESTIONS!

ONLY TWO? YOU ARE VERY LIMITED.

CAN YOU SHOW US A WAY OUT OF HERE THAT'S SAFE?

IF YOU WISH. AND THE SECOND?

CAN YOU DESTROY YOURSELF?

KNOWING--? I SAID--

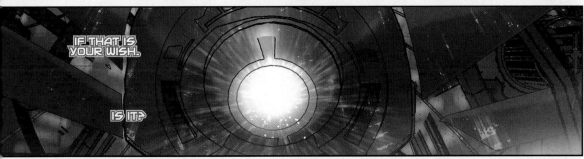

IF THAT IS YOUR WISH.

IS IT?

I'M SORRY, BUT...YES. IT IS.

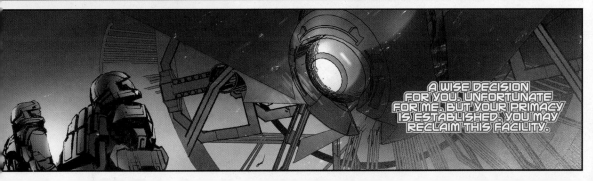

A WISE DECISION FOR YOU, UNFORTUNATE FOR ME, BUT YOUR PRIMACY IS ESTABLISHED. YOU MAY RECLAIM THIS FACILITY.

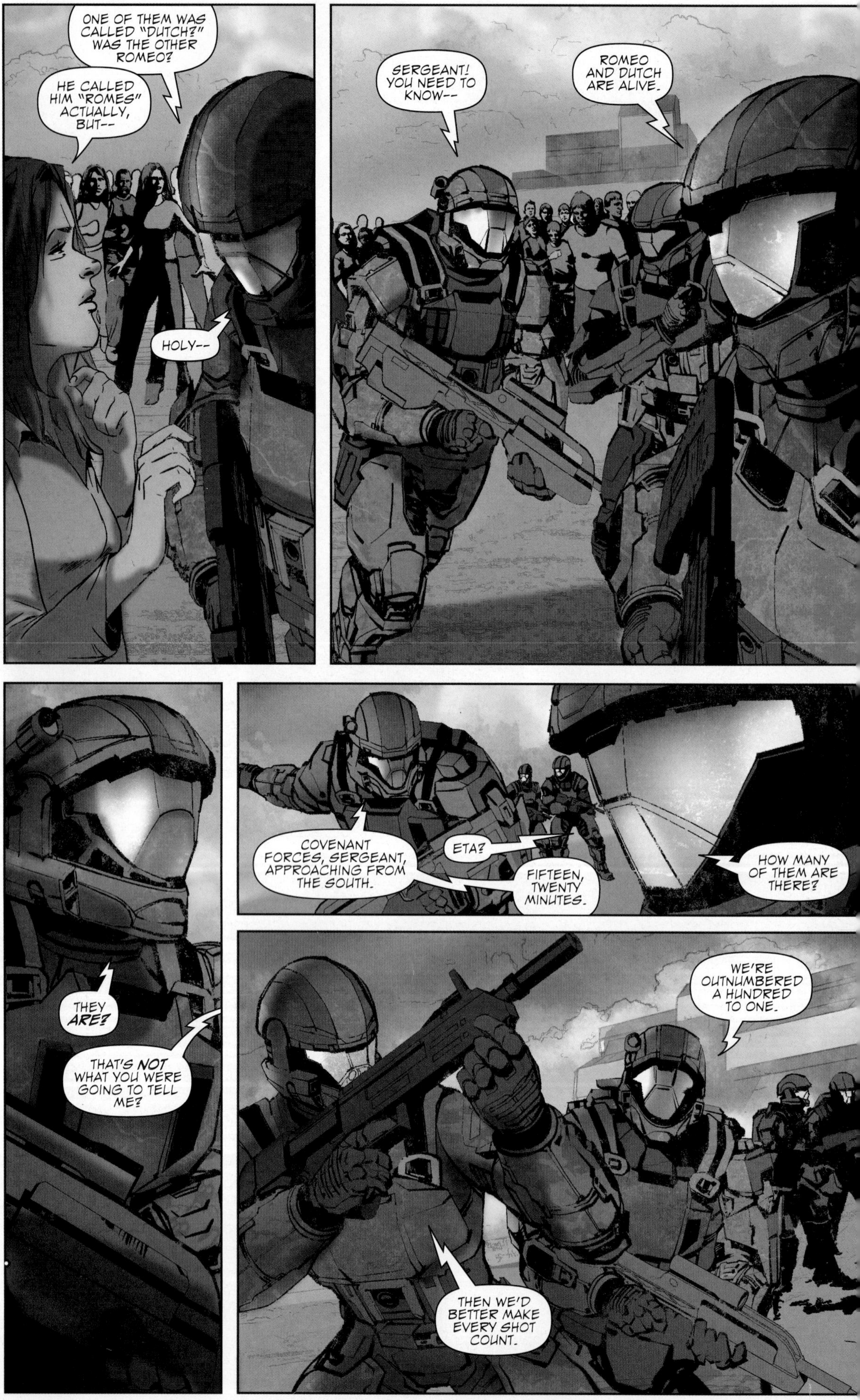
ONE OF THEM WAS CALLED "DUTCH?" WAS THE OTHER ROMEO?
HE CALLED HIM "ROMES" ACTUALLY, BUT--
HOLY--
SERGEANT! YOU NEED TO KNOW--
ROMEO AND DUTCH ARE ALIVE.
THEY ARE?
THAT'S NOT WHAT YOU WERE GOING TO TELL ME?
COVENANT FORCES, SERGEANT, APPROACHING FROM THE SOUTH.
ETA?
FIFTEEN, TWENTY MINUTES.
HOW MANY OF THEM ARE THERE?
WE'RE OUTNUMBERED A HUNDRED TO ONE.
THEN WE'D BETTER MAKE EVERY SHOT COUNT.

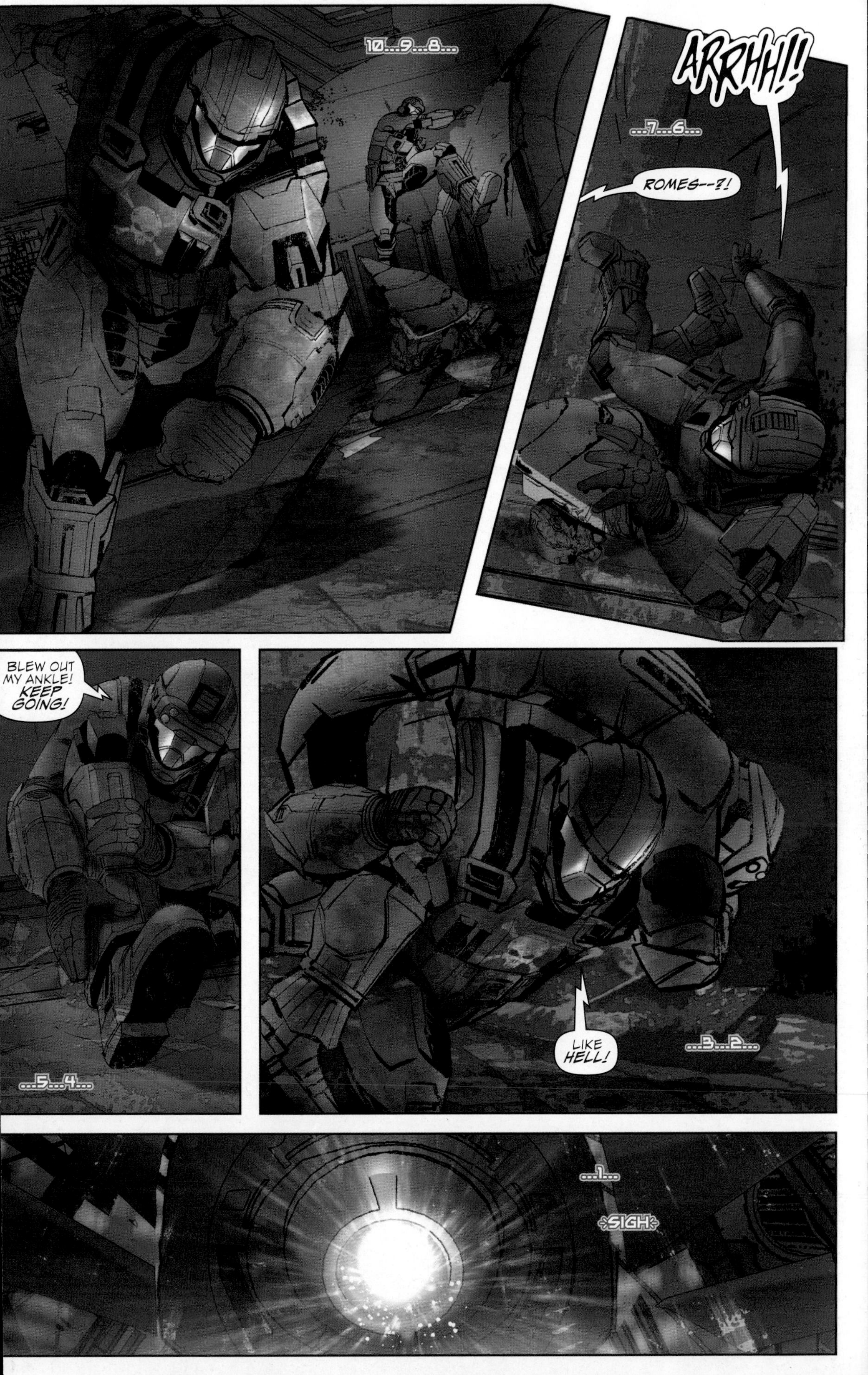
10...9...8...
ARRHH!!
...7...6...
ROMES--?!
BLEW OUT MY ANKLE! *KEEP GOING!*
...5...4...
LIKE *HELL!*
...3...2...
...1...
<SIGH>

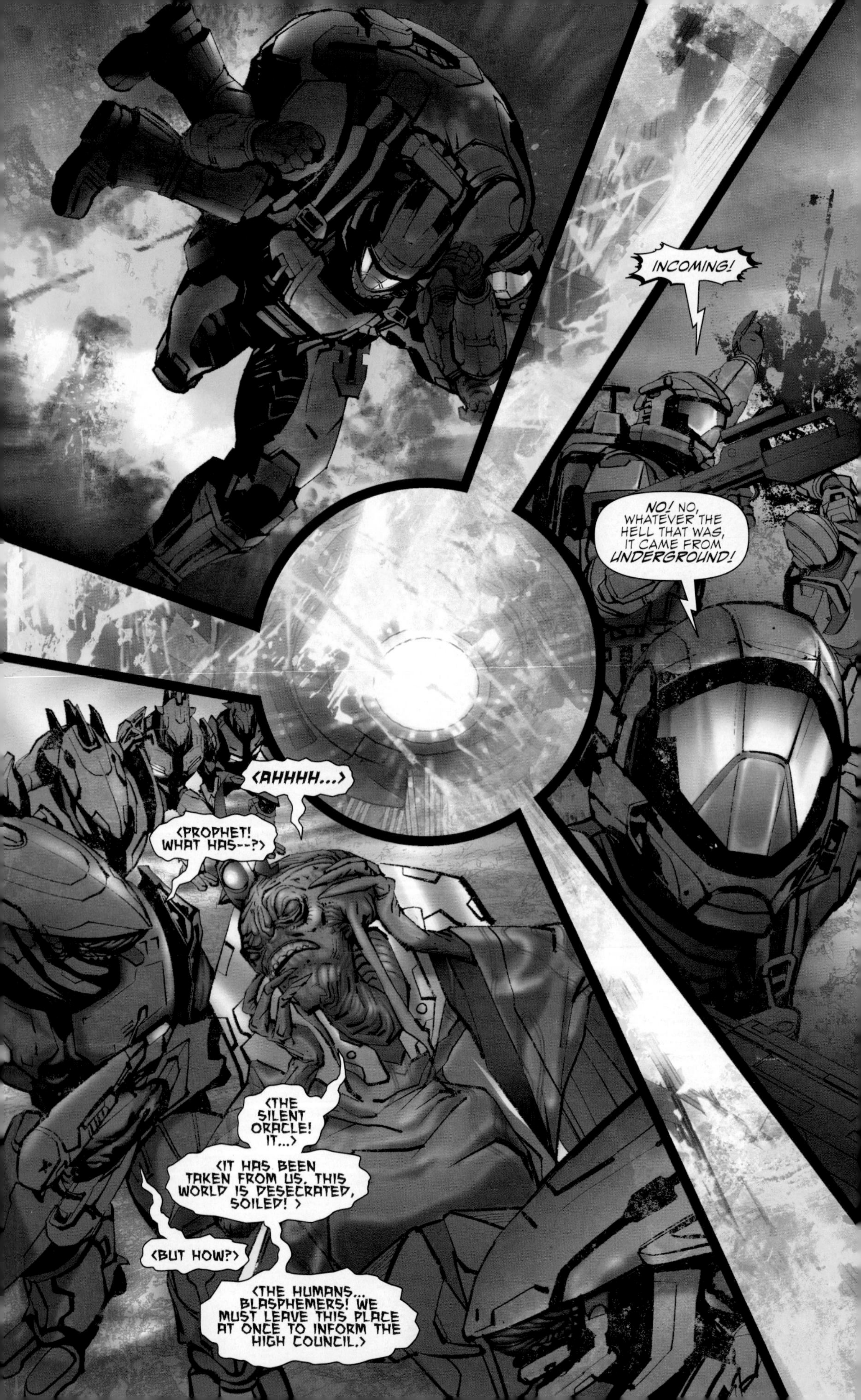
INCOMING!
NO! NO, WHATEVER THE HELL THAT WAS, IT CAME FROM UNDERGROUND!
<AHHHH...>
<PROPHET! WHAT HAS--?>
<THE SILENT ORACLE! IT...>
<IT HAS BEEN TAKEN FROM US. THIS WORLD IS DESECRATED, SOILED! >
<BUT HOW?>
<THE HUMANS... BLASPHEMERS! WE MUST LEAVE THIS PLACE AT ONCE TO INFORM THE HIGH COUNCIL.>

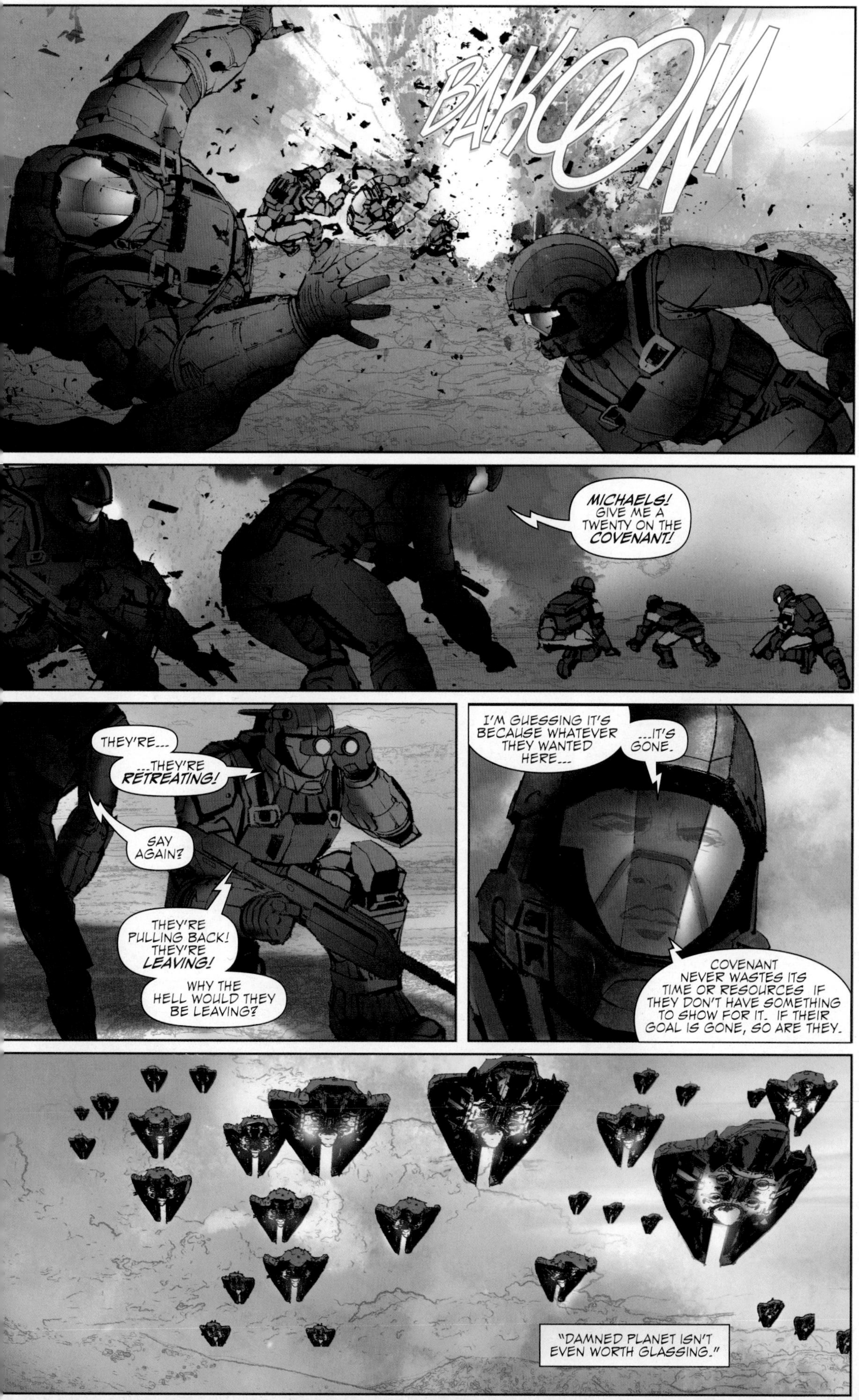
BAKOOM
MICHAELS! GIVE ME A TWENTY ON THE COVENANT!
THEY'RE...
...THEY'RE RETREATING!
SAY AGAIN?
THEY'RE PULLING BACK! THEY'RE LEAVING!
WHY THE HELL WOULD THEY BE LEAVING?
I'M GUESSING IT'S BECAUSE WHATEVER THEY WANTED HERE...
...IT'S GONE.
COVENANT NEVER WASTES ITS TIME OR RESOURCES IF THEY DON'T HAVE SOMETHING TO SHOW FOR IT. IF THEIR GOAL IS GONE, SO ARE THEY.
"DAMNED PLANET ISN'T EVEN WORTH GLASSING."

SARGE! SOMETHING'S MOVING DOWN THERE!

WEAPONS READY! FIND YOUR TARGET, MARINES!

=KOFF= AGH AND =KOFF= MILES.... REPORTING FOR DUTY.

SHOULD'VE KNOWN IF SOMETHING WAS BLOWING UP, *YOU TWO* WOULD BE INVOLVED.

HAUL THEIR ASSES OUT OF THERE AND FIND SOMETHING USEFUL FOR THEM TO DO.

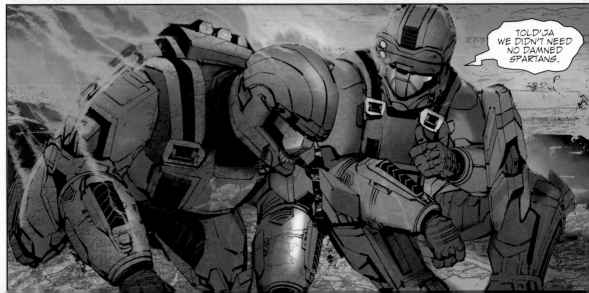

TOLD'JA WE DIDN'T NEED NO DAMNED SPARTANS.

BEING IN THE INFIRMARY, RECOVERING FROM A BUSTED ANKLE, SMOKE INHALATION...

...GIVES YOU A LOT OF TIME TO THINK ABOUT WHAT'S IMPORTANT.

SO... DUTCH... LOOK...

I'M NOT SURE IF SHE'S EVER GONNA FORGIVE ME, BUT--

SHE'LL GET OVER IT.

I DOUBT IT. SHE CARRIES A GRUDGE.

NEVER.

YOU DON'T KNOW HER LIKE I DO.

I...? ROMES, WHO'RE YOU TALKIN' ABOUT?

THE SARGE, 'CAUSE I PUT IN FOR A TRANSFER, TO BE ROTATED PLANETSIDE WITH YOU. I...THOUGHT YOU KNEW. WHY, WHO'RE YOU TALKING ABOUT?

GRETCH. WE AGREED THAT OUR SITUATION ISN'T PERFECT, BUT YOU'D BE DEAD WITHOUT ME. SO I WITHDREW MY TRANSFER REQUEST.

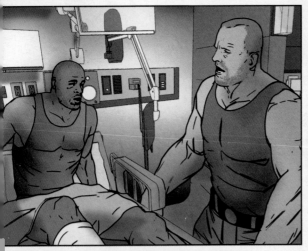

ROCK, PAPER, SCISSORS? WINNER'S DECISION STANDS, LOSER GOES WITH HIM.

FINE.

SCISSORS CUT PAPER.

DAMN.

TWO OUT OF THREE?

YEAH, OKAY.

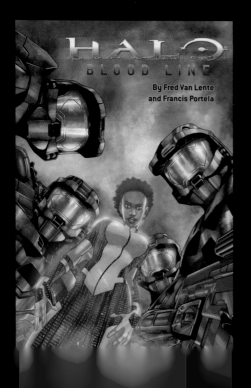